NEW ARENAS
FOR VIOLENCE

NEW ARENAS FOR VIOLENCE

Homicide in the American Workplace

Michael D. Kelleher

PRAEGER

Westport, Connecticut
London

Library of Congress Cataloging-in-Publication Data

Kelleher, Michael D.
    New arenas for violence : homicide in the American workplace /
Michael D. Kelleher.
      p. cm.
    Includes bibliographical references and index.
    ISBN 0–275–95652–0 (alk. paper)
    1. Violence in the workplace—United States. 2. Violence in the
workplace—Prevention. I. Title.
    HF5549.5.E43K45   1996
    658.4'73—dc20   96–16278

British Library Cataloguing in Publication Data is available.

Library of Congress Catalog Card Number: 96–16278
ISBN: 0–275–95652–0

First published in 1996

Praeger Publishers, 88 Post Road West, Westport, CT 06881
An imprint of Greenwood Publishing Group, Inc.

Printed in the United States of America

The paper used in this book complies with the
Permanent Paper Standard issued by the National
Information Standards Organization (Z39.48–1984).

10 9 8 7 6 5 4 3 2 1

For Cindy

Contents

Illustrations

Introduction

If you live in one of the more populous states, like California, your chances of being murdered at work are at least equal to those of being killed during your commute to or from your job site. If you are a gas station attendant, government employee, or retail store clerk, you have a higher probability of being murdered on the job than a police officer in your own community. If you are a secretary or clerk in an office, you are more likely to be murdered at work than a West Virginia miner is likely to be accidentally killed in an industry-related accident. If you work for a living, and most Americans do, you are a potential victim of one of the fastest growing areas of major crime in our society—occupational homicide.

This book examines the history, nature, and causal factors of occupational homicide—murder in the workplace—with a view to the development of a comprehensive understanding of the issue and the introduction of a prevention program that can help you and your coworkers create and maintain a safer work environment which will be less likely to become a breeding ground for violence or murder. A detailed understanding of occupational homicide will be presented through an examination of actual case histories of the crime and the application of analysis and prevention techniques that can be used to inform and train staff and managers. A new methodology of understanding and quantifying occupational homicide will be suggested, and the most efficacious methods of workplace violence prevention will be introduced. A new profile of the potentially violent worker will be developed through the examination of actual incidents of workplace homicide. This profiling system will emphasize ease of understanding and applicability to a wide variety of work environments. A new method of analyzing incidents of occupational homicide will be developed which can be used by workers and managers to learn more about this crime and assist in creating a safer work environment. Finally, the working profile of an organization that is committed to eliminating occupational homicide and workplace violence will be presented to help set a standard for individual safety in many different work environments.

Occupational homicide represents a new and unanticipated challenge to both staff and managers. The number of American workers murdered annually on the job has more than doubled since 1989, and this trend is increasing as we approach the year 2000. This book will show that a continuing increase in the number of annual workplace homicides is inevitable unless a widespread program of intervention and prevention is enacted throughout the American business community. Further, any such prevention program demands a comprehensive understanding of the nature of occupational homicide and requires a compendium of techniques to mitigate the growing menace of this crime.

Despite the demonstrable impact of this crime, very little information about occupational homicide has been made available to the American workforce. Through the combined influences of (1) a lack of accessible or accurate information about the subject, (2) the seemingly prevalent view that occupational homicide is beyond the jurisdiction of the workplace, and (3) an understandable reluctance to integrate this disturbing subject into existing training or workplace safety programs, an unnecessary vulnerability has been created in many American businesses. This book examines that vulnerability in detail and attempts to provide answers to the threat of workplace violence and murder through a practical and cost-effective prevention program.

The journey to an understanding of the crime begins with a definition of the nature of occupational homicide and a detailed look at its impact on society and the workplace. This is followed by an outline of early efforts to identify the issues surrounding the crime, an overview of important statistical information, and a history of workplace murder in America. The questions surrounding workplace murder are then developed in detail through an examination of case studies selected to provide a broad understanding of the crime, the perpetrators, and the failures of management systems to protect the work environment. The causal factors contributing to occupational homicide are examined in the context of sociological imperatives, change, cultural influences, financial and economic imperatives, and psychological factors. A profile of the potentially violent employee or client is then developed and detailed. Finally, a comprehensive system of intervention and prevention methodologies is presented.

Unique to this examination of occupational homicide are four elements that, together, provide the basis for protecting many different work environments from this crime.

1. A methodology of categorizing and interpreting occupational homicide in a manner consistent with the common understanding of the workplace by managers and staff. This method will allow members of the workforce to understand the crime from a practical point of view and, through this understanding, enable them to come to grips with the realities and probabilities of the issue.

2. A methodology of profiling potentially violent workers or clients that is consistent with the typical work environment and which relies on a foundation of existing knowledge among managers and staff. By training the workforce in the skill of identifying potentially violent individuals before they commit to violence, a higher level of overall workplace safety can be realized.

3. An understanding of occupational homicide that includes the contributing factors brought about by management action or inaction rather than focusing solely on the activities of the perpetrator. This will involve a new methodology of interpreting incidents of workplace violence and occupational homicide that establishes the importance of the interplay of the organization and its management and staff with the perpetrator in a violent event. It is a common misperception that an organization is simply a passive victim in an incident of violence or homicide. In reality, however, the actions or inaction of members of the workforce often contribute to the ensuing violence.

4. A compendium of prevention methodologies directed particularly toward the goal of mitigating workplace violence and occupational homicide in a variety of work environments. The emphasis in this book is on *practical* prevention techniques—those that are known to reduce violence.

Through an understanding of the nature and causes of occupational homicide and the development and implementation of a workplace violence prevention program, it may be possible to reduce the number of workers whose lives are needlessly lost each year because of this crime. The key concepts needed to accomplish this goal are an understanding of the issues, a concerned workforce and management team, and a commitment to action.

1

Murder in the Workplace

Occupational homicide—the act of murder in the workplace—represents a new and unanticipated challenge to staff and managers. The number of American workers murdered annually on the job has more than doubled since 1989 and, in some regions of the country, accounts for as many deaths each year as automobile accidents occurring during normal commuting hours. For reasons to be examined in this book, a continuing increase in the number of annual workplace homicides can be expected unless a widespread program of intervention and prevention is enacted throughout the American business community. Such a program must be practical, understandable and cost-effective if it is to take hold among the many forms of American labor.

Despite the increasingly lethal nature of the contemporary workplace, very little information about occupational homicide has been made available to the workforce, either in the context of an understanding of the problem or in the form of prevention methodologies. Although a few recent publications have made efforts to deal with the broader topic of violence in the workplace, American workers are left with virtually no resource to assist them in understanding the essential nature or causes of occupational homicide or how it can be prevented within their own organization. This lack of information leads, predictably, to the absence of preparation in most work environments.

The crime of occupational homicide is often viewed by the workforce as a matter for law enforcement or justice personnel and not as a crucial element in an organizational safety program. This is due, in part, to the fact there are no specific tools available to the workforce to (1) interpret occupational homicide or workplace violence in a manner consistent with their own experiences, (2) identify a potentially violent individual before a workplace incident evolves so that intervention measures are possible, (3) analyze incidents of workplace violence in a holistic manner such that the actions of the organization or its personnel are understood to be crucial in the evolving pattern of violence, and (4) have available a base of prevention/intervention methodologies suitable specifically to the prevention of this crime. In addition, it must be recognized that the subject itself is, at best, disturbing for both managers and staff. That it has not been broadly embraced by most workers as part of a continuing safety program is unfortunate but understandable.

The combined impetus of (1) a lack of information about the subject, (2) the prevalent view that occupational homicide is outside the jurisdiction of the typical workplace, (3) the absence of readily-accessible intervention/prevention programs, and (4) a reluctance to integrate this disturbing subject into existing training and safety programs creates an unnecessary vulnerability in many American businesses and presents a workplace safety problem of national proportions. In order to effectively mitigate this threat to the workplace, the workforce must be provided with the proper tools to ensure the safety of the work environment. These tools should address two major areas of concern: (1) a comprehensive understanding of the nature and impact of occupational homicide, and (2) specific methodologies to accomplish this understanding and enhance prevention possibilities.

In order to provide a comprehensive understanding of the nature and impact of occupational homicide, some fundamental questions must be addressed:

1. To what extent has this crime been studied, and what can be learned from the research?
2. To what extent does occupational homicide impact the American business community, and what is the probable future trend?
3. How pervasive is occupational homicide? Is it a general problem or one limited to certain industries, professions, or geographical areas?
4. Are organizations prepared to deal with incidents of occupational homicide? To what extent are organizations utilizing prevention methodologies? Is this an issue familiar to the typical American organization?
5. Are there formalized prevention programs available to workplace personnel to assist in the prevention or mitigation of the threat of occupational homicide? How can an organization acquire the prevention methodologies necessary to protect its staff and environment?
6. What is the true nature of occupational homicide? When the myths, stories, and media sensationalism are stripped away, what is left to be learned about this crime?
7. What is the role of the workplace manager in prevention? What is the role of staff? What are the staff responsibilities within the organization to aid in prevention? Do the actions or inaction of workplace personnel exacerbate potential violence?
8. Can an analysis of incidents of occupational homicide lead to the use of prevention techniques to avoid or mitigate future similar occurrences?
9. Can an analysis of incidents of occupational homicide provide a sufficient understanding of the issue? If not, what are the issues that require further research? Can these be illustrated from previous incidents of occupational homicide such that additional research can be undertaken productively?

10. Can the process of prevention and mitigation be initiated by the identification of tools for workplace managers and staff? What are these tools? Can they be provided in a form useful to individuals in the work environment?

To begin the process of providing specific tools for the use of workplace managers and staff, the following questions must also be addressed:

1. How can incidents of workplace violence and occupational homicide be categorized and defined in such a way as to provide for a meaningful understanding of the issue by managers and staff? Such a methodology must be specifically designed to be consistent with their common understanding of the workplace. The key test for any program of prevention must be one of practicality if it is to be enacted and sustained.
2. Can a potentially violent employee or client be identified *prior* to an act of violence such that appropriate intervention and prevention techniques are possible? Such a profile must rely on a foundation of existing knowledge among managers and staff, be understandable by all, and be easily communicated for training and educational purposes.
3. How can incidents of occupational homicide be analyzed holistically such that the contributing factors brought about by management action or inaction are appropriately viewed as important constituents in the evolving pattern of violence? Can the hypothesis that occupational homicide is not merely a singular act of violence but the result of a convergence of actions from multiple sources be proven valuable in helping workplace managers and staff understand the nature of the crime?
4. Can a base compendium of prevention methodologies be assembled that is directed primarily toward the goal of mitigating occupational homicide? Further, is it possible to define those policies and practices that lead to violence mitigation across a variety of work environments and assemble them into a practical form that is capable of implementation in the workplace?

This book will examine occupational homicide in detail in an effort to address each of these questions. The primary purpose of this study is to provide the tools of knowledge thought to be crucial to an understanding of occupational homicide and its prevention in the American work environment.

In a broad sense, this is a study of the unthinkable: an examination of violence that should never happen, yet frequently does. It is a glimpse into a part of the workplace that lies hidden from view yet remains a possibility, virtually anywhere, at anytime. For many individuals, this detailed examination of occupational homicide may be unsettling. It is clearly an unpleasant issue. For workplace managers and staff, however, it is not an abstract or idle subject. Many work environments will experience some form of violence within the next year. Some, unfortunately, will experience the horror of occupational homicide. There are, however, opportunities to improve the outlook for all working Americans. The impact of occupational homicide can be mitigated through an understanding of its causes and the application of measures designed to counteract or anticipate future incidents.

TERMS AND DEFINITIONS

The subject of occupational homicide has not been significantly explored, and therefore, a vocabulary unique to the crime has yet to evolve. For this study, the working definition of occupational homicide will be "the act of murder in the workplace." In this sense, any act of murder related to the job or job site will be considered an act of occupational homicide. However, in order to more precisely define this crime with a particular view to prevention methodologies it will be necessary to construct a more detailed definition.

Elements of this work will focus on case studies of occupational homicide with a view to exploring their nature and the opportunities they present for prevention techniques from the perspective of workplace personnel. To facilitate an understanding of this perspective, a new methodology of categorizing occupational homicide is required, which must be applicable to the workplace and understandable by managers and staff. It must, therefore, embody known and understood definitions common to the typical work environment. For these purposes, the method of Category Profile (CP) definitions, which were designed specifically to accommodate the typical workplace environment, will be used. The Category Profile method of crime definition is summarized in Table 1.1.

Table 1.1 : Category Profile Definitions

Category Profile	Category Definitions
I	Employee against employee
II	Employee against supervisor Supervisor against employee
III	Client against employee or supervisor Supervisor or employee against client
IV	Homicide by agenda or for political purposes
V	Indiscriminate homicide

The five Category Profile definitions have been designed to elucidate the nature of a violent incident from the variable perspectives of perpetrator, manager, staff and victim(s). Category Profiles I, II, and III define the interactive nature of the crime in relation to commonly understood workplace terminology. Category Profiles IV and V broaden the previous definitions to embrace motivations or action. This method of categorizing violent workplace incidents allows for a practical analysis and understanding of the event by workplace personnel and provides an easily understood technique that is useful in staff training and education.

SOURCES OF STATISTICAL INFORMATION

The National Institute for Occupational Safety and Health (NIOSH) is responsible for gathering statistical data about fatalities in the workplace. It is also charged with the dissemination of this data and of information about prevention programs. This agency has become the premier collection point for information about many forms of violence in the workplace, including occupational homicide. NIOSH data represents the most comprehensive pool of knowledge currently available on the subject. The agency has taken pains to adhere to a high standard of accuracy when collecting and disseminating information, thus making its publications reliable and informative.   Much of what can be measured about the impact of occupational homicide on the American workforce relies on the data collected by NIOSH over the past decade and a half.

NIOSH has carefully outlined their methods of operation and data management with each major publication. In its most recent report NIOSH used the following methods of information gathering and analysis.[1]

1. *Death Certificates.* Data was gathered by the National Traumatic Occupational Fatalities (NTOF) surveillance system. This software system was developed by NIOSH "to fill gaps in the knowledge of work-related injury deaths in the U.S. by providing a census of occupational injury deaths for all U.S. workers."[2] Death certificates were widely available for all states and for all workers who died during the survey period. Regardless of the work environment, NIOSH was able to assemble a broad base of worker death information without the constraints imposed by surveying other sources of information such as workers' compensation systems. NIOSH estimated that "death certificates captured 67% to 90% of all fatal work injuries."[3] This is a key point to remember when analyzing NIOSH data.

Although death certificates were the most reliable source of information available to the NIOSH surveillance system, they were not completely accurate; nor did they account for all worker fatalities, with up to 33% of workplace deaths not identified as such. It is therefore necessary to remember that the best statistics available from NIOSH represent a minimum of known fatalities in the workplace. The number of homicides is certainly greater than the NIOSH statistics indicate. The extent of this inaccuracy is, in the final analysis, unknown.

In dealing with the specifics of accuracy limitations, NIOSH noted that it was not always possible to "identify and retrieve the [death] certificates that met the study criteria."[4] For the period 1980-1989, for example, there were no published guidelines available to aid in the accurate completion of death certificates. This led to confusion when addressing the "Injury at Work?" question appearing on the certificates. Many responses received by NIOSH left this question unanswered; others were subject to an individual assessment of the interpretation of the question "Injury at Work?" Lacking guidelines, the responses provided on the death certificates could not be considered wholly reliable. Clearly, such data could easily be skewed by the introduction of false positives or false negatives, depending on the interpretation of the "Injury at Work?" section of the death certificate. After considerable analysis, NIOSH took the position that the 1980-1989 data probably represented the minimum number of work-related deaths in the United States.[5] This limitation continues with the present day data collection techniques.

2. *Occupation, Industry, and Cause of Death Coding.* NIOSH extracted occupational data from the narrative sections of the death certificates surveyed using software they developed. Cause of death was coded based on the International Classification of Diseases (ICD) categorization system. By determining the cause of death, NIOSH

analysts were able to more precisely define the probabilities of occupational homicide within industries and job categories. This technique became the basis for subsequent NIOSH publications.

3. *Employment Data.*   NIOSH analysts used several sources to obtain this data, including: County Business Patterns (CPB) census information, Census of Agriculture, Bureau of the Census, the Bureau of Labor Statistics, and a variety of state agency sources. This data, in conjunction with that derived from mapping techniques, provided NIOSH with the ability to determine the job categories most impacted by occupational homicide.

4. *Mapping.*   To map work-related fatalities, NIOSH used five categories for occupational fatality rates, ranging from "very high" (more than two standard deviations above the average rate) to "low" (more than one standard deviation below the average rate). Using this mapping technique, NIOSH analysts were able to identify those industries most significantly impacted by occupational homicide. The information derived from this aspect of the NIOSH study provided the basis for subsequent prevention recommendations targeting specific industries.

5. *Years of Potential Life Lost (YPLL).* The YPLL calculated by NIOSH was defined as "years of potential life lost before age 65 calculated for the 10-year (1980-1989) period."[6] This information was used to define losses to business and industry on a national scale.

Although other data sources were available for this study, some of which will be used in analyzing specific details of homicide in the workplace, the NIOSH data is generally regarded in the literature as the most comprehensive and reliable source of data available.

DIFFICULTIES OF LIMITED INFORMATION

A long-term longitudinal study of workplace violence, including occupational homicide, was initiated by NIOSH in 1983 and encompassed data for the period 1980 through 1989. The results of this study were released in 1993 by NIOSH and the Centers for Disease Control and Prevention (CDC); they represent the most comprehensive statistical analysis currently available on the subject. Analysts at NIOSH recognized, in this report, that a potentially significant limitation existed in determining the actual number of workplace deaths because a primary research methodology relied on information gathered by reviewing individual death certificates.   This method of information gathering resulted in a potentially significant understatement of workplace homicides of up to 33% for the decade under study.   Therefore, when considering occupational homicide statistics, it can be safely assumed that the number of annual occupational homicides cited represents an *absolute minimum* of those believed to occur. Of itself, this significant uncertainty in the potential impact of occupational homicide lends urgency to the argument for a more thorough understanding of the problem.

NIOSH is the most active organization currently engaged in gathering occupational homicide statistics on a national scale. Although other agencies at the state or local levels may gather similar statistics, results are not often published in a comprehensive or consistent manner that could provide the basis for further analysis. For this reason, and despite its known limitations, this study relies on the NIOSH data as the most comprehensive and accurate information available about the subject.

A secondary limitation to this study involves the lack of a comprehensive database of incidents of occupational homicide. Since the act of murder in the workplace demands an analysis of, not only the incident itself, but the motivations and profile of the perpetrator, as well as the actions of managers and staff prior to and during the incident, it will be necessary to examine a variety of case histories to search for patterns of possible analysis and understanding. In selecting case histories for this study, every effort has been made to identify reasonable and illustrative incidents without regard to the sensational nature of the case or its impact on the media. Nonetheless, subjective selections of case histories were required, and this in itself excludes other examples that could have been employed. Many incidents of occupational homicide have similar patterns and identifiable characteristics, others do not. Some incidents appear to be without reasonable explanation. The case studies selected for this book have been given significant consideration to ensure that they are (1) representative of the broad and identifiable issues surrounding occupational homicide, (2) reasonable and sufficient to illustrate corresponding prevention or intervention methodologies that could be practically employed in most organizations, and (3) of sufficient detail to be verifiable as to important issues and facts within the framework of the incident. In an effort to present a broad view of the issue, some incidents of occupational homicide are presented that clearly defy the general patterns recognizable in most workplace homicides. Even from such exceptional incidents, however, much can be learned. Overall, sufficient case histories of sufficient scope are presented to support a practical methodology of developing a profile of the typical workplace murderer as a key element in prevention.

AN EMERGING ISSUE

It must be emphasized that the issue of occupational homicide has received little research and is, in effect, an emerging issue. That there is a significant upward trend in the incidents of occupational homicide will be made evident in this volume. It can easily be demonstrated that the workplace in America has become increasingly violent in the last decade and, for a variety of reasons, it can be assumed that this trend will continue. This presents a social problem of considerable importance to the majority of American citizens.

Because of its nature as an emerging issue, occupational homicide presents many questions that remain unanswered. Although it can be argued that many incidents of occupational homicide may be mitigated by prevention or intervention techniques, there are cases of murder in the workplace that seem to defy all efforts at understanding or prevention. Several case studies presented in this book deal with such incidents in an effort to present unresolved issues clearly.   In addition, there is no system in place among American businesses to share information and resources in a combined effort to mitigate workplace violence. In an effort to address this important issue, it will be suggested that organizations, at the local level, combine resources and information to enhance their prevention efforts individually and severally. Finally, no formal system of investigating, analyzing, and responding to incidents of occupational homicide has yet evolved.   This study suggests elements useful to such a formal system but does not provide the complete framework for a comprehensive methodology, which may only be developed after more is known about this complex crime.

NOTES

1. National Institute for Occupational Safety and Health (NIOSH), *Fatal Injuries to Workers in the United States, 1980-1989*, Aug. 1993, 2.
2. NIOSH, 2.
3. NIOSH, 2.
4. NIOSH, 2.
5. NIOSH, 2
6. NIOSH, 4.

2

History of Occupational Homicide

A method of statistically examining homicide in the workplace was first developed in the 1980s in an effort to categorize this crime by utilizing Standard Industrial Classification (SIC) categories or the Alphabetic Index of Industries and Occupations produced by the U.S. Department of Commerce.[1,2] When viewed in this way, acts of violence in the workplace were summarized by professions, with a view to detailing risk within each job category. The method of using SIC categorization is today a common approach found in general survey results released by government agencies; it has the advantage of presenting key homicide data in a revealing and easily understood manner.

A series of longitudinal studies undertaken by NIOSH, examining workplace homicides for the period 1980-1989, used the SIC categories in Table 2.1 to summarize their results.[3]

Table 2.1: NIOSH SIC Categories

Taxicab establishments
Liquor stores
Gas stations
Detective/protective services
Justice/public order establishments
Grocery stores
Jewelry stores
Hotels/motels
Eating/drinking places

In addition to these categories, to further refine their data, NIOSH relied on the Bureau of Census occupational definitions as outlined in Table 2.2.[4]

Table 2.2: Bureau of Census Occupational Categories

Taxicab drivers/chauffeurs
Law enforcement officers
Hotel clerks
Gas station workers
Security guards
Stock handlers/baggers
Store owners/managers
Bartenders

These two categories (Table 2.1 and Table 2.2) have traditionally provided the basis for analyzing trends of workplace violence and relating occupational homicide to specific job sites or professions. Although effective as a broad risk-management technique, these categorizations failed to provide sufficient definition within a specific industry from which prevention methodologies could be easily developed. Their practical applicability for use by workplace personnel was absent.

A third, and more comprehensive, approach to categorization was employed by NIOSH in a detailed report released in August 1993.[5] In this report, NIOSH used multiple sources of employment data, resulting in a variety of job and workplace categorizations; this added depth to the previous results presented. Multiple information sources, such as the County Business Patterns (CBP) survey data, Census of Agriculture, and Bureau of Labor Statistics, allowed NIOSH to present its results in different ways, including illustration by broad industry definitions. These industry definitions are presented in Table 2.3.

Table 2.3: NIOSH Industry Definitions

Construction
Transportation/Communication/Public Utilities
Manufacturing
Agriculture/Forestry/Fishing
Services
Retail Trade
Public Administration
Mining
Wholesale Trade
Finance/Insurance/Real Estate

By using industry definitions, NIOSH was able to more effectively study a wide range of data for injuries and deaths in the workplace. In particular, this categorization method enabled NIOSH to employ specific coding techniques to a variety of causes of death in the workplace using the International

Classification of Diseases (ICD) E-code rubrics.[6] These E-codes encompassed several broad causes of death. They were further subdivided by ICD rubrics numbered E800-E989. Among these categories was "homicide" (E960-E969)—the focus of this study. The full NIOSH category titles are presented in Table 2.4.

Table 2.4: NIOSH Industry Rubric Titles

Rail Transport
Motor Vehicle
Water Transport
Air Transport
Poisoning
Fall
Fire
Nature/Environment
Drowning
Suffocation
Struck By Falling Object
Flying Object/Caught In Machine
Explosion
Electrocution
Suicide
Homicide
Other
Unknown/Undetermined

Throughout this examination of occupational homicide, the various categories employed by NIOSH will be used to help profile industries at risk. In addition, however, it is necessary to view workplace homicide data from a more understandable point of view dealing with risk within a typical work environment.

The primary goal of this study is to offer specific methodologies to properly interpret potential violence in the workplace and suggest preventative action. To do this effectively, one must view acts of violence in the workplace from the perspective of those who will be charged with its identification and prevention—workers, supervisors and management personnel. This study will, therefore, view historical data in a new way, which emphasizes this perspective—a view of occupational homicide from *within* the work environment. In order to accomplish this, the categories of occupational homicide outlined in Table 1.1 will be employed.

When case histories of occupational homicide are reviewed, they will each be assigned to one of the five categories in Table 1.1 and coded with a Category Profile (CP) identification number (I-V). Discussions of prevention will focus on management techniques that apply to one or more of these categories. It is hoped that, in this way, an entire workforce within an organization will be able to more effectively apply the recommended prevention methodologies through the use of a common perspective emanating from within the organization itself, regardless of its industry classification.

EMERGENCE OF WORKPLACE VIOLENCE

Prior to 1980, violence in the workplace was not recognized as an issue apart from that of general violence in society. Violent incidents at work were traditionally viewed as either matters of industrial safety or were relegated to the purview of law enforcement agencies. They were treated as exceptional incidents for all but those employment categories viewed as inherently dangerous and prone to violent occurrences (such as the military, law enforcement, security services, and prison guards). Beginning in the early 1980s, however, the traditional view of a safe workplace underwent a significant and rapid transformation.

Before 1980, such terms as "violence in the workplace," or the more contemporary terms "occupational violent crime" (OVC) or "occupational homicide" simply did not appear in the literature.[i] Few, if any, reference works dealing with crime, violence, industrial safety, personnel, human resource management, or the law offered significant information on this specific subject. Acts of violence that occurred in the workplace were broadly categorized into more traditional statistical groupings. Causal factors such as interpersonal conflict, intoxication, drug abuse, or violence in the pursuit of various crimes were often used to categorize an incident. Sometimes the type of weapon used in the commission of the crime was employed as a major category (this technique was particularly popular in governmental or law enforcement environments).[7] There was certainly no formal recognition of workplace violence or occupational homicide as an area of concern for management, scholars, researchers, the medical professions, the government, or law enforcement services.   Acts of homicide in the workplace were not differentiated from murder in society at large, despite the fact that homicide in society was increasing at an alarming rate and, presumably, also within the workplace. Figure 2.1 indicates the national trend in the per capita national crime rate from 1983 through 1992.[8]

---

i. OVC is defined as an "intentional battery, rape or homicide during the course of employment" (T. Hales, P. J. Seligman, S. C. Newman, and C. L. Timbrook, C. L., "Occupational Injuries Due to Violence," *Journal of Occupational Medicine*, [1988], *6*, 483).

Figure 2.1: Per Capita Crime Rate

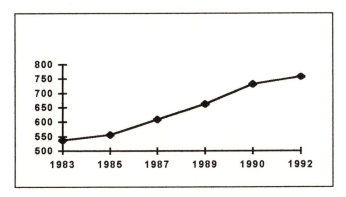

Because of the lack of statistical information, it is difficult to draw accurate conclusions about the pervasive nature of violent acts in the workplace before 1980. Certainly, one can assume that violence was to be found in the workplace before 1980. Prior to this time, however, there was insufficient information available from which to draw meaningful conclusions. As the decade progressed, though, it became clear that violence in the workplace was becoming a more frequent cause of injuries and death. Much of this new information was provided by NIOSH, beginning in the early 1980s.

American society experienced a general and dramatic upturn in violence in the mid-1980s, which resulted in an increase of 23.1% in violent crimes and 14.4% in forcible rape by the end of the decade.[9] This trend continued into the next decade. In 1990, approximately 37,000 Americans were killed by guns, and about 15,000 citizens were victims of homicide. Approximately 12,500 of these individuals were murdered with handguns, the weapon of choice of most perpetrators.[10] By 1992 the number of murder victims was in excess of 22,500.[11] A steady and frightening increase in the use of guns, particularly handguns, was evidenced in the years between 1980 and 1992 as indicated in Figure 2.2. This trend continues, unabated, in the 1990-2000 decade.[12]

In the past five years, there has also been a significant increase in the number and type of military style weapons being used to commit murder in society and the workplace. These new weapons contribute directly to the increase in the homicide rate in America. By 1993 the number of confirmed annual occupational homicides was at least 1,063; over 80% of these victims were killed with guns.[13] Many of these victims were murdered with military style weapons. Of the estimated 150,000 violent deaths that will occur in America in 1996, one third will be either homicide or suicide. The majority of these deaths will be caused by a gun, many of which will be military style weapons.

Clearly, the American workplace has suffered a significant impact from the general invasion of violence into society. Statistically, no information was available that could define the extent of the problem before 1980. Since 1980, however, data has been made available on an annual basis which demonstrates a continuing upward trend in occupational homicide as well as an alarming increase in indiscriminate homicides in the work environment.

Figure 2.2: Murder Weapons

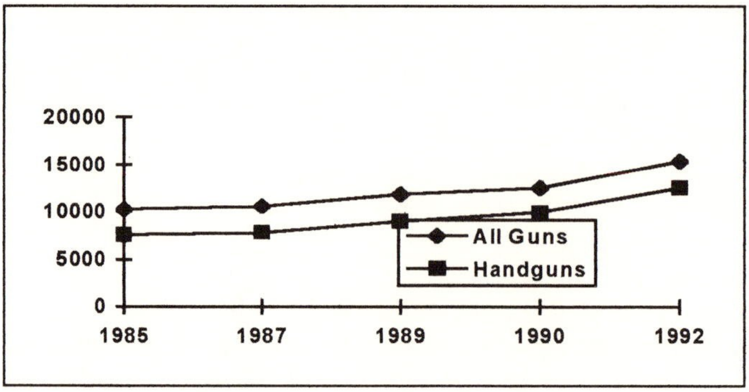

EARLY EFFORTS TO UNDERSTAND THE CRIME

There appears to have been little public awareness of the issues of workplace violence or occupational homicide until the mid-1980s. Media and government archives provide virtually no references to these categories of crime until the early 1980s, and then only in brief and disjointed form. Again, homicide in the workplace was dealt with as a series of singular incidents of violent crime, not as a categorical phenomenon. By 1986, however, the nation would awake to this new and formidable problem. The concept of violence in the workplace, and the recognition that homicide was a core component of this problem, would be established with permanence for every American worker by events in the small town of Edmond, Oklahoma, and through the efforts of a single government agency.

The first government agency to recognize and respond to the issue of general workplace violence was the U. S. Centers for Disease Control and Prevention (CDC) in Atlanta, Georgia. In 1983 the CDC provided funding for the development of a new program directed specifically at the collection of data and subsequent prevention of various forms of violence in American society.[14] This program included research into violence and death in the workplace. By its action in developing such a program, the CDC clearly identified violence as a societal problem of equal importance with any other threat to the well-being of American citizens with which it had historically grappled.

This was a departure from the CDC's traditional role, and one that required new leadership and a fresh approach. The CDC had traditionally developed many significant programs to reduce accidental injuries and deaths, some dating as far back as the 1950s (involving the automobile industry). However, the agency had never directly approached the prevention of violence as a programmatic issue. Before the early 1980s, the consensus of many medical professionals familiar with the traditional role of the CDC was that societal violence in general, and workplace violence in particular, was primarily a law enforcement issue.[15] These professionals were convinced that workplace violence should not be within the jurisdiction of a public agency such as the Centers for Disease Control. However, a key staff member in the CDC disagreed with this view.

The inaugural CDC violence prevention program was headed by Dr. Mark Rosenberg, a Harvard graduate with both a medical degree and a master's degree in public policy and the associate director of the CDC's National Center for Injury Control. Dr. Rosenberg's approach to violence as an area worthy of research was both innovative and refreshing because he brought a strong focus to the issue of violence prevention as a matter of public safety.[16] Dr. Rosenberg, in defining his personal view of the CDC program, made his position quite clear: "Some people charge that this public-health approach [to the prevention of violence] is really an attempt to pacify people. We're trying to do exactly the opposite—to get people to believe that they can change things and that they have much more power when they don't give up."[17]

The actions of Dr. Rosenberg in quickly launching and strongly guiding an innovative program of violence prevention gave clear notice that the subject of violence in the workplace was one that deserved wider attention, research, and community education. Although Rosenberg's efforts met with some strong opposition from other medical professionals, as well as a few special interest groups in Washington, D.C., his mandate was clear and his commitment unquestioned. The CDC began to actively dispense violence prevention grants, provide educational information, and gather statistical data as aggressively as possible, despite modest funding.

Agency efforts at collecting initial data on the subjects of workplace violence and occupational homicide were both effective and far-reaching, eventually drawing the attention of highly placed individuals in the Federal government. In 1984, C. Everett Koop, surgeon general of the U.S., stated that "violence in American public and private life has indeed assumed the proportions of an epidemic."[18] In making his statement, the surgeon general was reacting to the surveillance work undertaken by the CDC and its conclusion that workplace violence, including occupational homicide, was increasing at an alarming rate and must therefore be addressed as a public health issue.

The early efforts of the CDC were expanded each year and are carried on today by the National Center for Injury Control and the U.S. Department of Health and Human Services. The latter department includes the Centers for Disease Control and Prevention and the National Institute for Occupational Safety and Health—the two agencies most involved in the issues of workplace violence and occupational homicide. Of these agencies, NIOSH has become an abundant source of diverse information and statistical data on the specifics of violence in the workplace, providing regular reports and recommendations on the issues.

As events later in the 1980s would affirm, the early efforts undertaken by the CDC to support the program that was first led by Dr. Rosenberg were both significant and timely. One of the most horrendous incidents of mass violence ever experienced in the workplace occurred in 1986, and will be profiled in this study. The CDC and related agencies, because of their work on violence prevention begun three years earlier, were prepared to move ahead in their campaign to identify the causes of workplace violence by 1986. They were ready to offer violence prevention recommendations even as the Edmond, Oklahoma, post office massacre was still on the front pages of nearly every American newspaper.

Before 1986, most Americans were largely unaware of the issues of violence with which Dr. Rosenberg and his colleagues had become familiar. The imperative of national media attention that focused on the 1986 incident of occupational homicide in Oklahoma brought a new and frightening vision of potentially life-threatening violence to the attention of the general public. The dark nature of the post office massacre in Edmond was so unexpected and extreme that for many Americans, it changed forever their view of the sanctity and meaning of the workplace. For the CDC staff and Dr. Rosenberg, it must have provided a horrifying confirmation of what they had already recognized as a looming crisis of national importance.

A Public Awakening—The Edmond Post Office Massacre

Edmond, Oklahoma, is today a town typical of what many citizens mean when they use the term "mid-America." Located just north of Oklahoma City, in the central portion of the state, the community population is currently less than 50,000. At the time of the post office massacre, the population was under 35,000. To its residents, Edmond traditionally represented the best of what a mid-American community could offer in terms of family and work values.

Just after dawn, on August 20, 1986, Patrick Sherrill, a full-time substitute letter carrier, reported to the sprawling Edmond post office dressed in his usual blue uniform and carrying a mailbag over his shoulder. On this day, though, his mailbag concealed two loaded, .45-caliber pistols he had checked out from the National Guard Armory, where he was a member of the marksmanship team. He also carried in excess of 300 rounds of ammunition and a .22-caliber handgun, which was his own property.

Sherrill said nothing as he immediately walked up to the shift supervisor, Richard Esser, Jr., and shot him in the chest at close range. Still silent, Sherrill stalked more victims throughout the winding corridors of the Edmond post office. His rampage lasted for only ten minutes, but during that time, he managed to fire off 50 rounds and murder 14 employees. In a final act of violence, Sherrill turned one of the guns on himself and committed suicide.

This horrific crime inaugurated the era of the violent workplace in the press and the minds of many Americans. At the time, this incident was the third worst mass murder in American history, and one that shocked the public in a deeply personal way. There were relentless questions from across the nation, asking how and why this violence could have taken place in such an unlikely venue—such a peaceful mid-American town.

A postal union official blamed management for Sherrill's terrorism, but this position was not typical among post office employees interviewed by the press. A few employees said they thought that Sherrill's murderous rampage was an act of revenge, but others disagreed. The morning before the murders, Sherrill met with Esser and supervisor Bill Bland to discuss his work performance. Police sources stated that Bland threatened to terminate Sherrill; however, the U.S. Postal Service claimed this never had happened. If revenge was a motive for Sherrill, the details were not clear, and his actions were bizarre, seemingly without purpose.

Even if this horror was an act of revenge, why would an individual murder so many of his coworkers in an apparently indiscriminate manner? Where was the sense in such an act? To this day, such questions have not been answered satisfactorily despite other, similar workplace murders. Indiscriminate acts of murder are an unfortunate theme that will be seen to be repeated in other workplace slayings to be examined later in this book. Patrick Sherrill was, at the time, one of the most notoriously indiscriminate murderers in American history.

Sherrill was 44 years of age on August 20, 1986. He had lived on the same street for 20 years. According to his neighbors, Patrick Sherrill was sometimes referred to as "Crazy Pat" because of his strange behavior in the neighborhood. For example, at times, he would mow his lawn at midnight, peer into neighbor's windows while wearing combat fatigues, or tie up neighborhood dogs with baling wire. He was, by many neighborhood accounts, a loner and a strange individual.

In the workplace, Sherrill was viewed by coworkers as often angry and frequently depressed. There was no real evidence that his work performance had ever been seriously questioned even though it was obvious to many coworkers that he was a "problem" employee. A few of his coworkers described Sherrill as quiet and pleasant, but a person who preferred his own company to the usual workplace socialization. Other coworkers described him as a habitual complainer and a consistent nonperformer. Sherrill was, at best, enigmatic and not well understood by anyone who knew him. This would later prove to be a common profile for a potentially lethal employee.

Patrick Sherrill's mother, with whom he had lived all his life, died in 1974; after that, he lived alone. There was no evidence of unusual or traumatic incidents in his life before the post office killings. If some event in his personal life triggered Sherrill's actions on that August morning, no one knows of it or has offered it. It was known that Sherrill was scheduled to meet with his supervisor the morning of the murders to discuss performance issues. The supervisor, however, had no plans for formal disciplinary action. On the night before the murders, Sherrill made a call to his union representative to discuss a possible transfer to another post office location. Apparently, nothing came of that conversation. The fact that Sherrill made such a call, though, indicates that he had most likely not yet committed himself to murder as the only resolution to the issues troubling him.

Before taking the job as a letter carrier, Sherrill, an ex-Marine sharpshooter, held a number of short-term jobs as a file clerk, stockroom worker, and bicycle repairman. Two years before the shootings, Sherrill joined the National Guard. Because of his position on the marksmanship team, Sherrill was able to borrow handguns from the National Guard armory at his discretion. These were the weapons he used to murder his fellow employees. Sherrill was also able to check out a supply of "wadcutters"—special bullets with flat noses that expand when they enter a human target. This was the ammunition he used at the post office which accounted for so many fatal injuries. Throughout his life, Sherrill apparently held a strong fascination for weapons and was highly proficient in their use. He was also in a position to acquire them quickly and easily. These elements will be seen to be common to many workplace murderers.

A psychiatrist, who had never met or spoke with Sherrill, believed that the pattern of his life, and particularly his actions at the Edmond post office, indicated "factitious posttraumatic stress disorder." This was a disorder that, at the time, was thought to be relatively prevalent among Viet Nam war veterans, like Sherrill. Still, individuals who knew Sherrill personally and saw him on a frequent basis thought this unlikely. The most prevalent view of Sherrill's behavior indicated that he may have exhibited signs of depression. He had no history of mental illness, and in truth, no one knew if he was suffering from a psychological disorder, whether mild or severe. One of his former neighbors offered the following response when asked to describe Sherrill's mental state at the time of the killings: "He wasn't Rambo," insists Charles Thigpen, a onetime neighbor who remembers him [Sherrill] as a shy but gentle man who liked the words thank you and please. "We live in a time when we want quick answers. And since Pat's not alive to defend himself, they don't have to be the right answers."[19]

The fact is that no one was able to specifically account for Sherrill's actions, despite evidence that he exhibited several behavioral warning signs indicating potential violence. He left no clue behind, and said nothing during his rampage that would help elucidate his motives. He murdered at least one individual against whom he could have held a grudge (although this is not certain) and many others who were apparently selected at random or for reasons that can never be known.

The Edmond post office massacre is a Category Profile (CP) I, II, and V multiple homicide—not a rare or singular event. However, to relegate it to a simple category and dismiss it is to miss its true and lasting impact on American society. Of primary importance, the Sherrill case proved to be one of the prototypical scenarios for developing a predictable series of behavioral criteria common to workplace murderers.

The killings in Edmond received national press and television coverage. To this day, when asked, many individuals are able to recall the incident, if not the details.   Although violent crimes, including homicide, had been under scrutiny for some time by such organizations as the Centers for Disease Control, the public had little awareness of the potential threat inherent in the most seemingly safe job site, in what should have been among the most secure of American towns.   Sherrill's actions in 1986 permanently changed the American tradition of a workplace that is safe from the ultimate crime.   It is not an overstatement to say that a wave of concern swept America in the wake of the Edmond killings.   If such a heinous event could befall a quiet, safe town like Edmond, at a job site completely unprepared for any threat of violence, it could certainly occur in many other towns and cities throughout the nation.

For the purposes of this study, the actions of Patrick Sherrill establish an understanding of the true nature of occupational homicide and the impact it can have in the workplace and society.   Sherrill's background leads to an examination of points in common with other workplace murderers.   His actions just before and during the killings, in conjunction with other case histories of the crime, will help to formulate realistic prevention measures.   The hard truth that underlies this incident, though, cannot be ignored or, perhaps, ever fully comprehended.   Innocent individuals were ruthlessly murdered for actions they took in the workplace that were simply consistent with their job responsibilities.

A STATISTICAL VIEW OF WORKPLACE VIOLENCE (1980-1989)

From 1980 through 1989, 63,589 American workers died from injuries while working, and of these, 62,289 (98%) were in the civilian labor force. The third leading cause of death in the workplace for this period was homicide, representing 12% of all fatalities, as indicated in Figure 2.3.   This significant number of fatalities in the workplace translates to an annual occupational fatality rate of 7.0 individuals per 100,000 workers (all causes).   The actual number of workers who died by homicide during this decade was at least 7,600. During this period, the leading cause of death for females in the workplace was homicide.   These female victims accounted for 41% of all homicide fatalities.

When homicide data was examined by industry classification for the same period, it was found that occupational homicide represented the leading cause of death in six of the ten NIOSH industrial categories.   These are noted with an asterisk in Table 2.6.[20]

The total average annual rate of workplace homicides per 100,000 population for workers was 0.85, or about half of the annual rate for the single most prevalent cause of death—motor vehicles—for the decade ending in 1989.

When homicide data was examined by occupational classification it was found that occupational homicide was the leading cause of death in 6 of the 11

NIOSH occupational categories. These are noted with an asterisk in Table 2.7.[21]

Figure 2.3: Causes of Occupational Death
(as a Percentage of All Workplace Fatalities, 1980-1989)

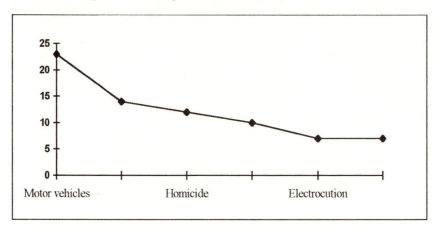

Of all homicide victims, 80% were male. Although homicide was the leading cause of death in the workplace for females, male workers were three times more likely to be murdered at work than their female counterparts. Half of the victims of homicide were between the ages of 25 and 44 years. Approximately 75% of homicide victims were white, 19% were black, and 6% were described as other races. The most frequently used weapon was some type of gun, which accounted for a full 75% to 80% of all occupational homicides. Only 14% of fatalities were caused by a knife or other cutting weapon.

Some places of work presented a significantly higher risk of homicide than others. NIOSH provided data on nine general work environments, with corresponding numbers and rates of homicide summarized in Table 2.7.[22]

VIOLENCE IN THE WORKPLACE TODAY

Violence in the workplace is now at epidemic levels, according to data provided by the U.S. Department of Justice and Bureau of Justice Statistics. In a report released in July 1994, the Bureau of Justice Statistics offered the following data:[23]

1. About 1 million individuals are the victims of some form of violent crime in the workplace each year. This represents approximately 15% of all violent crimes committed annually in America. Approximately 60% of these violent crimes were categorized as "simple assault" by the Department of Justice.
2. Of all workplace violent crimes reported, over 80% were committed by males; 40% were committed by complete strangers to the victims, 35% by casual acquaintances, 19% by individuals well known to the victims, and 1% by relatives of the victims.

3. Over half the incidents (56%) were not reported to police, although 26% were reported to at least one official in the workplace.
4. In 62% of workplace violent crimes, the perpetrator was not armed; in 30% of the incidents, the perpetrator was armed with a handgun.
5. In 84% of the incidents, there were no reported injuries; 10% required medical intervention.
6. Of all violent incidents, 61% occurred in private companies, 30% in government agencies, and 8% to individuals who were self-employed. At the time of this survey, 18% of the workforce was employed by the government.
7. It is estimated that violent crime in the workplace caused some 500,000 employees to miss 1.751 million days of work annually, or an average of 3.5 days per incident. This missed work equated to approximately $55 million in lost wages.

Table 2.5: Annual Fatalities (by Industry)

Industry Classification	Fatalities per 100,000 population
Agriculture/Forestry/Fishing	0.57
Mining	0.48
Construction	0.65
Manufacturing	0.27
Transportation/Commerce/Utilities	1.47 *
Wholesale Trade	0.19 *
Retail Trade	1.66 *
Finance/Insurance/Real Estate	0.39 *
Service	0.61 *
Public Administration	1.54 *

* Leading cause of death is occupational homicide.

Table 2.6: Annual Fatalities (by Occupation)

Occupational Classification	Fatalities per 100,000 Population
Executive/Administrative/Managerial	0.90 *
Professional/Specialist	0.26 *
Technical/Support	0.12
Sales	1.36 *
Clerical	0.18 *
Service	0.97 *
Farm/Forestry/Fishing	0.49
Crafts	0.42
Machine Operators	0.20
Transportation	1.50 *
Laborers	1.48

* Leading cause of death is occupational homicide.

Table 2.7: Workplace Homicide Data

Workplace	Homicides	Rate per 100,000 Population
Taxicab establishments	287	26.9
Liquor stores	115	8.0
Gas stations	304	5.6
Protective services	152	5.0
Justice/public order	640	3.4
Grocery stores	806	3.2
Jewelry stores	56	3.2
Hotels/motels	153	1.5
Eating/drinking places	734	1.5

In April 1994, *USA Today Magazine* reported on the results of a survey undertaken by the Society for Human Resource Management (SHRM). These results provided an additional view of violence in the workplace from the point of view of human resource managers.[24] The total number of responses to the survey was 479. Although this information cannot be considered as reliable as the data provided by NIOSH (due to the subjectivity of some of the questions), the results are illuminating and give a certain feel for violence in the workplace today. The SHRM survey revealed the following information:[ii]

1. Regarding violent incidents in the workplace:
    1.1. 33% of all managers surveyed experienced at least one violent incident in the workplace.
    1.2. 32% of these managers noted that one or more of the acts had occurred since 1989.
    1.3. 54% of these managers reported between two and five acts of violence in the five years prior to the survey.
2. Regarding the type of violence experienced:
    2.1. 75% of the reported incidents were fistfights.
    2.2. 17% of the incidents were shootings.
    2.3. 8% of the incidents were stabbings.
    2.4. 6% of the incidents were sexual assaults.
3. Regarding the victims of the incidents:
    3.1. 54% of the incidents were employee against employee.
    3.2. 13% of the incidents were employee against a supervisor.
    3.3. 7% of the incidents were clients against worker(s).
4. Regarding the sex of the perpetrator:

---

ii. The survey results shown here have been categorized to best suit the purpose of this study. The categories used are not present in the original *USA Today Magazine* article.

4.1. 80% of all violent acts were committed by males.
5. Regarding the injuries sustained by the victims:
   5.1. 22% of the incidents involved serious harm.
   5.2. 42% of the incidents required medical intervention.
6. Regarding the reasons for the violent incidents:
   6.1. 38% were attributed to "personality conflicts."
   6.2. 15% were attributed to "marital or family problems."
   6.3. 10% were attributed to "drug or alcohol abuse."
   6.4. .7% were nonspecific as to attribution.
   6.5 .7% were attributed to "firing or layoff."
7. Regarding crisis management programs:
   7.1. 28% of the organizations had a crisis management program in place prior to the violent incident.
   7.2. 12% of the organizations implemented a crisis management program after the violent incident occurred.
8. Regarding the effect of a violent incident on the workplace:
   8.1. 41% of the organizations reported increased stress levels in the workplace after a violent incident.
   8.2. 20% reported "higher levels of paranoia."
   8.3. 18% reported "increased distrust" among employees.

This survey did not focus on homicide to the exclusion of other forms of violence in the workplace, and therefore, the results of the survey indicate a good deal about the prevalence, nature, and result of violent workplace incidents generally. If the responses are considered to be substantially reliable, this survey clearly indicates that the American workplace is becoming even more violent than was determined by the original NIOSH survey information.

NIOSH data advised that 2 million Americans reported being physically attacked at work in 1992. The estimated medical cost of these injuries was $13.5 billion.[25] The estimated number of employees injured in 1993 was more than 2.2 million.[26] There have been at least 750 workers murdered in the workplace each year between 1980 and 1989, and this number continues to grow.[27] By 1992, the annual number of occupational homicides in the United States exceeded 1,000. In that same year there were over 111,000 significantly violent incidents, which cost employers an estimated $6.2 billion in lost wages, medical, and support costs.[28]

Additional information about occupational homicide and violence in the workplace has been sporadically reported by a variety of media and other sources. These reports, although varying in their consistency and reliability, each tend to support the data previously presented and indicate that the workplace has become more dangerous in the 1990s than it was in the 1980s.

In 1992 the National Crime Victimization Survey disclosed that over 650,000 workers were assaulted while at work; this represented about 11% of all violent crimes committed in the United States that year. In the same year, Northwestern Life Insurance Company surveyed 600 full-time employees to learn more about workplace violence. The survey noted that 3% of workers had been physically attacked, 7% had been threatened, and 19% had been harassed.[29]

Information in the media, though scattered, also supports the conclusion that workplace violence is growing at an alarming rate:

1. In February 1994, *Safety and Health Magazine* stated that, in 1992, approximately 2 million Americans reported being physically attacked at work. These incidents resulted in $13.5 billion in medical costs.[30]
2. *Business and Society Review*, in their Spring 1994 issue, reported that in 1992, 17% of all fatal injuries in the workplace resulted from occupational homicide. Over 80% of these victims were killed with guns.[31]
3. *Psychology Today*, in their January/February 1994 issue, stated there were "more than 2,000 [violent] incidents in American post offices in the last four years alone."[32] This number is considered to be conservative.
4. In an article specifically aimed at workplace homicide within the U. S. Postal Service, *Training and Development* magazine noted that 36 workers had been killed and an additional 20 injured at postal premises around the nation between 1986 and 1993.[33]
5. The September 1994 issue of *Redbook* magazine sported a major headline that read, "Shootings are the #2 cause of death in the workplace."[34] Although no citation was specifically provided for this piece of information, the statistic appeared to be supported by other publications available in the latter half of 1994 and early 1995.
6. In August 1994, the California Department of Industrial Relations released a detailed report on workplace homicide. In that report the department noted that 195 Californians were victims of workplace homicide in 1993, a 22% increase from the previous year. During the same year, 125 workers died in traffic accidents. Thus, for the first time in California history, murder surpassed traffic accidents as a cause of death in the workplace. The report also stated that women in the workplace were increasingly becoming at risk because domestic violence was frequently spilling over to the job site. Nearly half the women who died on the job in 1993 were victims of occupational homicide.

Americans are now beginning to fully understand that workplace violence is a problem of national scope which can effect anyone. In a TIME/Cable Network News (CNN) general population poll taken in April 1994, 37% of those surveyed cited workplace violence as a growing problem in the nation. Of the respondents, 18% had personally witnessed some form of workplace violence, and the same number (18%) feared for their own safety at work.[35] This growing awareness represents the first step in an organization's ability to enact strong violence prevention techniques in the workplace.

IMPACT OF OCCUPATIONAL HOMICIDE

Even a cursory review of current occupational homicide statistics can be chilling. Regardless of profession, a worker is more likely to be murdered on the job than to be fatally injured by a fall, electrocution, or being struck by a falling object. If the worker is employed in an office without dangerous machinery and is not using a vehicle, he or she is more likely to be murdered at work than to be killed by any other cause. In some states, such as California, a worker is just as likely to be murdered on the job as to die in an automobile accident while commuting to or from work.

The single employment profile of a typical office employee accounts for a vast number of American workers who are currently at risk on the job. Because many of the new jobs being created in America are targeted for just this kind of work environment, the implication for an increase in future workplace homicides cannot be ignored. Table 2.8 indicates those occupations that are expected to experience an increase of at least 100,000 new jobs by the year 2000 and are therefore at increased risk for workplace violence.[36] Many of these occupations are typically found within the common definition of an "office workplace environment."

Table 2.8: Projected Job Growth to the Year 2000

Occupation	Numerical Growth	% Growth
Medical assistants	104,000	70.0
Home health aids	207,000	63.3
Medical secretaries	120,000	58.0
Financial services	109,000	54.8
Systems analysts	214,000	53.3
Programmers	250,000	48.1
Electronic engineers	176,000	40.1
Receptionists	331,000	39.8
Registered nurses	613,000	38.9
Practical nurses	229,000	36.6
Guards	256,000	32.3
Nursing aids	378,000	31.9
Lawyers	180,000	31.0
Waiters/waitresses	551,000	30.9
Food service managers	161,000	28.8
Child care workers	186,000	27.8
Cooks	155,000	27.2

A retail store employee or government worker is not only more likely to die from homicide in the workplace than any other cause but is almost four times more likely to be murdered on the job than a miner is likely to be killed in an industrial accident. A taxicab driver is five times more likely to be murdered at work than a police officer. A gas station attendant has a slightly worse outlook for survivability than a police officer when occupational homicide is the cause of death. With the significant increase in government and service jobs in the past two decades and the outlook for continued growth in these areas, is it not reasonable to assume an even worse scenario by the next century?

On a national basis, at least one-third of American workplaces have experienced some form of violence in the past five years. Two thirds of these incidents were among employees and supervisors. Somewhere between 7% and 33% of other violent incidents involved clients in one manner or another. Most workplace murderers are male, as are their victims. However, a female in the workplace is more likely to be murdered on the job than to die from any other cause. Most shocking of all is the fact that more than 50% of the NIOSH industry classifications and over 50% of the NIOSH occupational classifications indicate homicide as the leading cause of death in the workplace.

By conservative estimate, over 1,400 Americans will be victims of occupational homicide this year. In many states, such as California, workplace homicide may again be the leading cause of employee death. This mortality rate is double that experienced by American workers less than ten years ago. While occupational fatalities for reasons other than homicide have decreased during the past ten years, murder has shown an alarming and unrelenting increase. There is little reason to expect a reversal of this trend in the near future. If the current rate of annual increase continues, it is possible that over 2,500 Americans will be victims of occupational homicide in the year 2000. The impact of these murders on the families of the victims, employers, coworkers, and society is largely inestimable, but clearly horrific.

Years of Potential Life Lost

The National Institute for Occupational Safety and Health (NIOSH) defined a methodology to account for the number of years of work lost by the premature death of a worker. This calculation, known as *years of potential life lost* (YPLL), is defined as: 65 years minus worker age at the time of death. The result of this calculation, or years of potential life lost, represents the number of years a worker would have been expected to be employed until the assumed retirement age of 65 years.

Assuming that the average age of an occupational homicide victim is 35 years, the YPPL for that individual is 30 years. The YPPL for a 40-year-old victim would be 25 years. Assuming that the median age of all occupational homicide victims is 35 years, and assuming 1,400 homicides during the course of a year, the national YPPL would be 42,000 years for that 12 month period.

Such large losses are of considerable economic and social impact when considered on a national scale. Not considered in this calculation is the additional work loss that can be attributed to organizational shifting necessary to manage the resultant workplace crisis, additional employee and survivor support, establishment of emergency work procedures to ensure business survival, and the eventual replacement of the victims in the workforce.

Costs of Organizational Change

An organization that experiences occupational homicide is affected in ways that are largely unforeseen and rarely mitigated by planning. Costs incurred by the organization can be staggering and often involve all the following areas:[37]

1. reestablishment of workplace security,
2. reorganization and general repair of premises,
3. losses suffered through business interruption,
4. loss of good public relations,
5. a general decrease in workplace productivity,
6. a general increase in employee absences,
7. a general increase in employee turnover,
8. a general increase in worker's compensation costs,
9. a general increase in employee medical costs,
10. a general increase in insurance premium costs,
11. unforeseen, and often significant, legal fees,
12. cost of additional medical support or counseling for employees and families, and
13. a general increase in employee benefits costs.

It is probable that any organization experiencing a workplace homicide will face most, if not all, of these additional financial obligations. The extent of each of these costs can not be determined prior to an incident and, in many cases, will be substantial.

General Cost Impact

It is difficult to precisely measure the cost impact of violence in the workplace and studies that address this issue tend to vary wildly in their dollar cost estimates. Regardless of the study selected, however, there is agreement that the costs are both staggering and increasing each year at an alarming rate.

In 1993 a joint study was undertaken by the National Safe Workplace Institute and Behavior Analysts and Consultants, Inc., to determine the dollar effects of workplace violence. The report issued by these organizations stated that more than $4 billion was spent by American companies in dealing with the effects of workplace violence. The estimated medical costs incurred by victims of workplace violence in 1992 was in excess of $13.5 billion; the estimate for 1993 was in excess of $15 billion. In addition to this, the report noted that employers can often pay in excess of $250,000 directly to the victims of workplace violence for each single incident.[38] A study by Liability Consultants, Inc., recently reported that "a jury typically awards $2.2 million for a workplace related death and $1.8 for a [workplace] rape."[39]

Liability Issues

Employers who fail to take adequate workplace safety measures can be held liable for certain violent acts committed by employees. Organizational liability in this area can be very broad and include direct or indirect management involvement such as the failure to perform background checks before hiring a violent employee or failing to provide an adequate violence prevention program for staff.[40] Workplace incidents such as threats, physical altercations, or incidents of intimidation may also pave the way for later employer liability in the event of a murder in the workplace.[41]

Management Review, in March 1994, reported the following statement regarding employer liability for workplace violence:

Courts have ruled that employers owe a duty of care toward their employees, customers and business associates to take reasonable steps to prevent violence on their premises and by their employees. Employers who ignore potential workplace violence may well find themselves involved in negligence suits for failing to provide a reasonably safe workplace or for hiring and supervising an employee who turns violent.

For example, in Illinois, an employer was found liable for negligent hiring and supervision when its doorman, who had been in previous fights, assaulted a patron. And, in Virginia, a church was found liable when an employee with a recent conviction for child molestation raped a 10-year-old. Other ideas of liability may be presented as well. For example, in California, workers' compensation liability for any employee injured in an attack can also include payment for psychological trauma.

In Minnesota, for instance, an employer was found liable for negligent supervision, retention and hiring after it hired an employee with a previous manslaughter conviction who made a death threat and then murdered a coworker while off-duty. [42]

The liability of employers was well established in the late 1980s by a series of verdicts dealing with the issue of wrongful death in the workplace. The view that employers may be liable for many forms of workplace violence is now well established in law and quick to be recognized by juries.

One of the largest wrongful death verdicts in the state of California occurred in 1989 and centered on the issue of occupational homicide. On July 10, 1980, a security guard, who worked for the Bank of America in Los Angeles, was shot to death during a robbery attempt. He was 38 years old at the time of the homicide. The decedent's wife sued the employer, contending the following points of negligence:

1. the bank should have provided two full-time security guards rather than the one full-time and one part-time guards employed;
2. the bank should not have assigned non-security tasks to the guards while they were on duty;
3. the bank should not have provided stools for use by the guards in that this created an additional hazard; and,
4. the bank's negligent security contributed to the decedent's death.

The trial was held in 1989 and lasted 11 days. After 4 days of deliberation, the jury awarded the decedent's wife and children a total settlement in excess of $7 million.[43] Clearly, the jury felt the defendant was negligent in the extreme. On the face of this case summary, however, it is difficult to explain the degree of negligence that must have been apparent to the jurors. Although awards of this nature are rare, there is sufficient precedent to show that any employer may be held liable for occupational homicide, even after having made a good-faith effort to provide a safe workplace.

BEHAVIORAL CHARACTERISTICS OF THE VIOLENT WORKER

Because occupational homicide cuts across virtually every aspect of American society, it is emerging as a subject of importance to psychologists and psychiatrists as well as organizational managers. As questions arise about this issue, a singular theme can be identified—is it possible to identify potentially violent workers or clients before they commit to action?   An aid to understanding the warning signs of potential violence can be found in the behavioral sciences.

Homicide is defined by the California Penal Code, Section 187, as "the killing of a human being, or a fetus, with malice aforethought."[44]   It is the most heinous of crimes, but often, the behavior and motivations of the perpetrator are not well understood.   How, then, can a potentially violent individual be identified in time to prevent the crime in the workplace?

From a clinical viewpoint, the risk of homicide is great in persons suffering from psychosis that is characterized by persecutory delusions, particularly if such delusions have become focused upon a single individual. Risk is also high when an individual has a history of violence, displays a pattern of defiance of authority, or suffers from an antisocial personality disorder. Further increasing the risk are activities such as substance or alcohol abuse, a history of jealous obsessions, or unresolved sexual conflicts.[45]

Although this is a rather sterile and short view of factors that increase the risk of a homicidal act, they provide a common point of understanding that can lead to a possible prediction of violence. Later in this study several profiles of the potentially violent employee will be offered.   These profiles provide a practical checklist of warning signs often observed in persons prone to violent acts. At the heart of these profiles will be found many of the characteristics just enumerated as high risk factors for homicidal behavior.

Regardless of the source of potential violence or the venue in which it may occur, a rudimentary understanding of the behavioral dynamics of the violent individual can be helpful. As will be seen from the case histories that follow, it often happens that the individual who is prone to a violent act exhibits predictable patterns of behavior before the crime is committed. It is important to remember, however, that such predictable patterns of behavior are not always in evidence or, if present, not always readily observable in the workplace. On the balance, though, an awareness of key behavioral patterns exhibited by potentially violent individuals can be beneficial in protecting employees and the organization since many perpetrators telegraph their aggressive intentions well before they act on them.

The Importance of a Profile

To help ensure a safe workplace, staff must be skilled in identifying potential violence among employees, former employees, or clients. To some degree, this skill can be learned from a careful study of historical incidents of occupational homicide, in combination with knowledge gained from the behavioral sciences. In an ideal violence prevention program, all workers possess well-developed recognition skills combined with a coordinated effort between management and staff to recognize potential violence and provide positive, proactive intervention for affected individuals. This unified process must, however, always start with an individual worker's ability to recognize the profile of potential violence.

Ten behavioral criteria have been recognized in the literature as significant indicators that are generally associated with individuals who may become violent.[46] These criteria are comprised of identifiable behavioral characteristics, an understanding of which can greatly increase the likelihood of identifying an individual who poses a threat to others. These characteristics are so common to the violent individual that it is rare to discover an incident of workplace violence or occupational homicide that has not been preceded by one or more of the warning signs.[47]

Although these criteria are of great value because of their reliability, some are of a technical nature. Several of the categories deal with complex modalities of behavior, which demand considerable training to detect with a high degree of accuracy. Other behavior patterns are more easily understood and recognized, however. An understanding of each of these categories of behavior does, however, provide a strong basis for recognizing a potentially violent individual.

In presenting the criteria, an emphasis will be placed on definitions of use to workplace personnel to assist them in recognizing potentially violent behavior and aid in training staff in the recognition process. Each element will be defined and evaluated with respect to its potential importance to workplace managers and staff. The focus here will not be on a complete understanding of complex behavior patterns, but rather on the importance of the recognition process:

1. *History of Violence.* This is generally considered to be one of the most reliable predictors of potential violence. If an individual has a history of violence, he or she is much more likely to commit violent acts in the future.

   Evaluation: It is not always possible to know the history of an individual to surety. Nor is it inevitable that an individual with a violent history will necessarily act violently in the future. A history of violence must, however, be of significant concern to workplace personnel. Screening of prospective employees may disclose previous violent crimes or activities. However, sometimes an individual's prior violent past may remain hidden despite background research or screening. The background of clients may typically be unknown except in certain specialized professions. As relationships develop in the workplace, an individual's violent past may become known to coworkers; or, on the other hand, it may be something that is never discussed.   Although historical knowledge is a primary indicator of future violence, such knowledge implies information that is often difficult to obtain and typically not shared voluntarily by individuals.   Nonetheless, this element is considered to be of such importance that, whenever possible and legal, efforts should be made to disclose a history of violence before an individual is employed. If, in the course of employment, it becomes apparent that a worker has a clearly violent history, the resulting information should be shared with management so that maximum safety in the workplace can be assured.   No doubt, such a recommendation may prove distasteful to some employees who fear they may develop a reputation as a "snitch" among the workforce.   Further thought on the matter, though, should make it clear that there is a higher goal to judiciously sharing such information.   Of crucial importance is a clear message from management that any information provided by workers will be held in confidence and used only to benefit and protect the workplace and the employees.

2.   *Psychosis*.   Psychosis includes a number of disorders that are complex and difficult to interpret for those not trained in psychiatry or psychology.   Such terms as *schizophrenia* or *paranoia*—elements that can be included in the broad definition of psychosis—are used in workplace conversations frequently, but they are generally not understood, or are misunderstood, by members of the workforce.

Psychosis can be defined as a "loss of contact with reality" or a "loss of the ability to process experience appropriately."[48]   Although not identical, these two brief definitions provide a basic understanding of psychosis.   This general disorder encompasses specific ailments such as paranoid states, major affective disorders, and schizophrenia.   A psychosis may last for only a few hours or days, in which case it is considered transient, or it may last for many months or years.

Some of the more pronounced manifestations of psychosis are:[49]

1.   disordered thought process,
2.   loose or disjointed associations in speech,
3.   extreme ambivalence,
4.   inappropriate or flat facial expression,
5.   hallucinations (if schizophrenic),
6.   verbalizing with thoughts (if schizophrenic), and
7.   bizarre and sometimes persistent delusions.

Evaluation: From the point of view of a manager or worker, someone suffering from a psychosis will generally exhibit behavior that is quite obviously strange and uncomfortable to others.   The behavior is sometimes quite bizarre and nearly always a point of conversation in the workplace.   Perhaps the behavior will instill fear in others, or it may be seen as humorous or eccentric but unsavory.   Workers displaying this type of behavior are typically avoided by coworkers if their disability is at all evident.   Employees may simply try to ignore such behavior and make an effort to avoid becoming involved.   Nonetheless, the potential for violence may be inherent in the behavior displayed; thus, the behavior itself should never be ignored.   The important underlying concepts to keep in mind when attempting to recognize psychosis are "loss of contact with reality" or "loss of the ability to process experience appropriately."   Should a worker exhibit extremes of behavior, such as grandiose ideas, delusions of persecution, an inability to distinguish fantasy from reality, jealous rages, bizarre sexual attractions or relations, or uncontrollable mood swings, there may be reason to suspect a psychological disorder.   Such warning signs are indicators of potential violence which may erupt unpredictably and with lethal effect. A psychotic individual is one who requires prompt and professional intervention for his or her own sake and that of other workers.

3. *Romance Obsession (Erotomania).* This category can also be considered a form of psychosis, and one that is more common than would be expected by most individuals. This disorder has received national publicity in recent years due to the stalking, and even murder, of prominent figures in the entertainment industry.

The layperson's understanding of erotomania is that it is a romantic or sexual attraction, but this is not the case. Erotomania is an obsessive state of erotic delusion in which idealized love reaches almost spiritual dimensions. Often, the object of this malformed attraction is unaware of its extent or, in the beginning, even its existence. Suffering from such a disorder, an individual may resort to spying on or stalking his or her target. He or she may send love letters, taped conversations, or gifts. Frequent telephone calls may occur.

Evaluation: When the person who is the object of this obsession fails to respond or responds negatively, violence can be the result. The highly publicized case of Richard Farley is a classic example of the extreme violence that can result from this disorder: "Laura Black finally filed a temporary restraining order against Richard Farley, former coworker and unemployed computer technician, after almost three years of romantic harassment. Farley could not stand the suffering she put him through and entered his former workplace. Firing over 110 rounds of ammunition, he killed seven individuals and wounded three others. Laura Black, although wounded, survived."[50]

This disorder has become the focus of much attention in recent years and has been well documented in the media. The Richard Farley case is one that points out the kind of indiscriminate violence that can result from erotomania, although mass murder is not a common result of this disorder. Even without a complete understanding of the nature of erotomania, the warning signs exhibited by an individual suffering from this disorder are typically clear and frequent. The key point in recognizing this disorder is the awareness of a persistent and unrelenting obsession with another individual as manifested in behavior that is clearly abnormal in scope and duration.

4. *Chemical Dependence.* Chemical dependence that leads to criminal behavior or violence is a subject well known in American society and in the American workplace. The behavioral characteristics of a person under the influence of drugs or alcohol are also generally well known. Because the problem of substance abuse is of national scope and touches the lives of so many Americans, many organizations provide a variety of information resources and assistance programs to their employees. Many federal and state agencies also provide current information to help managers identify workers with chemical dependence disorders; several of these agencies will assist with intervention programs or referrals as appropriate.

Evaluation: A large number of drugs exist, and are readily available, that create states of aggression in the user. Other substances may induce feelings of paranoia or depression. The effects of alcohol are well documented. When alcohol is taken in conjunction with drugs, the combination makes for a potentially lethal result. Drugs and alcohol impair reasoning, reduce inhibitions and can induce extremely aggressive or violent behavior. Fortunately, many companies provide training in recognizing substance abuse and dealing with it as a physiological condition. It is not uncommon for larger organizations to provide intervention programs or rehabilitation programs to assist employees who become victims of substance abuse.

This benefit is not as common in smaller businesses. Substance abuse is such a pervasive problem in the workplace that this study will devote a separate section to the subject, which will identify commonly abused substances and briefly outline their effects so that identification of the problem in the workplace can be more successful.

5. *Depression.* By many accounts, depression is the most common psychological disorder in the United States. Counselors and therapists estimate that as many as one in seven individuals suffering from depression will commit a violent act against others or themselves. Although depression is a common ailment, it may be difficult to detect by someone other than a medical professional. Table 2.9 offers an outline of some of the most common behavior patterns associated with depression:[51]

Table 2.9: Signs of Depression

Loss of interest in usual activities
Decreased energy levels
Difficulty sleeping
Feelings of worthlessness or guilt
Thoughts of death of suicide
Expressions of despair or hopelessness
Sorrowful appearance
Increased irritability
Change in appetite
Possible psychomotor agitation
Loss of usual efficiency levels
Inappropriate levels of guilt
Deterioration of physical appearance

Evaluation: It is unfortunate that depression, like other mental illnesses, is generally not dealt with proactively by employers. Since it is such a common and potentially devastating disorder, depression intervention and assistance should be given a high priority in any employee wellness program. Once again, employee assistance programs can provide the support needed to successfully intervene with a worker who is suffering from depression. Many medical benefit programs also encompass at least some form of out-patient treatment or evaluative procedure to take the first critical steps necessary to assist a worker suffering from this disorder. Depression is a serious illness, and one that implies intervention by a professional in order to be overcome.

6. *The Pathological Blamer.* The pathological blamer views the world as progenitor of all his or her problems. Regardless of the situation, this individual will find some person who is at fault or some organization upon which to cast blame. In addition to laying blame, the individual will commonly make threats to "get even" for the wrong that was suffered. The pathological blamer will refuse to admit mistakes or misjudgments, always looking to another for the cause of his or her problems.

Evaluation: For those who have spent some time in the workforce, this behavior pattern will, at first, seem familiar and common. There is, however, an order-of-magnitude difference between the employee who complains and the pathological blamer, who may commit an act of violence. The pathological blamer is often relentless in casting blame, intimidating in assigning fault, and threatening when speaking of consequences.   Supervisors or managers may sometimes interpret employee comments as complaints when the employee is simply trying to ensure that his or her point is heard and understood. Supervisors should be very careful to listen attentively and understand any employee comment so as to separate important and unimportant issues. Obviously, there is a substantial difference between an employee who blames a specific individual or group for an obvious grievance and one who blames indiscriminately. Still, those who cast blame and make any type of threat should always be taken seriously by management personnel and coworkers. The pathological blamer can quickly become a violent employee if ignored.

Thomas Harpley, a security consultant quoted in *Occupational Hazards* magazine, provided this observation about the pathological blamer: "Ten years ago, I would have interpreted those comments [constantly blaming] as someone blowing off steam. Now, I encourage employers to take them seriously because that is one of the primary warning signs of a person who is on the verge of acting out. They very often make comments about previous workplace violence incidents that have been publicized."[52]

The most reliable test of this issue must be a commonsense approach to the subject of concern expressed by an employee. Should an individual constantly blame the organization, or its members, for a wide variety of nonspecific or irrelevant matters, it is possible that the behavior is pathological. If this is the case, the organization may be at risk. On the other hand, many acts of blaming can have a root cause that is valid and should be addressed. Although the distinction between legitimate complaints and irrelevant blaming may seem vague in theory, it becomes quite clear from a daily management perspective. Pathological blamers are constant complainers whose sufferings, no matter how unrelated, are almost always attributed to the organization or its employees. Should the blaming become threatening or hostile, the most prudent course is to take it seriously and act to protect the staff and organization accordingly.

7. *Impaired Neurological Functioning.* This category will generally not be of significant benefit to workplace personnel without the application of a commonsense approach to knowing the behavioral characteristics of familiar employees or clients. The subject of impaired neurological functioning is complex and technical, with wide ranging variances in behavior patterns.   Individuals suffering from a neurological disorder may demonstrate hyperactivity, aggression, or lack of inhibition.

Evaluation: Generally, for the supervisor or manager, these patterns of behavior can not be assigned to a specific category with assurance; nor is such an assignment at all necessary. Ironically, the best guide for detecting abnormal behavior is often a simple feeling or instinct by, or in, the observer. If an observed behavior is uncomfortably aggressive or unusual and starts to form a pattern, it may be a warning sign of potential violence.   Previously unrecognized sources of neurologically related health risks are now beginning to be researched and documented. For example, it is possible that some workers, when exposed to certain solvents in the workplace, can suffer health consequences that include violent personality changes. Some of these solvents can be absorbed by employees through their lungs or skin and, with chronic exposure, this can result in erratic or extremely violent behavior. Although these incidents are not frequent, the hazards posed by certain chemical substances used in the workplace require the attention of safety and risk management personnel, as well as health staff.[53] This specialized area of concern can be researched using the resources of the Occupational Safety and Health Administration (OSHA) at the federal level or one of several safety and illness prevention agencies common to the various states in America. References to organizations which may be of assistance in this area are provided in the Appendix.

8. *Elevated Frustration with the Environment.* Should an employee begin to express a growing frustration generally or frustration with elements outside the workplace, it may represent an early warning sign of potential violence. Individuals must deal with a variety of situations and environments apart from the workplace. Sometimes employees bring these concerns with them to the job site. It is simply not possible for all individuals to wholly separate their experiences on the job from those away from work. Should an employee show a significant and sustained level of frustration with elements outside the employment arena, it is possible that violence resulting from these frustrations could occur at work.

  Evaluation: In recent years, violence resulting from deteriorating personal relationships outside of work, which is then acted on at the job site, has become common in the media; it is often referred to as "spillover" violence. Relationships of importance often exist in the work environment and may provide the necessary support system for individuals experiencing frustrations away from the job. Employees who do not benefit from these work relationships may experience, and express, increasing frustrations but have no viable way of finding assistance. The astute use of an employee assistance program may prove crucial in addressing this issue with an effected employee. Many of these programs provide a support vehicle for employees suffering from disruption outside the workplace which may spill over to the job site; they are usually capable of making referrals for long-term counseling, if needed.

9. *Interest in Weapons.* As several of the case histories in this study will demonstrate, an unusual interest in weapons or paramilitary topics can often be found in those who commit murder in the workplace. Individuals who collect a variety of weapons that are traditionally designed for use in the military or law enforcement services are sometimes providing a clear warning sign of potentially violent behavior. When this interest develops to the level of a fascination, or fetish, there is evidence of imminent and unpredictable danger.

  Evaluation: Americans treasure the right to bear arms, and the mere fact that an individual collects weapons does not indicate a potential problem. At what point an interest in weapons collection becomes unhealthy is difficult to assess. An individual who brings weapons to the job site, displays an obvious fetish for weapons or paramilitary subjects, or discusses these issues as a predominant theme may be exhibiting critical behavioral warning signs. It is possible that a thorough assessment of an individual in the pre-hiring process may disclose a history of this type of behavior. This is also a category of behavior that can benefit from the positive flow of information from staff to management in a combined effort to protect the work environment.

10. *Personality Disorders.* This is a difficult category and one best left to the medical profession for absolute determination and analysis. Even so, there are situations arising in the workplace that may indicate that an employee is suffering from a disorder requiring professional intervention. Such a disorder, if ignored, could result in violence. When the personality of a known worker changes radically and remains changed for some period of time, this may be a warning sign of potential trouble.

Personality is a set of behavior patterns that are generally consistent and help define an individual over a long period of time. When this consistency slips away—when personality patterns change radically and the change is more than fleeting—there may be cause for concern. Two specific types of personality disorder that have a strong relationship to workplace violence are termed *antisocial* and *borderline*.

A. *Antisocial Personality Disorder:* Individuals suffering from this disorder are commonly referred to as *sociopaths*. This disorder is most often found in males. The characteristics of a sociopath include extremely aggressive behavior, irritability, a delight with intimidating others, little or no social conscience about wrongdoing, destructive tendencies, and a highly impulsive nature. These individuals often own weapons and are interested in paramilitary subjects. Sociopaths are likely to lie easily, and have a poor or erratic work history, demonstrate poor job performance, and experience recurring periods of unemployment. They are usually unable to sustain a close relationship with others, and are prone to both domestic and workplace violence.[54]

B. *Borderline Personality Disorder:* These individuals tend to be highly unstable in their work habits and home lives. They are unable to set a direction for themselves or make decisions that give their lives proper direction. A person suffering from borderline personality disorder will exhibit a great deal of uncertainty about many aspects of his or her life. They tend to be moody and irritable, yet may be quite effective at manipulating others. These individuals are preoccupied with their own personality and problems, rarely reaching out to others. They may act in erratic and unpredictable ways, often to their own detriment.[55]

Evaluation: These two disorders may seem familiar when considered in conjunction with several of the case histories to be presented. The kinds of behavior exhibited by both the sociopath (antisocial personality disorder) and the person suffering from borderline personality disorder are frequently found among individuals who commit murder in the workplace. Although it is true that workers, supervisors, and managers cannot be expected to accurately determine such fine distinctions of pathology, the more obvious aberrations in behavior can, and should, be recognized as key elements in any prevention program.

Understanding potentially violent behavior is an excellent deterrent to a workplace crisis. Once such behavior is recognized, knowledge of it must be shared with key management personnel so that appropriate intervention can take place. Coworkers should be encouraged to advise management if a member of their group exhibits questionable behavior or is consistently exhibiting the warning signs described in this section. To best accomplish this, workers should be trained to recognize potentially violent behavior and encouraged to seek help from the supervisory staff. The supervisory staff, in turn, must be trained in the proper methods of intervention and workplace safety. In order to overcome workers' fears of retaliation, management must have a support mechanism in place for those who come forward with reports of disruptive behavior. The key component is the ability of each worker to recognize the early warning signs of potential violence and act appropriately to protect the work environment.

From Unacceptable Behavior to Violence in the Workplace

An individual's relative tendency toward violence can be clarified by a scale of unacceptable behavior that begins with questionable performance issues and ultimately ends in a homicidal act. This is not to say that such a scale implies that all behavior indicative of potential violence will inevitably lead to murder. There is, however, reason to believe that as potentially violent behavior increases along the scale, the possibility of a homicidal act increases as well. Knowledge of this escalating scale of inappropriate behavior is especially valuable in the workplace where the behavior of employees is generally well known to coworkers and supervisors.[56]

Activities that may lead to violence or homicide by an employee can be defined by three stages of unacceptable behavior:

Level One. At this level there is a clear indication that intervention by management is needed to divert potential violence:

A. The employee is unwilling to take direction or refuses to act cooperatively with supervisors or managers.
B. The employee is involved in arguments with coworkers.
C. The employee exhibits anger or hostility when interacting with clients.
D. The employee is excessively profane and has a tendency to be provocative with others, especially regarding sexual matters.
E. The employee verbally harasses coworkers or clients.

Level Two. At this level the individual is no longer functioning effectively in the workplace and clearly poses a potential threat. Immediate and professional intervention is needed:

A. The employee argues openly and frequently with others, including coworkers, supervisors, managers and clients.
B. The employee is openly defiant of supervision and refuses to comply with organizational policies.
C. The employee is involved in the theft or destruction of company property.
D. The employee expresses the desire to physically harm others.
E. The employee threatens others in writing.
F. The employee complains frequently that he or she is the victim of poor supervision, inept management, or an organization focused on his or her destruction.

Level Three. The employee is out of control and violence is occurring in the workplace:

A. The employee is frequently angry and engages in physical altercations with others in the workplace.
B. The employee threatens suicide.
C. The employee engages in physically destructive acts in the workplace.
D. The employee engages in a violent crime, most often using a weapon, which may result in murder.

Evaluation: This scale of potential violence can assist a worker, supervisor, or manager in the process of identifying behavior that has the possibility of deteriorating significantly.   There is no sure way, however, of determining how severely an employee's behavior will deteriorate or when, if at all, he or she will become lethal.   The scale does provide a good indication of the pattern of potential violence, and therefore allows for the recognition of intervention opportunities.

Intervention should be the order of business for any employee exhibiting behavior indicated at Level One.   Clearly, an employee who has reached the second level of unacceptable behavior is already a threat to the workplace, and therefore, professional intervention must be immediate in order to protect lives and assets.   At the third level there is violence occurring in the workplace and the situation may already be out of the control of management.

Although this scale provides a valuable methodology to aid in the understanding of how violence may evolve over time, managers, especially, must be provided with even more specific indicators of potentially violent behavior in order to intervene effectively and in a timely manner.   Fortunately, there are other behavioral indicators which provide meaningful and practical information.

Indicators for Managers

In addition to the behavioral warning signs that are so often associated with a potentially violent employee, there are other indicators available to supervisors and managers.   These indicators are oriented to a manager's view of employee behavior and may be more easily utilized than some of the specific behavioral warning signs discussed previously.

An employee exhibiting these indicators is not necessarily an individual who is prone to violence; however, violence is always a possibility when these warning signs are evident, especially in multiple combinations.   These indicators are typical of an employee in difficulty; they strongly suggest that some kind of immediate intervention is needed:[57]

Excessive Tardiness or Absences.   Beyond simply missing work, an employee may also reduce his or her workday by leaving early, departing the work site without authorization, or presenting numerous excuses for otherwise shortening the workday.   This is a particularly significant indicator if it occurs in an individual who has been typically prompt and committed to a full workday.

Increased Need for Supervision.   An employee typically requires less supervision as he or she becomes more proficient at work.   An employee who starts to exhibit an increased need for supervision or with whom the supervisor must spend an unprecedented amount of time may be signaling a need for help.   Managers should be alert to such a change and consider offering professional intervention if the situation so warrants.

Reduced Productivity. If a previously efficient and productive employee experiences a sudden or sustained drop in performance, there is reason for concern. This is a classic warning sign of dissatisfaction, and the manager should meet with the employee to determine a mutually beneficial course of action.

Inconsistency. As in the case of reduced productivity, an employee exhibiting inconsistent work habits may be in need of intervention. Employees are typically quite consistent in their work habits, and should this change, the manager has reason to suspect that there is in need of assistance.

Strained Workplace Relationships. Many of the classic behavioral warning signs may be identified under the category of strained relationships on the job. Should a worker begin to display disruptive behavior in the workplace, it is imperative that the manager intervene as quickly as possible in order to diffuse a potentially violent situation. This indicator should be taken quite seriously. A worker who exhibits disruptive behavior is in need of immediate counseling and, if appropriate, professional employee assistance.

Inability to Concentrate. An inability to concentrate may indicate a worker who is distracted and in trouble. Employee counseling is indicated.

Violation of Safety Procedures. Safety procedures may be violated due to carelessness, insufficient training, or stress. If an employee who has traditionally adhered to safety procedures is suddenly involved in accidents or safety violations, stress may be indicated. This may be a serious situation that requires the intervention of professional employee assistance personnel. Stress is a significant contributor to workplace violence.

Changes in Health or Hygiene. An employee who suddenly begins to disregard personal health or grooming may be signaling for help.

Unusual Behavior. A sustained change in behavior is often an indication that an employee is having difficulty. Common sense is the best way to judge this issue. Workers are typically quite familiar with the personalities of their peers and are often quick to notice significant changes. The work environment should be managed in such a way as to ensure trust and open communication so that workers undergoing a difficult time may be offered prompt assistance.

Fascination with Weapons. Fascination with weapons is a classic behavioral warning sign that should be easily recognized by coworkers and managers.

Substance Abuse. Substance abuse is such a prevalent problem in the American workplace that it has been given separate consideration in this study. It is important that every organization have some methodology in place to identify and assist an employee who has become the victim of drug or alcohol abuse.

Stress. Stress is a serious and widespread problem in the workplace. As with substance abuse, an organization should have procedures in place to identify workers who are victims of stress and provide an effective intervention program. The implementation of stress mitigation and personal wellness programs should also be considered by employers.

Excuses and Blaming. This is a classic behavioral warning sign that is often easy to identify yet is just as often ignored by managers. A worker who engages in this behavior is often signaling for assistance: he or she may require counseling and, possibly, professional intervention.

Depression. Depression is a common ailment in America, but not all individuals suffering from depression are prone to violence. If, however, the depression is evident for a sustained period of time a violent outcome is a possibility and professional intervention is recommended.

Evaluation: Several of these indicators for managers are alternative ways of interpreting the key behavioral warning signs associated with potential violence. They are almost always warning signs of an employee who requires help. An astute manager will often be quite aware of these indicators through experience and instinct. These tools—experience and instinct—are valuable components of good management and should never be ignored. Any employee who exhibits one or more of these indicators must be assumed to be in need of assistance or intervention. Managers must be alert to these indirect pleas for help and provide a positive and timely response in order to ensure a safe and secure work environment.

Substance Abuse and Violence

As most workers, managers and supervisors know, substance abuse in the workplace is a problem of epidemic proportions in America. It is a situation that often leads to violence and sometimes to death. A major component in a positive intervention program designed to assist employees is the early recognition of a substance abuse problem and the arrangement for appropriate professional support. The first, and most important, step in providing proactive intervention is the ability to recognize a substance abuse problem in the workplace.

Outlined below are some of the most commonly abused substances and their primary effects:[58]

Alcohol. This is a depressant that affects the central nervous system. It can have a tranquilizing effect on some people but stimulates others to aggressive, and even violent, behavior. Alcohol affects the brain in such a way as to diminish self-control and other appropriate social behavior. When such a condition prevails in the individual, aggressive behavior can be the result. If misused over long periods, alcohol can permanently damage the liver, heart, and brain. Taken in large quantities over short periods of time, alcohol can cause death.

Marijuana. This substance increases the heart rate, impairs short-term memory, reduces reaction time and the ability to concentrate, and induces feelings of euphoria. Because marijuana is smoked, it can be particularly harmful to the lungs if used over a prolonged period of time. Individuals with heart conditions are at high risk if they use this drug. It is also thought that marijuana may reduce fertility. In some cases, the drug may induce an acute panic (anxiety) reaction in the user which, in turn, may lead to violent behavior.

Hallucinogens ("Psychedelics").   The effects of these substances vary widely with the individual. Hallucinogens generally alter the personality of the user, cause abnormal reactions and vision, alter depth perception, and induce illusions or hallucinations. High doses of a hallucinogen may cause tremors, recurrent memories ("flashbacks"), loss of control of the thought process, anxiety, depression, and even signs of organic brain damage. Bizarre behavior is often associated with their use. Unexpected, violent reactions can occur in some individuals.

Phencyclidine ("PCP").   The effects vary with the dosage and range from euphoria to extremely violent and bizarre behavior. When violence occurs, it may be directed at others or oneself. Severe injuries and death are often associated with the use of PCP because of the violent reactions it can induce. PCP can also cause a schizophrenic-like psychosis that can last for days or weeks.

Stimulants (Amphetamines).   This is a class of drug that stimulates the central nervous system. The effects vary with the dosage but generally include increased activity and alertness, anxiety, mood swings, and paranoid thoughts. Even small doses can be toxic to some individuals. Frequent use can lead to brain damage and death. Long-term users develop rashes, gum disease, and severe damage to fingernails and hair. Some stimulants may lead to eventual death. Violent reactions are common and include extreme suspicion, paranoid states of behavior, and bizarre, physically aggressive outbursts.

Included in this category are cocaine ("freebase" or "crack") and crystal methamphetamine ("ice"). These drugs produce effects similar to those mentioned above, and both produce strong dependence on use. Criminal behavior is often associated with the use of cocaine in its various forms.

Sedatives (Tranquilizers).   These substances depress the central nervous system and represent the most commonly misused drug in America. Sedatives can be lethal because of their effects and the danger of overdose. Individuals using sedatives exhibit slurred speech, drowsiness, vague memory and impaired judgment. When taken in conjunction with alcohol, sedatives can be fatal or can lead to aggressive or violent behavior. Sedatives create dependence, and some sedatives create withdrawal difficulties more severe than with heroin.

Narcotics (Heroin, Codeine).   Effects of narcotics vary with the dosage which, if too high, can cause death. These drugs cause euphoria, sleepiness, and impaired physical and mental reactions and may induce unpredictable and violent reactions as the need for more of the drug is asserted. The use of narcotics by injection also subjects the user to secondary infections and disease. There are a wide variety of physical side effects caused by the use of narcotics.

Recognizing the Potentially Violent Employee

Recently, a number of profiles have appeared in the literature that attempt to briefly define the characteristics of a potentially violent employee or client. Since one of the objectives of this study is to provide a profile designed for the use of workplace personnel, a review of the existing profiles will provide appropriate background to this important topic. Once again, as appropriate, an evaluation of the profile is appended to its description so that its relative importance to this study can be assessed.

A popular psychological view of the potentially violent employee involves a three-part profile that defines (1) general characteristics, (2) characteristics specific to a nonlethal employee, and (3) characteristics specific to a lethal employee:[59]

1. General characteristics of a violent worker:
    A. a white male, age 25 to 50;
    B. demonstrates low self-esteem;
    C. is considered a loner; and
    D. has a fascination with weapons.
2. A worker who may commit *nonlethal* violence demonstrates these additional characteristics:
    A. under the age of 30;
    B. has a history of some violence; and
    C. abuses drugs or alcohol.
3. A worker who may commit *lethal* violence demonstrates these additional characteristics:
    A. over the age of 30;
    B. indicates no history of violence or substance abuse; and
    C. shows indications of paranoia or delusions and is unable to appropriately release frustration.

Evaluation: A thorough study of many case histories of workplace violence indicates that this profile, although sometimes accurate, attempts to go too far in defining "nonlethal" and "lethal" employee groups. As demonstrated by the case studies in this book, it is not certain that *all* violent employees are fascinated with weapons; neither is it accurate to assume that substance abuse is only found in employees under the age of 30. It is certainly inaccurate to say that only lethal employees demonstrate psychological disorders by exhibiting delusional or paranoid behavior. The evidence presented by actual cases of occupational homicide indicates that characteristics of either the nonlethal or lethal employee group are interchangeable and not predictable to a certainty. It is best not to attempt to specifically define the characteristics of a nonlethal or lethal employee. To do so is to risk underestimating a potentially lethal situation by interpreting presumed nonlethal characteristics that in fact are not wholly reliable. The more prudent and practical approach is to define potential violence with less specificity to grouping and seek a higher probability of predicating individual acts of violence. The characteristics outlined herein, when taken together without regard to nonlethal or lethal grouping, are, however, indicators of potential violence and should never be ignored.

Dr. Michael Mantell, assistant clinical professor of psychiatry for the School of Medicine at the University of California, San Diego, offered a more complete list of the characteristics of the potentially violent employee, which focuses primarily on attitudes and behavior. Such an individual:[60]

1. exhibits a disgruntled attitude regarding perceived injustices in the workplace.
2. is likely to be socially isolated—a loner.
3. is likely to exhibit poor self-esteem.
4. "cries for help of some kind."
5. demonstrates a fascination with military or paramilitary subjects.
6. may be a gun or weapon collector.
7. may demonstrate difficulties with temper control.
8. may have made threats against coworkers, supervisors or the organization.
9. demonstrates few, if any, healthy outlets for rage.
10. may demonstrate excessive interest in media reports of violence, especially violence in the workplace.
11. may have an unstable family life.
12. may cause fear or unrest among coworkers and supervisors.
13. may have been involved in chronic labor-management disputes.
14. may exhibit numerous unresolved physical or emotional injuries or have a history of numerous unresolved physical or emotional claims against the organization.
15. may complain regularly about poor working conditions or an unsatisfactory working environment.
16. may complain of heightened stress at work.
17. will be a male between the ages of 30 and 40 years.
18. may demonstrate a migratory job history.
19. may demonstrate drug and/or alcohol abuse.
20. may exhibit psychiatric impairment.

Evaluation: As can be seen from this extensive list of characteristics, Dr. Mantell expanded considerably on the previous profile and provided more finite characteristics by which to identify a potentially violent worker. This profile can be considered generally satisfactory except that it tends to be overly specific in key areas (such as the estimated age of the perpetrator). As will be demonstrated in the case studies that follow (Chapter 3), a more effective profile will tend to provide less specificity in some areas as a precaution so that overreliance on its use will not blind management to potential perpetrators who do not seem to fit the criteria.

At least two management journals have offered alternative profiles of potential workplace murderers in an attempt to educate managers about the issue. As with the profiles already offered here, some of the information is reliable, but some can lead to assumptions of safety where danger exists.

For example, a profile offered by National Trauma Services identified the typical violent worker as (1) white, (2) male, (3) middle-aged, (4) a user of unusual weapons, and (5) a "religious or political proselyte."[61]

Evaluation: The first two elements of this profile are reliable; the third is uncertain, although believed to be probable; the last two elements are not completely reliable predictors of violence, and they imply the exclusion of a variety of other, more common, indicators. A study of occupational homicide data as presented by NIOSH indicates that the most frequently used weapon is a handgun (although there is recent evidence that weapons with greater destructive potential are becoming more prevalent). Most workplace murderers use weapons that are readily available and with which they have some familiarity. Moreover, religious or political proselytizing, although an indicator of potential violence, is not the only warning sign to be considered; nor is it even among the most common.

Another profile offered to managers and supervisors included the following characteristics:[62]

1. male, age 25 to 40 years,
2. a loner,
3. owner of lethal weapons,
4. has a history of interpersonal problems,
5. exhibits self-destructive behavior, and
6. exhibits introversion after complaining or asking for assistance.

Evaluation: As in the previous examples, much of this profile is true; however, important behavioral warning signs are excluded. If interpreted to the exclusion of other possibilities, this profile could lead workplace personnel to overlook potential violence that did not match the specifics of the profile. It is certain that some violent workers will match this profile; however, it is also likely that many will not.

A leading American researcher into workplace violence is S. Anthony Baron, whose profile of the employee most likely to commit murder in the workplace includes these characteristics:[63]

1. a male, aged 25 to 40 years,
2. has a history of violence,
3. tends to be a loner,
4. owns several weapons,
5. has requested some form of assistance in the past,
6. exhibits frequent anger,
7. has a history of conflict with others,
8. has a history of family or marital problems,
9. after periods of verbalizing anger will become withdrawn,
10. is paranoid, and
11. exhibits self-destructive behavior such as drug or alcohol abuse.

Evaluation: It is important to recognize that there are a number of exceptions to this profile among the thousands of case histories of occupational homicide. Several of the incidents reviewed later in this volume show that the perpetrators were not involved in drug or alcohol abuse, did not have a history of violence and, in some cases, were not in the age range indicated in the profile. Overall, however, this profile fits well with the incidents of occupational homicide researched for this study. Nonetheless, one should not assume that the absence of a characteristic or two indicates that an individual is incapable of murder. It is valid to accept this profile as generally accurate so long as it is not taken too literally. Many tragic workplace homicides clearly indicate that a profile that is too specific or interpreted too rigidly can be misleading, at best. With this word of caution, however, Baron's profile is the most accurate of those reviewed in the literature.

One purpose of this work is to offer a new working profile for practical use by workplace managers and staff which is based on a variety of sources of data used in this study. This proposed profile will draw on the best of the elements now extant in the profiles offered in this chapter combined with what can be learned from detailed case studies and other research outlined in this volume.

NOTES

1. U. S. Office of Management and Budget, *Standard Industrial Classification Manual*, 1987.

2. U. S. Department of Commerce, *1980 Census of the Population: Alphabetic Index of Industries and Occupations* (Washington, D.C.: U.S. Department of Commerce,1982), 2.

3. National Institute for Occupational Safety and Health (NIOSH), *Request for Assistance in Preventing Homicide in the Workplace*, (Cincinnati, OH: NIOSH,1993), 3.

4. NIOSH, *Request for Assistance*, 4.

5. National Institute for Occupational Safety and Health, *Fatal Injuries to Workers in the United States, 1980-1989: A Decade of Surveillance* (Cincinnati, OH: NIOSH, 1993).

6. NIOSH, *Fatal Injuries to Workers*, App. 3.

7. Federal Bureau of Investigation (FBI), *Uniform Crime Report for 1990 and 1992*.

8. FBI, 1990.

9. FBI, 1990.

10. FBI, 1992.

11, FBI, 1990 and 1992.

12. FBI, 1990 and 1992.

13. Janice Windau and Guy Toscano, "Murder, Inc.: Homicide in the American Workplace," *Business and Society Review*, no. 89 (1994): 58.

14. Richard Blow, "A Social Disease," *Mother Jones*, Dec. 1992, Internet.

15. Blow.

16. Blow.

17. Blow.

18. Janice L. Thomas, "Occupational Violent Crime: Research on an Emerging Issue," *Journal of Safety Research* 23, no. 2 (1992): 55.

19. Daniel Pedersen, "10 Minutes of Madness," *Newsweek*, 1 Sept. 1986, 18.

20, NIOSH, 4.

21. NIOSH, 4.

22. NIOSH, 4.

23. Ronet Bachman, *Violence and Theft in the Workplace*, Washington, D.C.: U.S. Department of Justice, Bureau of Justice Statistics, 15 Jul. 1994.

24. "Violent Incidents on the Rise," *USA Today Magazine*, 122, no. 2587 (1994): 5.

25. Jim Castelli, "On-the-Job Violence Becomes Epidemic," *Safety and Health*, 149, no. 2 (1994): 85.

26. Tom Dunkel, "Newest Danger Zone," *Working Woman*, 19, no. 8 (1994): 38.

27. Jolie Solomon and Patricia King, "Waging War in the Workplace," *Newsweek*, 122, no. 3 (1994), 30.

28. S. Anthony Baron, "Workplace Violence" (Crisis Solutions International, seminar, 1994), 12.

29. Department of Industrial Relations (Division of Occupational   Safety and Health, California), *Cal/OSHA Guidelines for Workplace Security*, 15 Aug. 1994, 8.

30. Castelli, 85.

31. Windau and Toscano, 58.

32. "It's Personnel as Well as Personal," *Psychology Today*, 27, no. 1 (1994): 20.

33. "Murder at the Post Office," *Training and Development*, 48, no. 1 (1994): 29.

34. "Shootings are the #2 Cause of Death in the Workplace," *Redbook*, (unattributed informational insert), Sept. 1994, 95.

35. Anastasia Toufexis, "Workers Who Fight Firing with Fire," *Time*, 143, no. 17 (1994): 34.

36. Bureau of Labor Statistics, U. S. Department of Labor, *Microsoft Bookshelf*, Redmond, WA., 1994 ed.

37. Baron, 17.

38. "Over the Edge," *Security Management*, 37, no. 12 (1993): 12.

39. Daniel Weisberg, "Preparing for the Unthinkable," *Management Review*, 83, no. 3 (1994): 58.

40. William E. Lissy, "Workplace Violence," *Supervision*, 55, no. 4 (1994): 20.

41. James H. Quirk, "HR Managers Face Legal Aspects of Workplace Violence," *HRMagazine*, 38, no. 11 (1993): 115.

42. Quirk, 115.

43. *Jury Verdicts Weekly*, 2 May 1989: 20.

44. H. H. Goldman, ed., *Review of General Psychiatry* (Norwalk, VA: Appleton Lange/Prentice Hall, 1988), 654.

45. Goldman, 654.

46. Eugene D. Wheeler and S. Anthony Baron, *Violence in Our Schools, Hospitals and Public Places* (Ventura, CA: Pathfinder, 1994), 166-171.

47. Wheeler and Baron, 166.

48. Goldman, 671.

49. Goldman, 671.

50. Wheeler and Baron, 166.

51. American Psychiatric Association, *Diagnostic and Statistical Manual of Mental Disorders, 4th ed.* (Washington, D. C.: American Psychiatric Association), 320.

52. J. Branch Walton, "Dealing with Dangerous Employees," *Occupational Hazards* 37, no. 9 (1993): 81.

53. John J. Prince, "Fuming over Workplace Violence," *Security Management* 37, no. 3 (1993): 64.

54. American Psychiatric Association, 645.

55. American Psychiatric Association, 650.

56. Baron, 28-30.

57. S. Anthony Baron, *Violence in the Workplace* (Ventura, CA: Pathfinder, 1993), 50-52.

58. National Institute on Drug Abuse, *Microsoft Bookshelf*, 1994 ed., (Redmond, WA: Microsoft, 1994).

59. "It's Personnel as Well as Personal," *Psychology Today*, 27, no. 1 (1994): 21.

60. Michael Mantell, *Ticking Bombs—Defusing Violence in the Workplace* (New York: Irwin), 79-89.

61. Peggy Stuart, "Murder on the Job," *Personnel Journal*, 71, no. 2 (1992): 72.

62. George Milite, "Workplace Violence," *Supervisory Management*, 38, no. 9 (1993): 1.

63. Baron, 89.

3

Case Studies of Occupational Homicide

In order to better understand the nature of occupational homicide, a number of case studies will be presented. These actual incidents will serve as a basis for analysis leading to the goal of formulating practical measures of workplace violence prevention. In each case, the facts of the incident will be provided and the event itself classified according to Category Profile (CP) and, where meaningful, NIOSH industry and occupation classification. Following the synopsis of each incident, observations of consequence to the event will be offered in order to develop a more comprehensive understanding of the crime. Finally, each case will be briefly analyzed in relation to its implications for possible prevention. These implications represent areas of concern that could be used in prevention methodologies for similar, future incidents.

This method of analysis is comprised of three components designed to demonstrate the interplay of perpetrator with the organization, its management, and staff. This formula for analysis is offered as an effective way to analyze incidents of occupational homicide so that the actions (or failure to act) of all parties can considered. The key elements of the analysis process are:

1. *Facts of the Case*: a brief synopsis of the incident that identifies actions, individuals, and circumstances, to the extent they are known and verifiable.
2. *Observations*: elements of importance to the incident that may be separate from the incident itself but nonetheless impart value to an understanding of the event.
3. *Implications for Prevention*: an analysis of action (or failure to act) that can be attributed to the perpetrator, organization, its personnel, or others, and that may have value in future prevention methodologies.

These elements are, in order, each more subjective than its precedent. Element 1 can be considered factual, while element 2 may contain information not substantiated but considered important to an understanding of the event. Element 3 is subject to interpretation because it is often a conclusion and is evaluative in nature.   It is offered to provide the basis for future violence prevention opportunities or for a more complete understanding of the actions outlined in the facts of the case.   It is hoped that this method of incident analysis will provide a practical framework for workplace personnel and other interested parties to use to study the nature and causes of occupational homicide in a more systematic and holistic manner than now exists in the literature.

Since occupational homicide is both prevalent and increasing, there are literally thousands of possible case histories that could have been included in this study.   Those offered here have been selected without regard for their sometimes sensational nature or their impact in the media.   Rather, they are intended to provide a cross-section of the varied kinds of incidents that have occurred, and continue to occur, in many American places of work.   These case histories, taken together, formulate a brief composite portrait of occupational homicide so that the issue may be understood from as broad a perspective as possible.   Employing this perspective will assist in constructing recommendations for prevention that are applicable to many different organizations.

UNIVERSITY OF SOUTHERN CALIFORNIA HOSPITAL

Case Study Number: 1
Location: Los Angeles, California
Date of Incident: February 8, 1993
Category Profile: CP III (client against employee or supervisor)
                          CP V (indiscriminate homicide, attempted)
NIOSH Classification: Service industry
                          Professional/Specialist occupation

Facts of the Case: The incident took place in an extremely busy ambulatory care unit on a Monday, at 12:20 in the afternoon.[iii]   At the time of the incident there were over 100 patients waiting to be assisted.   An angry patient, who was wearing a bulky camouflage jacket and fatigues, began pacing the floor in an agitated state and demanding medical attention in a loud voice. After some time in this agitated state, the patient walked over to a group of three doctors standing near the office door and fired seven shots.   The three doctors, who were standing close together in conversation, were all critically wounded.   The perpetrator then ran to a nearby X-ray room, took two female

---

iii. This case is exceptional in that none of the victims were fatally injured. Had such an incident taken place other than in the immediate proximity of an emergency room of an outstanding hospital, it is likely that one or more of the victims would have died.

hostages, handcuffed them to himself, and barricaded himself and his hostages inside the room. After some five hours of negotiations, the perpetrator released his hostages unharmed and surrendered to authorities. He was armed with a .44-caliber Magnum revolver, a .38-caliber automatic pistol, a sawed-off rifle and a ten-inch Marine Corps knife. The three critically wounded doctors recovered, thanks to the immediate intervention of the emergency room staff.[1] Neither of the hostages was injured.

Observations: Even though the doctors working in this environment later stated that they were not surprised at the violence that had occurred, clearly, no one in the care unit was prepared for the actual event as there were apparently very few, if any, security measures in effect at the time of the incident. The patient came into the offices heavily armed and became obviously agitated. There is no evidence that anyone working in the care unit approached the patient or communicated with him in any way, despite his pacing and loud demands, which reportedly went on for some ten minutes before he began shooting. Dressed in pseudo military clothing and presenting the picture he did, one must wonder if the staff was so accustomed to strange behavior by patients that this individual's obvious indications of potential violence were simply ignored. During hostage negotiations the patient told police that he grew tired of waiting for attention and that he wanted satisfaction. He also told the negotiators that he did not know any of his victims, although hospital records later disclosed that one of the doctors had treated him twice previously.

The perpetrator had lived alone in a "skid row" hotel for five years prior to the shooting. He collected weapons and military artifacts, although he himself never served in the military. There were no reports of drugs or alcohol present, and the patient had no prior criminal record or history of mental disorder. Those who knew the patient viewed him as not hostile or aggressive, but as a loner.

Implications for Prevention: The background of this individual is clearly similar to that of Patrick Sherrill (see Edmond Post Office Massacre in the previous chapter), although Sherrill apparently functioned more productively in society. They were both loners with a clear interest in—perhaps a fetish for—weapons and military paraphernalia. In both cases the perpetrators victimized individuals whom they either did not know at all or against whom they apparently held no personal vendetta. In this case it seems evident that the shooter gave several obvious indications that he was angry and frustrated. When his behavior elicited no reaction or satisfaction from the hospital staff, he took matters into his own hands. Since he was a previous patient at the hospital, and presumably had had other negative experiences waiting for medical attention in a busy facility, he visited this day armed and expecting the worst. He was evidently prepared to do indiscriminate violence, and gave warning of his growing aggression.

A question immediately arises regarding intervention. Had some member of the hospital staff taken proactive measures to communicate with this individual and assuage his growing anger, could the violence that followed have been prevented? Other questions regarding security and staff training to deal with hostile clients must also be considered in this case.

A work environment must be as secure as practical, given the nature of the work performed. This is particularly important if the organization serves a wide variety of clients, each on an infrequent basis. A proactive interest in clients, especially those who are upset or uncooperative, is a necessary element in violence prevention. The observation and recognition of behavioral warning signs that are indicative of aggression are also crucial to any violence prevention program. If a potentially violent incident is developing, it simply makes good sense to get assistance and arrange for intervention as quickly as possible. To ignore an obviously agitated client is, at best, an unwise practice. In this case it was a near-lethal oversight.

FAIRVIEW DEVELOPMENTAL CENTER

Case Study Number: 2
Location: Costa Mesa, California
Date of Incident: 1991
Category Profile: CP II (employee against supervisor)
                          CP V (indiscriminate homicide)
NIOSH Classification: Service industry
                          Managerial occupation

Facts of the Case: A painter, who was angry with management for not alleviating poor staff morale and tension in his division, shot and killed a facilities supervisor and wounded two others.[2]

Observations: Although very little detail is included in this report, there is sufficient information available from which an emerging pattern can be seen. The perpetrator was male, as is true in 80% or more of workplace homicides. He used a gun, also characteristic of approximately 80% of such incidents. Once again, as in the previous case, he apparently attempted to murder individuals against whom he held no personal grudge, although this is not definitive from the information provided. It can be assumed that the perpetrator felt that his grievances had not been sufficiently heard or understood and that he felt compelled to take the actions he did.

Implications for Prevention: The question of security in this case study remains an issue. The perpetrator was able to enter his place of work with a weapon and murder a supervisor by shooting him at close range. Certainly the workplace is not an appropriate place for weapons. Any comprehensive violence prevention program must address methods of ensuring that weapons are not brought to the job site and that basic security is in place.

The question of management's ability to communicate effectively with employees must be considered in this case. Even a completely invalid grievance should allow for nonviolent solutions in the workplace. Many organizations provide formal grievance procedures to assist in settling workplace disputes. Although this is a positive step, many such grievance procedures evolve into a "court of last resort" that is formal, intimidating and impersonal. In such a forum there is little opportunity for the parties to develop a complete understanding of opposing positions. In some cases, a formal grievance procedure can polarize parties to such an extent that the work environment suffers. Although there is a place for formalizing a grievance, it is often more productive to attempt to resolve a dispute with discussion, true understanding, and a willingness to compromise. The most ill-informed action would be to dismiss an employee concern as irrational or determine a grievance to be meaningless without a complete understanding of the issues and their importance to the grievant.

Managers and supervisors must not only be able to effectively listen, they must be proactive in resolving workplace disputes before violence occurs. Supervisors cannot rely on passive tactics or the implementation of rigid personnel policies in an environment where human dynamics is always at center stage. They must actively manage the staff on a continuing basis in order to maintain organizational integrity and a positive work environment. Training staff, managers and supervisors in the process of conflict resolution provides an excellent defense against potential workplace violence.

Recent Similar Cases

Incidents of workplace murder attributed to workplace stress, poor working conditions or low morale are abundant. On August 29, 1995, a postal employee reported to work with a handgun which he used to shoot two coworkers who he claimed were his friends. The shooter was a 53-year-old male who had worked at the same location for about 20 years and had an exemplary service record. The only complaint he expressed at the time of the incident concerned the stressful working environment he experienced daily at the post office.

Another postal worker, who was described as "quiet and unassuming" reported to work as usual on July 10, 1995. He, also, was carrying a handgun. On the job for 22 years, the 58-year-old man shot and killed his supervisor, then peacefully turned himself over to coworkers to await his arrest. His chief complaint was low morale.

SCHUYLER COUNTY CHILD SUPPORT AGENCY

Case Study Number:	3
Location:	Watkins Glen, New York
Date of Incident:	October 15, 1992
Category Profile:	CP III (client against employee/supervisor)
	CP V (indiscriminate homicide)
NIOSH Classification:	Public Administration industry
	Professional/Specialist occupation

Facts of the Case: John T. Miller was charged with back child support payments in excess of $6,700 for a child he claimed he had not parented. A county family service agency began to withhold portions of the amount due from his paycheck. He retaliated against the agency by walking into the backdoor of the office and using a handgun to kill four of the five employees on duty. Miller had visited the office the day before the shooting, but gave no overt appearance of hostility. The agency staff had often approached management with their concerns about potentially violent clients; however, management had taken no action to protect the employees.

Observations: This incident is significant for a number of points. The public administration classification used by NIOSH has the second highest per capita rate of all industry classifications for workplace homicide, at 1.54 individuals per 100,000 workers (1980-1989 data). It is outranked only by the retail trade classification, at 1.66 per 100,000 workers (1980-1989 data). Government services are traditionally viewed with disdain by many Americans who see them as staffed by individuals who are unconcerned and lack motivation. True or not, this is a view so common to the American citizenry as to require no further supporting evidence. Perhaps this (perceived) historically inferior approach to the welfare of clients lies at the heart of much frustration with such agencies. On the other hand, many government agencies are in the uncomfortable business of enforcing laws, codes and regulations with large numbers of unfamiliar clients. Certainly a client on the "other side" of the law presents the potential for violent retaliation—a fact that such agencies should take seriously in terms of violence prevention and intervention.

Implications for Prevention: This case points out an apparent lack of concern by the management of the agency for the basic security of their employees. Here is what was disclosed about the work environment at this agency after the murders occurred:[3] "The child support staff had asked for greater security for their unit, but never got it. Beverly Clickner, who had an office next to the child support unit, said, "We're threatened all the time, and sometimes we're not taken very seriously. Upham [a fifth social worker who survived the attack by Miller] reported that there was no way to lock their office doors from [the] inside, no escape routes, and visitors could gain entrance by way of a back door as Miller did."[4]

Evidently, this organization was not prepared for the possibility of violence in the workplace. In addition, if the employee comments are to be taken at face value, the agency management was not sufficiently responsive to staff concerns about potential violence. When such concerns are expressed by staff, it is incumbent upon management to take them seriously and, if appropriate, institute corrective action. In this case it seems that staff made more than one attempt to bring the issue of potential workplace violence to management. Certainly it would seem reasonable to expect management to take some action to investigate the extent of the problem and mitigate the possible consequences.

Apparently, this was an organization that experienced many warning signs of potential violence yet failed to take minimum precautions such as prohibiting entry to the offices from a backdoor. One can also assume that the communication lines between management and staff were weak, at best.

Questions also arise about client services and how they were implemented. Were employees trained to deal with angry or potentially violent clients? Was the staff familiar with conflict resolution techniques and their application? Had the staff been trained to recognize the warning signs of potential violence?

Employees are a primary source of information about the workplace environment. Management must keep communication lines open and act upon important employee recommendations. Although office environments have traditionally been viewed as safe, this is clearly not the case, as the statistical evidence presented earlier demonstrates. Many office environments, such as those in this incident, are among the most potentially dangerous in terms of possible workplace violence. Managers must make efforts to prepare staff for threats to the safety of the workplace. Primary among the measures to be undertaken is the establishment of a working environment that allows employees to express their concerns to a management team willing to accept their appropriate suggestions.

Recent Similar Cases

A related case of homicide in the public administration job category occurred on April 27, 1995, at the Richmond Housing Authority in Richmond, California. After a housing authority employee was fired from his job, he immediately left the offices for his car in the agency parking lot. He retrieved a handgun from the automobile and returned to the offices, where he shot and killed his supervisor and a coworker standing nearby. The 38-year-old perpetrator then quietly surrendered to arriving police officers. Although the perpetrator was a former employee and an individual who was reacting to the termination of his employment, the kind of violence that ensued is surprisingly common in the public administration sector. One may speculate that the impersonal impact of bureaucracy experienced by many clients of public administration agencies has a similarly negative effect on its employees.

EXXON CORPORATION

Case Study Number: 4
Location: Trenton, New Jersey
Date of Incident: April 29, 1992
Category Profile: CP IV (homicide by agenda)
NIOSH Classification: Commerce industry
                          Executive occupation

Facts of the Case: Sidney Reso, president of Exxon Corporation International, was abducted from the driveway of his home as he left for work on April 29, 1992, by Arthur Seale and his spouse, Irene. Arthur was a former police officer and current security consultant for Exxon. During the abduction attempt, Reso was shot and subsequently died on May 3, 1992. Arthur Seale buried him in a shallow grave in a nearby state park. The Seales were arrested on June 19, 1992, and Irene Seal cooperated with authorities, pleading guilty to extortion charges. Arthur Seale received a maximum sentence of 95 years in prison.[5]

Observations: Cases such as this tend to garner a great deal of publicity in the press, yet relative to other categories of workplace homicide, they are rare. Considering that Arthur Seale was a security consultant for Exxon, it is possible that he had access to confidential personnel information that aided him in planning the crime. Perhaps the two men were even known to each other. Would the information to which Seale had access have included personal data about key management members such as the president of the corporation? Since Seale was only a consultant to Exxon, we must assume that somewhere in the organization, some other member of management had control over sensitive personnel information. How was this information protected? Limited access to confidential employee information is a crucial point in violence prevention.

Implications for Prevention: This case raises several interesting questions. What security measures were in place in the organization to thwart an attempted abduction of a key member of management? Were members of top management briefed on basic security precautions or provided any other form of information that would help to prevent abductions? Was Arthur Seale's background checked carefully and completely before he was given a contract with the corporation? Did Seale undergo a comprehensive interview process to determine if a predilection for violent behavior was in evidence?

An organizational violence prevention plan should outline basic security provisions for key management personnel who may be targeted for economic or political motives. Organizational security measures should also adequately protect confidential personnel information. These are specialized areas of prevention that must be considered in dealing with key personnel in an organization. Unfortunately, methods of violence prevention may overlook such areas of concern.

Violence prevention measures must often extend beyond the workplace and must take into account the protection of employees even while away from the work environment. Security measures must also extend to the protection of information that may put an employee at risk. Of paramount importance is the knowledge gained about an individual prior to employment in any capacity. Taking precautions such as thorough background investigations and comprehensive interviewing techniques can provide an excellent deterrent to potential violence. A reliance on minimum background information is an unsafe personnel practice, regardless of the contemplated nature of the relationship.

CENTRAL INTELLIGENCE AGENCY

Case Study Number: 5
Location: Washington, D. C.
Date of Incident: January 12, 1993
Category Profile: CP IV (homicide by agenda)
NIOSH Classification: Public Administration industry
                          Professional/Specialist occupation

Facts of the Case: The suspect, Mir Aimal Kansi, has never been apprehended. Kansi parked his car in the left turn lane outside the entrance to Central Intelligence Agency (CIA) headquarters. He walked between rows of cars waiting to enter the premises and opened fire on several vehicles, using an AK-47 assault rifle. After the shooting, Kansi fled to his car and sped away. Two male CIA employees were shot to death. Police were convinced that Kansi had specifically targeted CIA employees. A follow-up investigation located the murder weapon in Kansi's apartment. It was later determined that Kansi had worked for a courier service owned by the son of a former high-level CIA official.[6]

Observations: This is a singular case, and one that points out the limitless potential for violence in the workplace. From the case history there is no evidence of a prior warning of impending violence. The perpetrator was not an employee of the target organization and probably did not know his victims. It is possible there was a grudge motivation because of Kansi's employment connection—the fact the business for which he worked was owned by the son of an ex-CIA official. This is, admittedly, a tenuous connection and it forms a speculative hypothesis at best. Kansi is currently on the Federal Bureau of Investigation's "Most Wanted" list and is believed to have escaped to the Middle East. It is possible that Kansi's actions could be considered a form of terrorism.

Implications for Prevention: The point behind this incident is that preventative measures, no matter how thorough, may still be inadequate. If an organization such as the CIA was unable to foresee or prevent an incident such as this, it is probable that the typical American business would be subject to even greater exposure. In the final analysis, it is impossible to prepare for all eventualities in the workplace. To try to do so would be tantamount to crippling the typical organization. There is an inherent risk in the workplace, as there is in society. This risk should be fully recognized and accorded sufficient consideration in prevention planning. Any comprehensive violence prevention program must attempt to account for the unexpected and even the bizarre. Planning for a workplace crisis through the development of a wide array of potential risk scenarios is an important element in workplace violence prevention.

A violence prevention program cannot remain static or ignore the unexpected. Such a program must continue to evolve as new information about occupational homicide becomes available. Although it is unlikely that a single organization can implement prevention techniques for all potential workplace threats, there is a great deal of benefit in sharing information about workplace violence experiences and developing prevention plans that deal with a wide variety of possibilities. Organizations tend to establish safety and prevention programs in isolation, suitable only for their unique work environments. However, a more integrated, holistic approach, employing the knowledge and resources of many organizations, would benefit all employers interested in violence prevention.

RICHARD J. DALY CENTER

Case Study Number: 6
Location: Chicago, Illinois
Date of Incident: January 11, 1984
Category Profile: CP IV (homicide by agenda)
NIOSH Classification: Public Administration industry
                          Executive/Administrative occupation

Facts of the Case: In 1984, the Richard J. Daly Center had a security program in place that included a metal detector and armed guards at the entrance to the courtroom area. Despite this fact, the guards allowed a man in a wheelchair, with a blanket on his lap, to enter the courtroom without either passing through the metal detector or having his belongings subjected to a cursory examination. The (apparently) disabled man smuggled a .38-caliber revolver into the courtroom under his blanket, and shot a judge and lawyer to death. It was later learned that he was angered about a post decree divorce proceeding with his ex-wife.[7]

Observations: This case precedes the infamous Edmond post office massacre by two years and, no doubt, was viewed as an isolated incident at the time. In 1984, the awareness of occupational homicide was not as general as it is today and the crime was certainly not considered commonplace. However, this incident took place in a courtroom—the scene of several homicides prior to the incident and a place where security had been the norm for some time. The courtroom area benefited from security measures that, on their face, appeared to be adequate. Regardless of the sophistication of the security systems or the presence of armed guards, prevention and protection can only be as effective as the adherence to the security program in place. Clearly, the guards in this case failed to follow what should have been obvious precautions. Considering the individual's apparent (or even obvious) disability, the guards were willing to allow entrance to the courtroom without any assurance of his intentions or any attempts at appropriate intervention. There is no evidence that the visitor was challenged in any way or that any conversation between him and the guards took place.

Implications for Prevention: The reaction of the guards to this individual may be understandable, but it was fatal. They apparently made assumptions about the nature and intent of the visitor, possibly because of his perceived disability, which proved to be horribly incorrect. Had they unfailingly followed the policy of courtroom security, this incident might have been avoided. This case points out the fact that assumptions about the appearance, motivations, or actions of others can often be incorrect and sometimes lethal. Equally dangerous is the failure to follow established security procedures.

Even with a comprehensive violence prevention program that incorporates solid security measures, there is risk in the workplace if procedures are ignored. Assumptions about the potential behavior of any individual are unwise and, in certain cases, quite dangerous. Much protection can be afforded by well-considered security procedures that are thoroughly understood and strictly obeyed.

Courthouse Security—Ten Years Later

Unfortunately, many of America's public places, such as courthouses, remain unsafe and unprotected more than ten years after the murders just profiled. On March 2, 1995, at the King County courthouse in Seattle, Washington, two women and a seven-month-old fetus were murdered by a gun-wielding husband while waiting for an annulment hearing. The perpetrator, a 47-year old white male (Timothy Blackwell), shot and killed his pregnant wife and her friend on the second floor of the courthouse. Although this was not, strictly speaking, a case of occupational homicide, the incident makes clear that security measures in many of America's public places remain inadequate.[8]

BROOKLYN FAMILY COURT

Case Study Number: 7
Location: Brooklyn, New York
Date of Incident: March 12, 1993
Category Profile: CP III (client against employee/supervisor)
NIOSH Classification: Not applicable [iv]

Facts of the Case: Max Almonor, at age 52, was involved in a dispute with his wife about visiting rights for their teenage daughter. Both Max and Danielle Almonor were parole officers. In March 1993, the Almonors were summoned to appear in family court for a visitation hearing.

---

iv. This case deals with client against client, which is not typical of the cases utilized in this study. However, this incident, like the previous case study, points out the fact that even institutions with sophisticated security measures are at risk when those measures are not applied diligently. In addition, this case points out the value of providing special employee assistance for certain high-stress jobs.

Law enforcement officials in New York were allowed to keep their weapons on their person while in the courthouse as long as they were on official business. Mr. Almonor, who was most likely known to the courthouse security personnel, displayed his badge and entered the courtroom with his weapon, a .38-caliber revolver, despite the fact he was not on official business. While in the court waiting room, Mr. and Mrs. Almonor got into an argument. Mr. Almonor drew his weapon and shot Danielle Almonor twice in the head, also wounding two bystanders. Mrs. Almonor was rushed to the hospital but was pronounced dead on arrival. After the shooting, Mr. Almonor surrendered his weapon to court security personnel without incident.[9]

Observations: It is clear that proper security measures were not followed and that invalid assumptions were made about the motivations and intentions of Max Almonor. He was a trusted "fellow" of the law enforcement community and, therefore, apparently presumed to present no security risk. Security personnel relaxed their normal procedures, and indirectly, may have aided in the murder of Mrs. Almonor. A more subtle issue in the case, though, lies in Max Almonor's profession and that of Mrs. Almonor. Both were parole officers—which is known to be an extremely stressful occupation. No doubt they were both overworked and dealt daily with individuals who, by their own actions or history, may have induced in the Almonors regular anxiety, stress and even fear for their own safety. Beyond this, it seems apparent that the couple faced the stress of being working partners with a teenager to look after. Perhaps, because of the apparent complexity of their lives and their jobs, the Almonor marriage collapsed, adding additional stress.

Implications for Prevention: A pressing question in this case is what could have been done to help these individuals before matters reached such a state that Mr. Almonor felt he had no option but to resort to homicide. Certainly, there must have been warning signs somewhere along his path to violence. Perhaps there were indications at their respective places of work. Given the stress of their job responsibilities, was there something that could have been done at the workplace to assist either, or both, of the Almonors? Was there an employee counseling program or employee assistance program in place? Perhaps an alert or interested supervisor could have seen indications of a problem developing with Mr. Almonor and suggested intervention. Although it is not legal, proper, or desirable for a supervisor to unduly intrude into the private affairs of an employee, there is an opportunity in the relationships that develop on the job to offer assistance when the need is apparent and desired. Beyond this, certain high-stress jobs, like that of Mr. and Mrs. Almonor, require special attention to ensure that employees remain as healthy, happy, and productive as possible.

The assumption of safety can be a deadly mistake. To compromise security measures, even for a seemingly positive purpose, is risky in the extreme. Likewise, the assumption that an employee can withstand the combined pressures of a complex home and work environment without support and assistance may also be a grave error. A forward-looking violence prevention program should include a component that proactively addresses employee wellness and deals with stress as a crucial issue.

DEARBORN POST OFFICE

Case Study Number: 8
Location: Dearborn, Michigan
Date of Incident: May 6, 1993
Category Profile: CP I (employee against employee)
                            CP V (indiscriminate homicide)
NIOSH Classification: Public Administration industry
                            Clerical occupation
                            Technical/Support occupation

Facts of the Case: Larry Jasion, age 45, was a postal mechanic who was angry because another employee had been promoted to a clerical job he desired. He had also been involved in a recent argument with a coworker about playing a radio in their shared work area.   When a vote of the employees in the surrounding work area was taken, Jasion's wish to play his radio was turned aside. Several days after the vote, Jasion entered his work area armed with a shotgun and handgun and shot three coworkers.   He then committed suicide with the handgun. The woman who had received the promotion Jasion coveted was critically injured, with two gunshot wounds to the head and one to the back. The coworker with whom he had the dispute about the radio was killed.

Jasion had been a post office employee for 24 years. Several weeks prior to the shootings he had filed a complaint with the Equal Employment Opportunity Commission (EEOC) because of his rejection for promotion. The postal inspector at the Dearborn post office verified that the issue of Jasion's rejection for promotion had been discussed with him and that he had been instructed how to file an appeal with the Equal Employment Opportunity Commission. No further personnel action was taken, nor did Jasion receive any counseling.

Observations: Discussions with post office employees indicated that Jasion was "an eccentric and embittered person" who frequently exhibited strange behavior on the job.[10] Post office officials noted that Jasion threatened his supervisor shortly after the Edmond post office killings by saying to him, "You're going to be next."[11] The threatened supervisor resigned in 1987, one year after Jasion's statement, citing fear that Jasion would make good on his threat. No personnel action was taken by post office management.

When a union official was interviewed after the shootings, he claimed that the murders could have been avoided. The union official noted that the woman who had been critically wounded had written a letter to the postmaster stating that Jasion had threatened her life on at least two occasions. This letter had allegedly been written some six weeks prior to the shootings, yet no action was taken by officials at the post office. According to the union official, "The union didn't even find out about the letter until two weeks after the shootings."[12]

Implications for Prevention: There are a number of key points contained in this case history. For example, Jasion clearly fits the most common profile of a violent employee (age, sex, type of weapon, etc.), as evidenced in previously discussed case histories. The perpetrator exhibited clear warning signs of mounting frustration and anger and, in fact, had embarked upon confrontational behavior in the workplace.

This case also elucidates issues that, on the surface, appear to be in conflict. Jasion was a long-term employee of the organization, yet "coworkers and authorities said [he] was an eccentric and embittered person." If this is true, and not merely an embellishment added after the shootings, how was such an employee able to acceptably perform his job for such an extraordinary length of time without the notice, and intervention, of management? One would expect that such an employee would demonstrate performance problems on the job, yet there is no indication of performance issues or management intervention. Is it possible that an employee who aroused this type of reaction in the workplace could have performed his duties satisfactorily for over two decades? It seems unlikely. On the other hand, this view of Jasion could have been taken, in retrospect, after his outburst of violence.

It was stated by a previous supervisor that Jasion had threatened bodily harm or death in the workplace some six or seven years before he committed the act. The supervisor claimed he took this threat so seriously that he had to quit his job. It appears as though the supervisor quit approximately one year after the threat. If the supervisor was indeed so afraid, why did he wait so long to quit his job? What, if any, other actions did he take? Was management ever informed, and if so, why did they fail to take any action? Did it seem easier to simply ignore the problem?

It is, of course, all too easy to second-guess the actions of management in response to an employee who may be posing problems in the workplace. Federal personnel regulations and labor law impose important and necessary individual safeguards that may sometimes constrain proactive solutions. Management must, however, give needed attention to potentially violent or disruptive behavior as soon as it is recognized. If Jasion made the statements claimed by the supervisor, and if he exhibited such strange behavior for such a long period of time, would this not be a signal to management that such an employee was in need of some assistance?

Regarding the promotion issue, it may be true that post office officials advised Jasion of his rights in seeking a grievance for the denied promotion, but did anyone in the organization ever closely listen to Jasion and make an attempt to diffuse a situation that could become violent?

From the case history it now seems obvious that Jasion was an employee who exhibited warning signs pointing to potential disruption in the workplace. One must wonder if the many supervisors Jasion may have encountered in his long work career were as unwilling to become involved in a solution as was the supervisor he threatened. Of even more importance, one must wonder about the kind of work environment at the post office that could allow such an obvious personnel problem to linger unanswered for so long.

There are many behavioral warning signs that indicate potential violence. They should be made common knowledge to both managers and staff, and should never be ignored. Personnel issues must be addressed in a timely manner so as to diffuse potential workplace violence. It is clear that managers especially must be proactive in working with employees to ensure that early warning signs of violence are not overlooked or ignored.

ACTS OF TERRORISM AGAINST THE WORKPLACE

Case Study Number: 9
Location: Multiple locations [v]
Date of Incident: From December 1989 until present
Category Profile: CP IV (homicide by agenda)
NIOSH Classification: Public Administration industry
                          Professional/Specialist occupations

Facts of the Case: A number of acts of terrorism have been carried out against judges and lawyers since 1989. These incidents are continuing to this day, although with diminished frequency. In just ten days in December 1989, five separate violent incidents occurred, including:[13]

1. A circuit court of appeals judge was killed in his home by a package bomb. The package contained no clues as to the sender, nor was a motive for the murder immediately evident.
2. A civil rights lawyer was killed in his home by a similar device under similar circumstances.
3. A mail bomb was sent to a courthouse in Atlanta. No one was injured.
4. A mail bomb was sent to the offices of the National Association for the Advancement of Colored People (NAACP) in Jacksonville, Florida. No one was injured in the incident.
5. A pipe bomb explosion critically injured a judge.

Observations: Although these incidents differ from the classic profile of workplace homicide, they clearly belong in this study. Evidently, the violence suffered by the judges, and others, was a direct result of their chosen profession and activities at work. In this sense, the individuals who died were victims of homicide in the workplace, regardless of where and how the murders took place.

Implications for Prevention: This form of violence is, in reality, terrorism.   The nature of these attacks is of such a quality as to make

---

v. This case history encompasses more than one incident since the murders were connected by the method of operation.

prevention extremely difficult and, perhaps, ultimately impossible. There is no obvious way to formulate an irrefutable link between the perpetrator and the victim, and no sure way to be clear about motivation. More troublesome than this, there is no way to predict the next act of violence. Although it is true that some measures of personal safety might have spared the number of lives lost, many potential victims might find the restrictions imposed by these measures too onerous to be tolerated. In the final analysis, one might be able to somewhat profile the perpetrators, but have little ability to stop the violence, short of the ultimate apprehension and imprisonment of the guilty individuals. To this day, no suspect has been arrested in any of these incidents.

This is a particular type of workplace homicide that places potential victims in an extremely defensive position with few positive options for prevention. A comprehensive and sophisticated personal safety program could provide some measure of protection but, even if tolerable, such a program could not possibly answer all eventualities.

In designing any violence prevention program, it is necessary to consider the nature of various jobs in the workplace. Many professions in American society convey highly charged symbolic meanings which in themselves can become focal points for violence. Those in such professions must be aware of, and account for, the additional risks that may be a part of their chosen career.

Recent Similar Cases

On April 19, 1995, the worst incident of this form (CP IV) of terrorism against the workplace took place in Oklahoma City, Oklahoma. On that day, the federal building was nearly completely destroyed by a home-made fertilizer bomb detonated from a van parked at the front of the multistory office building. In the ensuing explosion 167 individuals were killed, including children at an office day-care center, and another 460 persons were injured. The two suspects, Timothy McVeigh and Terry Nichols, are still awaiting trial in the case. This heinous act was one of pure terrorism, allegedly undertaken in retribution for the actions of the Federal Bureau of Investigation (FBI) and the Bureau of Alcohol, Tobacco and Firearms (ATF) against a religious sect, in which many members of the organization were killed, two years to the day previously.

SUBSTANCE ABUSE AND OCCUPATIONAL HOMICIDE

Case Study Number:	10
Location:	Unknown
Date of Incident:	Unknown
Category Profile:	CP I (employee against employee)
	CP II (employee against supervisor)
NIOSH Classification:	Public Administration industry

Facts of the Case: A government employee, 54 years old, was convinced that his coworkers and supervisor were ridiculing him. He believed they were preventing him from performing his job in a satisfactory way and that they frequently made unwanted sexual gestures at him. The employee was apparently suffering from depression and anxiety because of his negative experiences at work. He went to three different physicians for consultation, and each doctor prescribed barbiturates and amphetamines to alleviate his symptoms.   The employee then obtained multiple refills at different pharmacies. Although his wife was aware of his substance abuse, she did not notify any of the physicians or his employer. The employee, who was now severely addicted to the medications, soon received a poor performance evaluation.   He retaliated by shooting his supervisor and two coworkers to death. The individual was later found guilty of second-degree murder rather than first-degree murder, based largely on medical testimony at his trial indicating that he was chronically addicted to the medication prescribed by his doctors.[14]

Observations: Although this case history provides few specifics, it points out a workplace problem that is pervasive in American society—substance abuse. Many organizations now provide for some form of employee assistance when substance abuse is suspected. In such organizations, it is possible to use an assistance program to intervene and, perhaps save not only a life, but also a potentially valuable employee.

Implications for Prevention: It is unclear in this case whether or not intervention took place, although it seems unlikely given the facts. What is clear, though, is that this employee was exhibiting behavioral warning signs that affected his performance and indicated potential violence. Questions arise as to what procedures were in place at the organization to assist an employee experiencing the difficulties outlined in this case.

Despite the fact that the doctors involved may have acted irresponsibly in treating this individual, there may have been other possibilities to prevent the violence that ensued. Were the supervisors trained in recognizing the signs of substance abuse and in dealing with the problem? Was there an employee assistance program in place, and if so, how was it used? Did the employee develop any relationships with coworkers who might have been able to assist in an informed and nonthreatening way? Once again, as in other cases, what was the role of organizational security and why was it unable to prevent this violence? Although sparse in details, this case history, like many of those that have preceded it, leaves open the questions of involvement and intervention. Certainly someone in the organization witnessed the difficulties this employee was experiencing. Were his difficulties ignored because no one in the workplace cared to be involved? It is ironic in the extreme that workers can form life-long friendships based solely on their mutual experiences at work, yet prove unwilling to become personally involved when an employee is in obvious difficulty.

Once again, it is unwise to speculate and assume in a case such as this. The efforts taken by management, supervisors, and coworkers are simply not sufficiently known. The question that must always be asked is to what extent efforts were made to prevent potential violence through observation, understanding, and, where appropriate, positive intervention.

All organizations should support proactive and effective substance abuse programs for employees. Substance abuse is epidemic in the United States, so any worthy violence prevention program must deal with this issue in a clear and meaningful manner. Beyond this, managers should create a caring work environment wherein individuals are willing to support each other in times of need and involve managers when intervention is indicated.

PACIFIC SOUTHWEST AIRLINES

Case Study Number:	11
Location:	Near San Luis Obispo, California
Date of Incident:	December 9, 1987
Category Profile:	CP I (employee against employee)
	CP II (employee against supervisor)
	CP V (indiscriminate homicide)
NIOSH Classification:	Transportation industry
	Professional/Specialist occupation

Facts of the Case: David Burke was a 35-year-old father who worked for USAir, the parent company of Pacific Southwest Airlines (PSA), for over thirteen years in New York before moving to Los Angeles. On the West Coast he worked for PSA as a ticket agent. While he was stationed in New York, Burke had been investigated by the FBI and local police for narcotics sales and automobile theft but had never been charged formally. He was described as a genial, hard-working employee, but also as a person with an unpredictable, violent temper. On November 19, 1987, Burke was fired from his job by supervisor Raymond Thomson who accused him of stealing $69 in flight receipts from in-flight operations.

On December 9, 1987, Burke was able to board PSA flight 1771 on a scheduled run from Los Angeles to San Francisco, which originated in San Diego. Despite the fact Burke no longer had his PSA employee identification card, airport security personnel, knowing him by sight, allowed him to pass around security checkpoints and board the flight. The supervisor who terminated Burke, Raymond Thomson, was onboard on the same flight. What transpired while the airplane was en route was later reconstructed from the flight recorder and radio conversations.

While airborne over San Luis Obispo, Burke brandished a .44-Magnum revolver that he had smuggled aboard the airplane and shot Thomson. He then forced his way into the cockpit and shot the entire flight crew. The airplane subsequently plummeted to the ground, killing all 43 on board. Among the wreckage, the FBI located the revolver which Burke had borrowed from a friend, as well as a note written by Burke to Thomson. It had been scribbled on the back of an air sickness bag and read: "I think it's sort of ironical that we end up like this. I asked for some leniency for my family, remember? Well, I got none and you'll get none."[15]

Observations: The obvious tragedy in this case history is the loss of so many innocent lives. There is also a sense of the horrible that accompanies the way in which they died. These factors allow little or no sympathy for David Burke. This incident raised a furor nationwide, and in the Congress, regarding airline security measures. Clearly, this mass murder could have been avoided if even the most basic of established security measures had been followed by airline personnel. Reporter Mitchell Satchell, writing on the subject of airline security and this incident for *U.S. News and World Report* in 1987 wrote: "But how could such a large gun—recovered two days after the crash—have been smuggled aboard? USAir officials said they had confiscated Burke's employee badge. Still, the FBI said Burke was allowed to bypass security screening as a familiar airline employee." [16]

A year before this incident, a nationwide study of airline security was undertaken by the U.S. government. The study disclosed some disturbing trends:

1. At Dulles Airport, Washington, D.C., 25% of mock weapons used in the security examinations were successfully smuggled past airport security personnel.
2. About 25% of 9,000 airline employee identification cards were missing or otherwise unattributed in the airline personnel records.

Based on these national results, the Federal Aviation Administration (FAA) was told to immediately improve airline operations by increasing the quality of inspections and security procedures at airports nationwide.[17] Clearly, the anticipated improvements in security came too late for David Burke's victims.

Implications for Prevention: The failure of security procedures in the PSA case is obvious. Less certain are the personnel procedures in place at the time Burke was terminated from his job. Given Burke's history with USAir, it is possible that the organization was quick to use the opportunity of missing in-flight money to terminate him. This action may have been justified. However, the question that arises is one of methodology. Burke's brushes with the legal system and violent temper were probably known to airline management. In this regard, it would have been reasonable for management to take additional precautions when dealing with him. Did USAir and PSA have procedures in place for dealing with terminated employees in such a way as to diffuse potential retaliation in a situation where the individual was thought to be volatile? Was termination the only option available? If so, how was the process handled? Was Burke provided sufficient opportunity to protest the action and state his case?

Procedures for terminating employees must account for the possibility of retaliation. Sound personnel management demands that there be a process for dealing with an exiting employee that is at least as thorough as the employment process. The exit process must not leave the organization, its employees, or its client in peril. In the past decade there have been a number of workplace homicides attributed to employee terminations or layoffs. Given the uncertain state of the American economy, which often results in unexpected business reorganizations, the importance of the exit process for a terminated employee is crucial and cannot be underestimated. Admittedly, the PSA incident is an extreme example of the importance of properly handling employee terminations. There is, however, sufficient data from other workplace homicides to make a compelling case for strong personnel management techniques in this area.

The most innocuous breach of security can result in devastation. It is vital that employees be, not only fully aware of security procedures, but also committed to following them, even in uncomfortable situations. Security training and follow-up are crucial to any violence prevention program. Personnel procedures must be adequate at all points, particularly in dealing with terminations or layoffs.

Recent Similar Cases

The media abounds with cases of occupational homicide resulting from the actions of terminated employees. This is particularly true in the past few years. Here are some examples:

1. *December 15, 1995, Evandale, Ohio.* Gerald Clemons, 53, of Cleveland, returned to the Trans-Continental Systems office from which he had been fired a few days earlier. Brandishing two pistols, Clemons shot and killed three employees and wounded a fourth. A witness stated Clemons was "going after [someone] who had screwed him over." After the murders, Clemons surrendered quietly to authorities.[18]
2. *July 19, 1995, Los Angeles, California.* A city electrician with a 12-year work history shot and killed four of his supervisors when he learned he was facing dismissal for poor work performance. After the shootings, the killer, 42, surrendered to police without further incident. He was heard saying that he had specifically targeted the four victims because he "felt he was being picked on and singled out" by them and was about to lose his job.[19]
3. *May 18, 1995, Asheville, North Carolina.* An individual described as a "classic loner," who had just been fired from his job at a machine tool company, returned the next day with a rifle and a pistol. The perpetrator, who as 47 years old, killed three coworkers and wounded another four before surrendering to police.[20]
4. *April 4, 1995, Corpus Christi, Texas.* A terminated employee, 28 years old, walked into a refinery inspection company and killed five coworkers with a handgun before turning it on himself. He was carrying a 9-millimeter semiautomatic pistol and a .32-caliber revolver.[21]

Although most ex-employees who become violent do so immediately or very soon after they are terminated, there are exceptions to this pattern. The case of Jerry Hessler is an example of a discharged employee who became violent more than a year after his termination. Hessler was terminated from his job at a bank credit card center in Columbus, Ohio, in October 1994, following charges of sexual harassment. A year later, on the night of November 19-20, 1995, Hessler sought his revenge. Armed with a handgun and wearing a bullet-proof vest, Hessler forced his way into the homes of two ex-coworkers. During his rampage he fatally shot four individuals, including a 4-month-old girl, and seriously wounded two others. He was captured while attempting to flee Columbus in his automobile. Hessler was 38 years old at the time of the murders. Although this kind of delayed violent reaction is not typical, it has occurred with sufficient frequency to warrant being considered a real possibility in any violence prevention program.

ELGAR CORPORATION

Case Study Number:	12
Location:	San Diego, California
Date of Incident:	June 4, 1991
Category Profile:	CP II (employee against supervisor)
NIOSH Classification:	Manufacturing industry
	Professional/Specialist occupation

Facts of the Case: The Elgar Corporation, San Diego facility, employed approximately 300 individuals involved in the manufacturing of power electronics equipment. In early 1991 the company laid off five workers due to a fluctuation in their production level. One of the laid-off workers was Larry Hanson, a 41-year-old test technician, who was married and the father of two children. Hanson had worked for Elgar Corporation for three years prior to losing his job. It was the company's policy to lay employees off by ranking their job performance and eliminating workers from the bottom of the ranking list.

Between March and June of that year, Hanson was allowed to come back to the company headquarters several times to use the telephone and prepare his resume. The organization had no outplacement program or other formalized assistance program for employees who were terminated. According to the vice president for human resources, the company "had an open-door policy" regarding terminated employees.[22]

On June 4, 1991, in the afternoon, Hanson returned to the headquarters once again. On this visit he set off two remote-control pipe bombs, one of which started a fire in the building. He then approached the building reception area and shot out the company switchboard, severing all communications in the building and to outside services. He ran upstairs to the executive offices and shot the vice president/general manager, and the organization's regional sales manager. Both died at the site. Hanson was also looking for his former supervisor and the vice president of human resources, both of whom managed to avoid him. No warnings were given to any of the employees in the building, nor did law enforcement officials arrive on the scene until after Hanson had fled. Hanson fled on a mountain bicycle he had previously hidden at the scene.

He rode some distance away and then transferred to his automobile for a well-planned escape. Hanson later surrendered to authorities about 135 miles from the crime scene.

Observations: Hanson was known to his coworkers to be "a religious fanatic, a doomsayer and a survivalist."[23] He avoided other workers and was considered a loner; coworkers did what they could to avoid interacting with him. Hanson once said to his supervisor, "This is stressful—remember what happened at the Escondido post office." He was referring to an incident of occupational homicide that took place in a town just north of San Diego in August 1989, in which a 52-year-old postal worker murdered two coworkers and committed suicide.

Immediately after the tragedy, the organization made significant efforts to assist employees. Among the actions taken by the company were:

1. A telephone team was set up to keep employees and vendors informed of the status of the business.
2. Employees were told not to return to work until the premises were cleaned up and reorganized.
3. The organization called upon a public relations agency to help deal with the press.
4. A trauma team was established for the employees, which provided two weeks of intensive individual and group therapy. In addition, the trauma team offered 24-hour telephone assistance as well as help for the families of the staff who were traumatized by the incident. Long-term counseling was provided for employees in need.

Subsequent to the murders, the organization also took the following long-term actions:

1. In response to employee criticisms that the management acted in an uncaring manner about workers, the organization launched a program to improve communications throughout the workforce as well as between management and staff.
2. Office security was increased on a variety of fronts, including installation of a new card access entry system.
3. An emergency warning system was installed.

Implications for Prevention: This case was fairly well documented and provides a unique view of the actions taken by an organization after an incident of occupational homicide.[24] The Elgar Corporation tragedy also demonstrates a repeat of management mistakes that were apparent in previous case histories.

It is clear that management was either unaware of, or not sufficiently responsive to, the behavioral warning signs exhibited by Hanson to his coworkers. Still, management must have been cognizant of at least some difficulties with this employee since they had laid him off based on performance criteria. It is not clear how these performance criteria were established or used in the case of Larry Hanson. It is also not apparent that the corporation made any attempt at positive intervention when dealing with

Hanson's workplace behavior or performance. Management appears to have been aware of the fact that it was dealing with a troubled employee but apparently had no methodology in place to accommodate the situation.

It appears that communication lines between workers and management were weak. Workers knew Hanson and avoided him. The vice president for human resources for the corporation said that Hanson was not a problem employee and had showed no hostile intentions, but this was clearly not the view of Hanson's coworkers. Apparently, the common knowledge of Hanson's odd behavior was either not sufficiently recognized by management or else not taken seriously.

The company had an "open-door" policy for ex-employees, yet it provided no formal or structured services for those who were laid off. There was no employee assistance program for terminated employees and no outplacement program. Apparently, there were no formal services whatsoever to cover the eventuality of layoffs. It is also not clear how decisions regarding layoffs were made or communicated to workers. In general, personnel practices seem to have been inadequate. Security for this work site was also apparently inadequate.

After the incident, the company made a strong effort to assist employees with trauma counseling. These efforts were, no doubt, beneficial; an assumption can be made that they were also quite costly. There was no formal crisis management or trauma plan in place before the incident. Despite this, the company did as good of a job at post-incident employee assistance as could be expected. In addition, the organization made continuing efforts to improve security and, most important, communications. Unfortunately, it is apparent that the corporation had been completely unprepared for an incident of occupational homicide.

Creating a healthy work environment is crucial to violence prevention. The work environment must benefit from a number of integrated programs, including safety, security, trauma and crisis planning, employee assistance, outplacement programs, and, most important, a commitment to excellent communications. Management must work tirelessly at ensuring open and honest communications with staff. A threat made by an employee is always a serious matter and must never be ignored. Finally, management must create an environment in which workers know they are highly valued and trust management sufficiently to convey information that may indicate a threat to the workplace.

CLIENT RETALIATION

Case Study Number:	13
Location:	Burlingame, California
Date of Incident:	August 12, 1993
Category Profile:	CP III (client against employee/supervisor)
	CP V (indiscriminate homicide)

NIOSH Classification: Service industry
                          Professional/Specialist occupation

Facts of the Case: Balbir Singh Lally, 40 years of age, made his living by purchasing, remodeling, and selling single family homes in a middle-income area south of San Francisco. As was typical of many individuals in this line of work, Lally suffered through lean economic times and benefited significantly when home sales were brisk. It was an "up and down" business, with which Lally was familiar. Lally also had a relationship with a local, well known real estate broker, William J. Britton, and his son, John. The Brittons and Lally had been involved in joint real estate transactions in the past. In the late 1980s, Lally's business was doing well until he suffered a fire that destroyed his home. Following the fire, the local real estate market experienced a sudden and significant downturn. Lally was forced to file for bankruptcy and move into a smaller home in a low-income area of San Francisco. Things went from bad to worse for Lally, and he was unable to support his wife and two sons. The Brittons, realizing that Lally could not manage to keep his home, purchased it at a foreclosure sale. Lally pleaded with the Brittons for time to make payments and somehow save his home; he also refused to move out of the house when the Brittons made it clear that they would take possession. On August 12, 1993, in the late afternoon, Lally walked into the Britton's office. He waited for the receptionist and other Britton family members to leave, and then entered the inner offices, armed with a .38-caliber revolver. Lally shot and killed William Britton, aged 63 years, and wounded his son, John, aged 35 years. Lally then drove to a local beach and attempted to commit suicide by shooting himself in the chest. Although wounded, he then changed his mind about the suicide and flagged down a passing motorist for assistance. Lally was tried in 1994 and found guilty of first-degree murder and attempted murder.[25]

Observations: It is clear that the Brittons had every legal right to pursue the economic course of purchasing Lally's home at the foreclosure sale. It is equally obvious that Lally's actions were heinous and unwarranted. Despite these facts, this is a case in which many indications of impending violence were obvious. Lally was an individual who was greatly concerned about his failed ability to support his family; he was a man accustomed to the inconsistencies of his trade and probably felt that he could once again be successful, as in the past. According to the investigation that ensued, Lally pleaded frequently with the Brittons in an effort to keep his home. At one point he even threatened physical harm. Surely the Brittons knew, or suspected, that Lally was a man with little left to lose and willing to take extreme measures to protect himself and his family. Despite this knowledge, the Brittons pursued their course of action and apparently made no significant effort to ensure their own protection or settle the dispute with Lally.

Implications for Prevention: This case is disheartening in that the outcome seems preordained. Would it not have been possible for the parties to find some middle ground of commonality before violence became inevitable?

Violence is frequently the final result of a continuum of incidents, behaviors, and reactions, few or none of which are actually preordained. Intervention somewhere along this continuum can save lives by obviating the need for a violent reaction. This concept—intervention—lies at the heart of effective violence prevention methodologies.

Recent Similar Cases

Threats from clients or other nonworkers is a major concern for many American organizations. This form of violence is increasing each year, and individually, such acts are becoming more deadly. On December 8, 1995, in Harlem, a man who was apparently involved in protesting the closure of a neighborhood music shop entered the master-tenant's clothing store with a gun and arson materials. He immediately set the store on fire and began shooting at nearby workers. Eight individuals were killed, including the perpetrator, and another three were seriously wounded by gunfire.

THE QUESTION OF SANITY AND OCCUPATIONAL HOMICIDE

Case Study Number:	14
Location:	Milwaukee, Wisconsin
Date of Incident:	1990
Category Profile:	CP II (employee against supervisor)
NIOSH Classification:	Service industry
	Professional/Specialist occupation

Facts of the Case: Christopher Scarver received national notoriety in November 1994 when he was charged with the slaying of mass murderer Jeffrey Dahmer. At the time of Dahmer's killing, Scarver was already serving a life sentence for murdering his work supervisor in 1990. While incarcerated, Scarver had been heavily medicated with antipsychotic medication for an extended period of time.

Scarver, at age 25, was accepted into a job-training program in Milwaukee in 1990. He had no criminal record or history of violence at the time of his acceptance into the program. Shortly after beginning the program, Scarver fatally shot a job training supervisor four times in the head, forced the program manager to write him a check for $3,000, and fled the premises after also stealing a few dollars in petty cash. He was arrested a few hours later on the stoop of his girlfriend's apartment, without incident. Scarver immediately claimed he heard voices ordering him to commit the crimes. He also insisted he was "the chosen one" and "the son of God"—a theme Scarver was reported to have consistently used throughout his adult life. At his trial, Scarver offered an insanity plea as defense. Court appointed psychiatrists were divided on the nature of Scarver's disability but were in general agreement that he was psychotic. Nevertheless, Scarver was found competent to stand trial and, later, found guilty of the murder with which he was charged. He was placed in the Columbia Correctional Institution near Madison, Wisconsin.

In prison, Scarver was generally considered to be insane by the prison staff and other inmates. He was given continuing antipsychotic medication in an attempt to control his violent and erratic behavior. Despite this treatment, he severely beat other inmates, critically injuring at least one. In November 1994 Scarver attacked and killed two inmates who were assigned to a work patrol with him, one of whom was Jeffrey Dahmer.[26]

Observations: Behavioral warning signs are critical to avoiding potential violence, but only if they are recognized and used effectively. The case of Christopher Scarver demonstrates that the understanding of potentially violent behavior is, at best, an uncertain process. However, the effectiveness of recognizing behavioral warning signs to protect the workplace does not require a specific diagnosis or even a comprehensive understanding of behavior.

Scarver's extremely violent behavior, beginning with the murder of his supervisor in 1990, developed into an uncontrollable pattern throughout his imprisonment. His compulsion to act violently was clearly recognized by prison staff, who tried to control Scarver's outbursts through medication. Certainly, from a layman's point of view, Scarver could not be considered an individual who acted in a rational or sane manner. Nonetheless, psychiatrists were unable to come to an agreement about Scarver's diagnosis or an understanding of his actions. The result of this inability to determine how best to deal with Scarver's illness resulted in future violence.

Implications for Prevention: What should have been clearly understood by prison officials seems to have been overlooked. Why was an individual known to be as violent as Scarver allowed to mix with the general population of the prison without adequate supervision? One of the most predictable indicators of an individual's potential for violence is a history of violence. Although many inmates are violent, Scarver was known to be patently more violent than the typical member of the prison population. This issue should not have been ignored by prison officials since they had the advantage of knowing Scarver's violent history—an advantage not shared by his supervisor at the job-training center.

There are few specifics available about Scarver's behavior prior to his first violent act in 1990. It is possible, however, that Scarver demonstrated significant behavioral warning signs prior to murdering his supervisor. This would be especially likely to be true if he was psychotic. The question arises as to whether or not Scarver's coworkers would have been able to prevent the workplace violence that occurred had they been trained in the recognition of behavioral warning signs and the use of intervention techniques. A specific diagnosis of Scarver's illness would not have been necessary to trigger some form of intervention had key behavioral warning signs been in evidence and staff training in place. As discussed earlier in this study, it is often the case that one or more key behavioral warning signs are demonstrated by a potentially violent individual prior to the actual criminal act.

ASSAULT WEAPONS AND ILLEGAL WEAPONS

Case Study Number:	15
Location:	Washington, D. C.
Date of Incident:	November 22, 1994
Category Profile:	CP V (indiscriminate homicide)
NIOSH Classification:	Service industry
	Professional/Specialist occupation

Facts of the Case: Bennie Lee Lawson, a 25 year-old male suspect in a triple murder incident in the Nation's capitol, walked into the District of Columbia police headquarters on November 22, 1994, armed with a semiautomatic TEC-9 assault weapon. This weapon had been specifically banned by Congress earlier in 1994, with legislation aimed at reducing crime. It was the same weapon used by Gian Luigi Ferri in 1993 at a San Francisco law firm when he attacked a busy workplace and murdered eight individuals, finally committing suicide with the same gun. Lawson was able to hide the weapon successfully and make his way to the third floor of police headquarters, where the homicide division was located. It was thought that Lawson was specifically stalking homicide detectives who had earlier questioned him about the recent triple murder. Lawson drew his weapon and began firing indiscriminately, killing a detective, two FBI agents, and wounding others. He was shot and killed by other officers in the area.[27]

Observations: Beyond the obvious lack of security at the police headquarters in question, this case points out an increasingly common theme in recent workplace homicides—the use of weapons designed for maximum violence. The TEC-9 is a weapon made by Intratec Corporation, a Miami company founded by Cuban exiles, and is specifically designed as a weapon of war. It uses .9-millimeter (mm) ammunition and, at a minimum, carries a 36-round magazine. With its ability to fire large rounds rapidly, the use of this weapon is only too obvious—and deadly.

The availability of assault weapons has increased dramatically in recent years. Modern assault weapons are extremely powerful, deadly, and often superior to the handguns used by traditional law enforcement officials. Despite legislative attempts to regulate these weapons, their use in the workplace has become increasingly frequent in the past five years. Many recent incidents of indiscriminate workplace homicide reported in the press involved the use of these lethal, and often illegal, weapons.

Implications for Prevention: Weapons such as the TEC-9 have no place in American society, other than their possible use in the military. There has been recent movement in the Congress to outlaw many of these assault weapons. Still, such weapons are readily available and much desired by those driven to violence. It is clear that American political leaders must implement much stronger measures to ensure that assault weapons such as the TEC-9 are completely banished, whether by public or private sale and whether legally licensed or illegally obtained. The risk to public safety that these weapons present should not be tolerated by the American citizenry, either in the workplace or elsewhere.

A YEAR OF OCCUPATIONAL HOMICIDE IN ALASKA

Case Study Number: 16 [vi]
Location: Various locations in Alaska
Date of Incident: 1993 (multiple)
Category Profile: Various (multiple)
NIOSH Classification: Various (multiple)

Facts of the Case: Prior to 1993, the state of Alaska experienced an average of 2 workplace homicides each year.   By 1993, however, the third leading cause of death in the workplace was murder.   In that year, Alaska experienced 11 workplace homicides, or a rate of 4.1 murders per 100,000 workers.   This surge in occupational homicides prompted officials to investigate each case in detail and attempt to define parameters for the incidents.   The Alaskan investigation disclosed certain characteristics of occupational homicide that are quite common throughout the contiguous United States:[28]

1. All the victims were male, as were all the perpetrators.
2. The median age of the victims was 40 years, with a range of 22 to 50 years. The median age of the perpetrators was approximately the same.
3. Eight of the murders involved firearms.
4. Six of the 11 victims knew their assailants, 2 did not. In 3 cases it was unknown if there was a relationship between the victim and assailant.
5. In five of the incidents there was no other crime involved. In three of the incidents a robbery was in progress. No information was available for the other incidents.
6. The occupations of the victims were:
    A. maintenance personnel (2),
    B. taxicab driver (2),
    C. airline pilot (1),
    D. shopkeeper (1),
    E. forester (1),
    F. painter (1),
    G. army national guardsman (1),
    F. health aid (1), and
    G. security guard (1).

---

vi. This case study represents a compendium of incidents that occurred in Alaska in 1993.   It has been included to provide a broad overview of occupational homicide as an emerging issue.

7. Four of the incidents were caused when an argument escalated into violence, while at least two appeared to have been unprovoked acts of homicide. Information about the other incidents was unavailable.

Observations: The murders in Alaska are interesting in that they exhibit a typical cross-section of the general pattern of this crime throughout the contiguous United States. The profile of the victims and perpetrators, type and frequency of weapon, and variation in profession are all representative of the broader national experience of occupational homicide.

Implications for Prevention: The striking similarities in so many incidents of occupational homicide provide an opportunity to isolate elements that may provide a measure of forward-looking protection. Due to the significant coincidence of many of the characteristics of workplace murderers it is possible to construct a profile of the individual most likely to commit such a crime at the job site. Such a profile is an integral part of a successful violence prevention program.

CASES OF INDISCRIMINATE OR UNPREDICTABLE OCCUPATIONAL HOMICIDE

It is possible that many occupational homicides may be prevented by a judicious integration of workplace safety measures and an awareness of behavioral warning signs that can foster proactive intervention. Unfortunately, some homicides appear to be completely unpredictable or indiscriminate acts in which victims are selected at random or the perpetrator's motives are wholly unclear. Whether these acts are truly random or indiscriminate is not known to a certainty, usually because there is insufficient information available about the perpetrator or his motives. It is possible that, with sufficient study and understanding, many apparently random killings could provide information to aid in the prevention process. However, it is also true that there is no obvious way to protect workers from every potentially deadly situation. Violence prevention on such a broad basis is an issue beyond the sole jurisdiction of the workplace. At present, without a long-term study of all forms of violence that affects workers, the most to be attained is an awareness of the potential for homicide in the workplace. Perhaps this awareness can, in itself, provide the impetus for employers and employees to cooperatively engage in a serious violence prevention program that not only encompasses the workplace but extends to the practice of personal safety measures. An interdisciplinary approach, undertaken by organizations acting in a cooperative manner, could significantly enhance violence prevention on a national scale. Sadly, in America, such a cooperative venture is not on the immediate horizon.

The following case studies represent different aspects of indiscriminate or unpredictable homicide in the workplace. In the first case, victims were murdered indiscriminately but with a motivation that was at least somewhat clear, albeit heinous.[vii]   There is at least a possibility, however, that more effective management at the murderer's former workplace may have prevented the crime. This incident points out the interconnectedness of workplaces in America and how, through organizational coordination, commitment, and cooperation, workplace violence could be mitigated.

The second incident appears to have been completely unpredictable. The motivation of the perpetrator could not be determined and there was no apparent connection between the murderer and his victims. The nature of the organization, with its tradition of open access, would likely not allow for security measures that may have prevented the killings.

The case of John Taylor also represents the most unpredictable kind of occupational homicide. Taylor was a model employee with many friends who, for reasons completely unknown, became a vicious murderer. Taylor, like Patrick Sherrill, worked for the post office. Could the rather notorious work environment known to exist at the post office have played a part in John Taylor's unexplained act of homicide?

LUBY'S CAFETERIA

Case Study Number:	17
Location:	Killeen, Texas
Date of Incident:	October 23, 1991
Category Profile:	CP V (indiscriminate homicide)
NIOSH Classification:	Various

Facts of the Case: On Bosses' Day, 1991, in Killeen, Texas, a local cafeteria was serving about 200 patrons, mostly workers from the immediate area, who had gathered to treat their employers to lunch. George Hennard, 35 years old, smashed his pickup truck through the front window of the cafeteria, exited the vehicle, and began shooting individuals with two semiautomatic pistols. Hennard killed 23 people that afternoon, shooting most of them in the head at close range. His rampage would have been much worse had it not been for the fact that several policemen attending a conference were close to the cafeteria. These officers heard the shots, responded, and wounded Hennard, who then shot himself in the head.[29]

Observations: Hennard was unemployed—a former merchant marine who lived alone in a nearby town. In 1989 he was terminated from his position, charged with possession of marijuana. Recounting his feelings about losing his job, Hennard said to a judge, "It [the job] means a way of life, it means my livelihood. It means all I've got. It's all I know."[30]

---

vii. There is a possibility that the murderer targeted women; however, the murdered women appear to have been selected indiscriminately.

Hennard was reputed to have a deep hatred of women; fourteen of his victims in the cafeteria were female.   Several women from Hennard's hometown had received threatening phone calls or been harassed by him, and more than one resident had received threatening letters. He was in the habit of standing in front of his home and shouting obscenities at passing women. In many cases, the women notified local law enforcement officials, but no significant action against Hennard was ever taken. There was not, however, any apparent connection between Hennard and any of the victims in the cafeteria. Local officials simply attributed Hennard's actions to his hatred for women.

Implications for Prevention: If   the interpretation provided by local officials was correct—and that is uncertain—there was nothing an employer could have done to protect workers from the kind of insane violence that occurred. Employers and employees, gathered in an activity important to the morale and solidarity of the workplace, were randomly executed for reasons apparently unconnected with their occupations. This kind of situation would, of course, be unforeseen, and therefore, beyond reasonable homicide prevention methods. However, there are other possible explanations.

An unanswered question in this case is why Hennard chose this time and place to commit his outrageous crime. Was it significant that Hennard chose Bosses Day on which to commit his crimes? Was there a possibility that Hennard could have received positive intervention or assistance from his previous employer? He was known to have a substance abuse problem, but did his employer make any effort at intervention or referral? It is possible that Hennard's employer chose to be rid of a "problem employee" in the most expeditious manner possible rather than make an effort at intervention.

If Hennard was typical of a potentially violent individual, he would have displayed many behavioral warning signs that should have been apparent to his previous employer. Such behavior would have presented opportunities for intervention. Was Hennard's employer unwilling to intervene and work with him to solve the problem? Was there an organizational program in place to assist employees in difficulty?

Was Hennard's termination handled in such a way as to diffuse potential violence? It was abundantly clear that Hennard viewed his job as vital to his well-being. Was he provided with any support in the departure from his job such that, after rehabilitation, he would have an opportunity to return to work or was he left without any hope for the future—a man with nothing more to lose?

Although the Killeen victims were apparently unconnected with Hennard, perhaps his previous employer could have taken steps to prevent the violence that later occurred. It is possible that an act of intervention taken by Hennard's former employer could have made an interorganizational and life-saving connection. Organizations do not work in isolation; they are deeply, though subtly, interrelated.   A successful violence prevention program in any workplace may benefit other organizations and possibly prevent future incidents. An employer who ignores potential violence at work may, through luck or circumstance, escape a deadly result at the time; however, the next workplace may be indirectly victimized by the original employer's failure to act. In this sense, there may be far fewer indiscriminate acts of occupational homicide than the literature indicates. A caring, astute employer will not only view violence prevention as important to his or her organization, but vital to American business generally.

SACRAMENTO LIBRARY

Case Study Number:	18
Location:	Sacramento, California
Date of Incident:	April 18, 1993
Category Profile:	CP V (indiscriminate homicide)
NIOSH Classification:	Service industry
	Professional/Specialist occupation

Facts of the Case: The library in California's capitol was holding a grand opening celebration in April 1993. The staff of the library and a number of citizens and dignitaries were present for the ceremonies. Barrett Street, 38 years old and a regular patron for many years, entered the third floor of the library and killed two librarians with a gun. He was cornered on the roof of the building by officers where, after a brief conversation, he raised his weapon in a threatening manner. The officers immediately shot Street, who fell from the roof ledge and died. After investigating the crime, officials were unable to determine why Street had murdered the librarians. Street gave no prior indications of violence and made no coherent statements at the time of the murders.

Observations: A case such as this defies any attempt to recommend a course of prevention. Given the nature of the organization (a public facility, which is free and open to all) and no apparent motive or connection between the victims and the perpetrator, it is impossible to draw any useful conclusion from the crime. Truly unpredictable incidents such as this are exceptional and relatively rare.

Implications for Prevention: A tragedy such as this may only have been preventable through measures of protection so onerous as to negate the purpose of the organization. In such situations, one must look to areas other than the science of management for an understanding of motive or purpose. There is, unfortunately, little in terms of prevention that would be helpful in such a bizarre situation.

ORANGE GLEN POST OFFICE

Case Study Number:	19
Location:	Orange Glen, California
Date of Incident:	August 10, 1989
Category Profile:	CP I (employee against employee)

NIOSH Classification:
CP V (indiscriminate homicide)
Public Administration industry
Professional/Specialist occupation

Facts of the Case: John Taylor worked for the Orange Glen Post Office for 27 years. He had often received awards and commendations from management for excellent performance and customer service. Taylor was also highly regarded by coworkers; he was arguably the most likable employee at the Orange Glen station. One of Taylor's supervisors said about him, "If you were to make a composite of a model employee, you'd come up with John Taylor."[31]

On August 10, 1989, at the age of 57 years, Taylor reported early to work, as usual. He was in the habit of meeting two coworkers who also reported early so that they could spend a few moments chatting together before beginning their daily duties. On this morning, however, Taylor came armed with a .22-caliber semiautomatic handgun and a box of ammunition. Without speaking a word, Taylor approached the two coworkers and shot them to death. He then roamed the post office, randomly shooting other workers. During his rampage he fired over 20 rounds and finally shot himself in the head. When police later investigated the incident, they discovered that Taylor had murdered his wife before leaving for work by shooting her twice in the head while she slept.

Observations: Taylor's coworkers and supervisors were completely shocked by the murders; so were his neighbors and friends. He was universally considered a most unlikely candidate as a murderer. It was nearly impossible to find an individual who did not have a kind word to say about John Taylor. Still, there may have been some warning signs that were overlooked because of Taylor's benign personality and excellent work performance.

A coworker who knew Taylor well claimed that he had a drinking problem that he kept secret. The problem apparently never affected his work performance or his relationships with friends or coworkers. In fact, there was no hard evidence of such a problem, and it was not believed true by many who knew Taylor.

Shortly before the killings, Taylor expressed concern that postal inspectors were investigating him by "planting" money along his postal route. He consistently turned the found money in to the postal authorities and was assured by them that he was not under investigation.

At least one of his coworkers mentioned, after the murders, that Taylor was concerned about possible investigations of his activities by his employer. Was this paranoia or a delusional disorder, embellishment of the facts by the reporting individual, or just coincidence? Whatever the situation, no action was taken by the post office managers, and it was not known for certain what Taylor really thought about the situation. As his coworkers frequently attested, Taylor was not one to complain about things.

Friends and neighbors consistently stated that Taylor was deeply in love with his wife. They noted that Mr. and Mrs. Taylor were always in the company of each other and seemed quite happy. There was no evidence of significant domestic difficulty throughout the marriage. Was this relationship as strong as it seemed, or was Taylor simply able to give a troubled relationship a positive appearance?

Implications for Prevention: This case is an enigma.   There is some evidence of behavioral warning signs, but they are not consistent or obvious. If Taylor was exhibiting warning signs such as paranoia or frustration, they were extremely subtle or well controlled. He was a long-term, well-liked employee who apparently loved his work and his wife. However, for some reason, he committed unprovoked murder in the home and at the workplace.   It is impossible to review this case without considering the actions of Patrick Sherrill at the Edmond, Oklahoma, post office. Was it simply coincidence that both incidents took place at a post office—a work environment then known to be difficult at best? Since these murders, the U.S. Postal Service has taken strong measures to improve the work environment at the local post office level throughout America. Surely, the management of the postal service recognized something was terribly wrong on a national scale. Perhaps what was known to so many postal employees for so long should have encouraged management to undertake positive personnel changes long before men like Sherrill and Taylor committed their crimes.

SITUATIONAL WORKPLACE VIOLENCE

Case Study Number:	20
Location:	Michigan
Date of Incident:	September 12, 1994
Category Profile:	CP I (employee against employee)
	CP V (indiscriminate homicide)
NIOSH Classification:	Manufacturing industry
	Occupation uncertain

Facts of the Case: Oliver French, 47 years of age, worked at the Ford Motor Company Rouge Plant for 28 years. He was an active member of the United Auto Workers (UAW) 600 in a work unit representing maintenance and construction workers. On September 12, 1994, the union held a meeting to discuss work issues.   As the meeting was progressing, French dismissed himself.   He returned about 20 minutes later, armed with a .357-caliber Magnum handgun, and starting shooting. During his rampage, French killed two coworkers and wounded two others. It was later disclosed that French could give no more comprehensive motivation for his actions than that he feared union activities that could lead to a plant shutdown or the layoff of workers.[32]

Observations: At times, indiscriminate occupational homicide develops because of uniquely stressful situations arising in or around the work environment.   A common example of this type of violence surrounds the aggressive and hostile environment emanating from work-strike activities in certain industries.   In the midst of a heated and hostile management/union work dispute, it sometimes happens that individuals act out their violent predispositions indiscriminately.

Implications for Prevention: This type of indiscriminate violence can be considered situational in most cases, and therefore allows for intervention by the use of negotiation and conflict resolution strategies. Unfortunately, at times, both sides become polarized and unwilling to negotiate toward a common goal. When such a stalemate ensues, violence can be the result. In fact, as in this example, even the expectation of an event feared by a worker can trigger unexpected violence.

SYMBOLIC, INDISCRIMINATE VIOLENCE

Case Study Number:	21
Location:	New York City, New York
Date of Incident:	August 31, 1994
Category Profile:	CP V (indiscriminate homicide)
NIOSH Classification:	Communication industry
	Professional/Specialist occupation

Facts of the Case: William Tager, 46 years of age, attempted to enter the studio of the "Today" television program while it was being aired nationally. He was stopped at a stage entrance by a security guard. When the security guard took action to notify local law enforcement officials of the attempt to gain entrance, Tager removed a rifle from underneath his coat, subsequently shooting and killing the guard. Tager was later found to be incompetent to stand trial for the murder. Although Tager never gave a clear motive for his actions, his disjointed statements led investigators to conclude that he viewed this television station, or perhaps the program itself, as symbolically evil.

Observations: Some forms of indiscriminate violence seem to have an origin in the effect of symbols on certain individuals. In such a situation, the perpetrator, often without a clearly stated motive, appears to be striking out against a symbolic enemy and, unfortunately, murders indiscriminately as a result. The perpetrators of these crimes will sometimes later declare a political motivation to justify their actions or, at times, will be ultimately diagnosed as suffering from a disorder that deems them legally incompetent during the process of the crime.

Implications for Prevention: The implications are indeterminate.

A CASE OF LONG-TERM BEHAVIORAL WARNING SIGNS

Case Study Number:	22
Location:	Montreal, Canada
Date of Incident:	August 24, 1992
Category Profile:	CP I (employee against employee)
	CP V (indiscriminate homicide)

NIOSH Classification: Service industry (education)
                            Professional/Specialist occupation

Preamble: There are few cases in which detail is sufficient to examine the complete development of an incident of occupational homicide. Often, detailed history about the perpetrator or knowledge of the ongoing reactions of managers and coworkers is unknown. The case of Dr. Valery Fabrikant at Concordia University is an exception to this general lack of knowledge. This case presents a 13-year view of events that led inexorably to mass murder in the workplace. It has the advantage of offering an observation of both the perpetrator's behavior and the reactions of coworkers and managers as the brutal incident developed. In this way, the case of Dr. Fabrikant provides a real life example of how a potential workplace murderer acted out his growing compulsion towards violence while, at the same time, individuals in his environment tried to cope with a situation that wheeled out of control.

Fabrikant was a Russian émigré who traveled to Canada on Italian papers in 1979. He was reputed to be a recognized scientist in Russia who had published papers as far back as 1971. In reality, however, no one knew his background at all. He joined Concordia University in late 1979, and worked there for almost 13 years. On August 24, 1992, Fabrikant went on a murderous rampage, killing four fellow professors and wounding another. Unlike many workplace murderers, Fabrikant survived his crime and was tried in the courts.

This case is one that received a good deal of attention and was subject to intense investigation at Concordia University. A number of papers were written that outlined Dr. Fabrikant's actions as well as a variety of alleged misjudgments made by university officials in dealing with the professor.[33] Because of the attention this case received, it is possible to reconstruct many of the circumstances that led up to the tragedy in Montreal.

Facts of the Case: The chronology of the Fabrikant case begins with his arrival in Montreal in 1979:

December 18, 1979. Fabrikant arrives at the office of T. S. Sankar, chair of the Department of Mechanical Engineering, Concordia University. He has no appointment and is not known to Sankar, yet he insists on meeting with him personally about a job. It is Dr. Sankar's policy not to see applicants without a curriculum vitae (CV) and a prior appointment. Dr. Fabrikant tries to "talk his way in" but is rebuked. He leaves his CV and makes a future appointment.

December 19, 1979. Dr. Fabrikant returns to Dr. Sankar's office, once again, without an appointment. He is extremely persistent and eventually gets Dr. Sankar to meet with him. For some reason, Sankar gives Fabrikant a job on the spot, without any background check or reference material other than his CV and their conversation.

December 20, 1979. Fabrikant starts his new job on a work permit as Sankar's research assistant. He is given an annual salary of $7,000 per year.

August 1, 1980. Fabrikant is given the title of Research Associate. His annual salary is now $12,000, and Sankar appears to have been pleased with his performance.   Other members of the staff orally express concern about Fabrikant's aggressive and hostile behavior.

June 1, 1981. Sankar increases Fabrikant's pay to $16,000 per year and arranges for him to do some part-time teaching for an additional $2,080 per year.

May 27, 1982.   Sankar recommends to the dean that Fabrikant be appointed to the faculty position of Research Assistant Professor at an annual salary of $23,250. In the normal course of such an appointment, three letters of reference would be required. This requirement is waived in the case of Dr. Fabrikant, for reasons that are unclear. Research later indicates that there were never any letters of reference for Fabrikant on file at the university.

Also during 1982, Fabrikant is accused of rape by a female student, who reports the incident to a university ombudsperson. The woman is in such a psychological state, and apparently so afraid of Dr. Fabrikant, that she chooses not to pursue the matter further. Individuals later investigating the activities of Fabrikant were of the opinion that the rape probably took place, although legal action never resulted. No action was taken by the university.

Spring 1983.   Fabrikant enrolls in a French-language continuing education course (fee waived) at the university. He begins to show hostile and outrageous behavior in class, and particularly against the course instructor. Fabrikant repeatedly attacks the instructor, in writing and speech, in a vicious and humiliating manner. His behavior becomes so disruptive that he is barred from the course several times (orally, in writing, and by a legal order from the university).   Despite this, he attends class nonetheless and rips apart the documents forbidding his attendance in front of the instructor and students. Students withdraw from the class in fear and ask for assistance. The director of continuing education finally bars Fabrikant from all continuing education classes.

Fabrikant now takes the matter of the French-language course to a university ombudsperson and the rector. Fabrikant claims that his career has been irrevocably damaged because he is unable to take the course in question for free. He demands $1,000 so that he can take the French course elsewhere. He is twice refused in writing.

At the same time, Sankar is making efforts to get Fabrikant promoted to Research Associate Professor. In correspondence exchanged with the vice-rector academic, the latter writes that Fabrikant's behavior has "given cause for complaint in several quarters."

September 1, 1983. Fabrikant is promoted to Research Associate Professor.

September 27, 1983. Throughout this period, Fabrikant is still obsessively demanding $1,000 for the French course. The matter is finally brought to the university legal counsel, who notes that Fabrikant "continues to act in a completely irrational manner."   The issue is never completely resolved. Coworkers at the university continue to complain about Dr. Fabrikant's aggressive behavior.

June 1, 1984. Fabrikant's salary is increased to $27,000 per year.

June 1, 1985. Fabrikant's salary is increased to $30,000 per year.

October 1, 1986. Fabrikant's salary is increased to $37,500 per year. Although no formal documentation is available, Fabrikant has a unanimous reputation among his coworkers as an individual who is argumentative, aggressive, hostile, and unpredictable.

June 1, 1987. Fabrikant's salary is increased to $40,000 per year while coworkers and staff continue to complain about his behavior. It is reported that some colleagues at the university refuse to work with him.

November 1, 1987. Fabrikant's salary is increased to $42,000 per year, retroactive back to June 1, 1987.

April 29, 1988. Fabrikant attempts to cancel the purchase of an $8,400 laser printer ordered at his direction by Purchasing Services at the university. The reason he gives for the cancellation is because the delivery is a few days late. Fabrikant is told that the printer was shipped on April 27, two days earlier, and that the order cannot be canceled. Fabrikant becomes irrational and extremely hostile, refusing payment and demanding additional compensation because of the delay. He makes bizarre interpretations of the law to several coworkers and says he will charge the university rent for the printer.

May 18, 1988. Fabrikant receives a contract for two years, until May 31, 1990.

June 1, 1988. Fabrikant's salary is increased to $46,000 per year.

June 8, 1988. The manager of purchasing services warns university officials that the printer supplier is going to "cut off" the university because Fabrikant has refused to pay the bill for his purchase. He writes to the chair of the Mechanical Engineering Department for help and mentions that he wants co-signatures on all future requests from Fabrikant. In his letter to the chair, the manager notes that "this is not the first problem I've had with Dr. Fabrikant, who seems determined to see the inside of a courtroom."

The vice-rector is now dragged into the printer affair. Dr. Fabrikant has become irrational on the matter and is causing a great deal of disruption on a variety of fronts. To settle the matter and quiet Fabrikant, the vice-rector agrees to have the university warrant the printer for an additional year, bear the cost of any repairs, and allow a $2,000 overexpenditure as compensation.

June 19, 1988. The printer supplier refuses to do further business with the university.

January 19, 1989. Fabrikant writes to several coworkers complaining about a variety of things, many of a conspiratorial nature. In one letter he complains about "unfair treatment by the department over the years." Fabrikant is known to have made threats against several coworkers.

January 23, 1989. The university declines Fabrikant an early promotion to full professor. Fabrikant becomes obsessive about the issue and begins a vociferous campaign against coworkers and administrators. He claims that others in the university are benefiting from his research and that there is a general conspiracy against him. During this time, Fabrikant makes several threats of violence. One coworker recalls him saying, "I know how people get what they want, they shoot a lot of people." The university rector now arranges to have personal security because of Fabrikant's widespread threats.

April 1989. Officials of the university consult an outside psychiatrist on how to deal with Fabrikant. No decision on action is reached.

June 1, 1989. Fabrikant's pay is increased to $54,340 per year.

September 20, 1989. Fabrikant is recommended for a two-year contract, to extend until May 31, 1992.

November 15, 1989. The dean concurs with the recommendation for Fabrikant's contract renewal.

December 21, 1989. Fabrikant writes to the new vice-rector academic, asking a number of questions about tenure, teaching load, and clarification of his eligibility for a desired sabbatical leave.

January 23, 1990. Fabrikant receives a reply to his letter of December 21, 1989, but the reply is generally unresponsive.

February 1, 1990. Fabrikant writes again, in a hostile and irritable manner, and demands confirmation of some answers he proposes on his own. He later receives a response that rebukes his approach but does not deal with the issues originally raised in the December 21, 1989, letter.

Spring 1990. Fabrikant is refused promotion to the rank of Research Professor. No reasons are given.

June 26, 1990. Fabrikant appeals the refusal to the University Appeals Board. His appeal is later denied.

Summer-Fall 1990. Complaints about Fabrikant's bizarre and aggressive behavior continue to be voluminous. A large number of internal memoranda now appear that discuss his dismissal for disruptive conduct.

September 12, 1990.   The chair of the Department of Mechanical Engineering recommends that Fabrikant be appointed to a regular tenure-track position of Associate Professor. On the same date, a letter is written from the rector to Fabrikant implying that Fabrikant has been pestering too many individuals about his voluminous concerns. The letter rebukes Fabrikant and states that his behavior is inappropriate.

Fall 1990. Fabrikant begins a vitriolic campaign of letter writing and verbal accusations directed against coworkers. Although a few of Fabrikant's complaints have some merit, most are false and outrageous. This campaign continues until the shootings in August 1992. A sense of fear is prominent among Fabrikant's coworkers throughout this period.

October 18, 1990. The vice-rector academic warns Fabrikant that she believes he is harassing her and her staff. In this letter, she threatens disciplinary action.

October 30, 1990. The Personnel Committee meets to consider what can be done with Fabrikant. No decision is reached.

October 31, 1990. University officials meet with an outside psychiatrist to further discuss Fabrikant and how to deal with his behavior. No action is taken.

December 4, 1990. Fabrikant is offered a two-year probationary appointment as Associate Professor at a salary of $56,677 per year. No conditions regarding his behavior are attached to the offer.

December 11, 1990. Fabrikant accepts the offer, which was made retroactive for six months.

November 7, 1991. Four senior department members write to the secretary general of the university asking for an emergency suspension of Fabrikant. No action is taken.

November 18, 1991. The Personnel Committee recommends not to renew Fabrikant's appointment at the end of his contract, in May 1992.

November 20, 1991. The University Intervention Team suggests that an outside individual be recruited to handle the Fabrikant situation. No further action is taken on this issue.

November 21, 1991. Fabrikant's request for a sabbatical leave is formally denied again.

December 12, 1991. The vice-rector academic agrees to allow Fabrikant an additional one-year renewal on his contract, with a set of four conditions. One of the conditions requires Fabrikant to correct his behavioral problems.

January 1992. Reports from coworkers indicate that Fabrikant's behavior has become even more bizarre and extreme. He is now verbally attacking a large number of individuals both within and outside the university.

January 15-23, 1992. A verbal and written battle breaks out between Fabrikant and university officials regarding his refusal to prove his credentials and questions about conflicting statements in his CV. Fabrikant is accused of falsifying his credentials.

Winter-Spring 1992. Fabrikant begins a war of words using electronic mail on the Internet and letters to anyone who appears receptive. He attacks coworkers with wild accusations and threats. Fabrikant has become so hostile and aggressive that some faculty members have installed "panic buttons" on their desks; others have doubled the locks on their office doors because they fear he might make good on his continuing threats of violence.[34]

April 21, 1992. The university writes to Fabrikant, implying disciplinary action if his aggressive behavior continues. No additional action is taken.

June 11, 1992. The chair of the board of governors of the university suggests that an independent inquiry be carried out to determine the validity, if any, of Fabrikant's charges about coworker misconduct. No mention is made of Fabrikant's behavior.

June 22, 1992. Fabrikant tries to get an employer endorsement from the university for his request to carry and transport a handgun on the university grounds.

June 23, 1992. Senior university officials meet to discuss Fabrikant's request about a weapon. They recommend that Fabrikant be immediately suspended, but no action is taken.

July 14, 1992. Fabrikant's request for an endorsement to carry a handgun is formally and forcefully declined by the university.

July-August 1992. Fabrikant continues his verbal and written attacks in an unrelenting manner. He is now risking contempt of court for comments made against a justice in various electronic mail messages, and he is facing a number of lawsuits resulting from other, similar actions.

August 21, 1992. The university's legal counsel writes to Fabrikant regarding his various public statements about coworkers and officials. He is warned of legal ramifications and his job is threatened, but no other action is taken.

August 24, 1992. Fabrikant comes to the ninth floor of Concordia University's Hall Building in downtown Montreal and begins shooting and taking hostages. He is armed with three handguns and a briefcase full of ammunition. Two staff members are mortally wounded, two are killed at the scene, and a fifth is wounded but survives. The 53-year-old Fabrikant is arrested after terrorizing the University for an hour and a half.

Spring-Summer 1993. Fabrikant is placed on trial after two court-appointed psychiatrists determine he is sane, but hostile and paranoid. During the course of the trial, Fabrikant receives six contempt-of-court citations. He hires, then fires, ten lawyers. At the end of the trial, he is acting as his own attorney. Throughout the trial, Dr. Fabrikant insists he was sane at the time of the murders and maintains he was provoked by the actions of his coworkers and the university staff. The superior court jury finds him guilty on four counts of murder, and he is sentenced to life imprisonment.

Observations: Fabrikant worked at Concordia University for nearly 13 years and, throughout his tenure, perpetually exhibited behavioral warning signs of violence. The university often ignored or overlooked nearly constant telegraphing by Fabrikant that he was an individual who represented a threat to the workplace. In fact, as the chronology demonstrates, the university often rewarded the professor, on one hand, while meeting to decide how to deal with him, on the other.

Implications for Prevention: The point of this chronology is not to attack or second-guess the decisions or actions of university officials. The objective here is to delineate the variety of ways in which behavior can provide clear warning signs of trouble. The sad, underlying theme in this case history is the nagging question, "Why didn't they *do* something before it was too late?"

There is little need to add commentary to this dark chronology. It serves as a primary example of an individual who, in the end, was completely out of control. There were many warning signs given by Fabrikant, making his case one of the best documented of its kind. Much could have been done, but was not. The management paralysis that gripped the university authorities was, in retrospect, horrifying and inexplicable. One is left to wonder if this tragedy could have been averted had the university been committed to an informed, proactive violence prevention program.

A CASE OF NEAR-TERM BEHAVIORAL WARNING SIGNS

Case Study Number:	23
Location:	Louisville, Kentucky
Date of Incident:	September 14, 1989
Category Profile:	CP I (employee against employee)
	CP II (employee against supervisor)
	CP V (indiscriminate homicide)
NIOSH Classification:	Manufacturing industry
	Professional/Specialist occupation

Facts of the Case: Joseph "Rock" Wesbecker was a 47-year-old pressman who had worked for the Standard Gravure Corporation for twenty years. For most of those years, Wesbecker was considered to be a model employee and was popular with coworkers. However, in the mid-1980s, things began to change when he experienced marital problems which eventually ended his marriage.

By 1988, due to the failure of his marriage and the stress of a poorly managed work environment, Wesbecker was in severe emotional trouble. He had become an erratic and unpredictable employee. Coworkers were no longer comfortable with Wesbecker and, it seemed, he had lost most of his friends. He became a collector of weapons and a persistent reader of paramilitary magazines; his aggressive and angry speech surprised and alienated his former friends. The once-gregarious Wesbecker now resorted to tactics of intimidation and threats of violence in the workplace.

During this time, Wesbecker approached management and asked to be placed in a less stressful job because he was suffering from depression. He even produced a doctor's certification to support his request. The company ignored both his request and the doctor's recommendation. Wesbecker was furious over the company's rejection of his request for a reassignment, and he let his coworkers and management know about it in no uncertain terms. He complained to the union and tried to engage their help, but he was unsuccessful in persuading the corporation to reassign him.

Wesbecker, now suffering from manic depression, was forced to take a disability leave at 60% of normal pay. At the time he went on leave, it was clear to his coworkers that Wesbecker was angry, violent, and intent on revenge. He had often vocalized his intentions to "get even" with the corporation which he viewed as a partner in his distress and the cause of widespread poor morale in the workplace.

In September 1989, 13 months after Wesbecker had been placed on leave, he returned to the Standard Gravure Corporation. Entering the premises, he confronted a long-time coworker with the greeting: "I told them I'd be back. Get out of my way, John. I told them I'd be back."[35] Wesbecker was armed with two semiautomatic 9-millimeter handguns, a .38-caliber revolver, a bayonet, and over 20 boxes of ammunition.

Wesbecker entered the building and made his way to the executive offices on the third floor. On his arrival, he shot a receptionist and another employee standing in the area. He continued shooting randomly until he had killed seven workers and wounded an additional fifteen. At the end of his rampage Wesbecker shot himself in the head.

Observations: Several years after the shootings at the Standard Gravure Corporation, a lawsuit was brought against the drug manufacturer, Eli Lilly Corporation, which centered around Wesbecker's actions. It was disclosed that Wesbecker had been taking the antidepressant medication Prozac for approximately one month prior to his murderous rampage. The lawsuit against Eli Lilly claimed that this medication was the cause of Wesbecker's actions. In December 1994, the jury hearing the case rejected the lawsuit, determining that Wesbecker's actions were not related to the medication.[36]

Implications for Prevention: The case of Joseph Wesbecker provides another clear example of the profile of a lethal employee.[37] In this case, the employer was well aware of the fact that a long-term, valued employee was experiencing difficulties; yet the organization chose to ignore the obvious. The result was horrific.

This tragedy should have been avoided by the corporation management. Wesbecker was a loyal employee who had performed well for two decades. When he was faced with a crisis in his life and approached his employer for assistance, the organization abandoned him. By their actions in ignoring Wesbecker's pleas for help, those in charge at the Standard Gravure Corporation helped set the stage for murder. With nothing left in his life but his job, and with obvious ties and commitments to his employer, Wesbecker felt he had no option but to take revenge. Certainly, he had given all the warning signs of what was to come. Unfortunately, they fell on deaf and, perhaps, uncaring, ears.

SUMMARY OF THE CASE STUDIES

These case studies provide a cross-section of occurrences of murder in the workplace. They are, of course, a small sample of the many work-related homicides that have occurred. Still, these cases are representative of the issue of occupational homicide and therefore provide a starting point to help support a workable profile of the potentially violent employee.

A summary of some of the key case studies provides an interesting, encapsulated view of the many similarities to be found among the perpetrators who have been examined (see Table 3.1).
must possess an especially firm understanding of the workings of occupational homicide from both the perpetrator's point of view and the organizational standpoint

Table 3.1: Summary of Key Case Studies

Case	Sex		Age	Category Profile					Behavioral Warning Signs									
	M	F		I	II	III	IV	V	1	2	3	4	5	6	7	8	9	10
1	X		?			X		X								X	X	
2	X		?			X		X								X		
3	X		?			X		X								X		
4	X	X	?				X											X
5	X		?				X		uncertain									
6	X		?				X		uncertain									
7	X		52			X							X			X		
8	X		45	X			X								X	X		
9	?		?				X		uncertain									
10	X		54	X	X									X				X
11	X		35	X	X		X		X			X			X			
12	X		41	X										X		X		
13	X		40				X								X	X		
14	X		25		X				X	X								
15	X		25				X		uncertain									
16	X		40	multiple incidents					multiple incidents									
17	X		35				X							X		X		X
18	X		38				X		uncertain									
19	X		57	X			X		uncertain									
20	X		47	X			X									X		
21	X		46				X		X									
22	X		53	X			X									X		
P [viii]	X		25-55				X									X		

Key: Behavioral Warning Signs

1. history of violence
2. psychosis
3. erotomania
4. chemical dependence
5. depression
6. pathological blamer
7. impaired neurological functioning
8. elevated frustration
9. interest in weapons
10. personality disorder

Category Profiles

I. Employee against employee
II. Employee against supervisor, supervisor against employee
III. Client against employee, employee against client
IV. Homicide by agenda or for political purposes
V. Indiscriminate homicide

[viii] Represents the most common profile among the case studies presented.

FINDINGS FROM THE CASE STUDIES

As demonstrated in these case studies, an incident of murder in the workplace is often a complex web of human interactions that requires a knowledge not only of the perpetrator's activities, but also those of the organization and its personnel in order to fully understand what has occurred. Such an incident is often a story of failed prevention or, sometimes, failed management. From a practical point of view, a worker, supervisor or manager can best prevent workplace violence and occupational homicide by understanding those patterns that seem to be repeated in many tragic incidents. Even though murder in the workplace is not a wholly predictable event, and sometimes strikes despite preparation and understanding, there are trails to follow and warning signs that are frequently evident.

Homicides in the workplace that are of type CP I (employee against employee) and CP II (employee and supervisor) are among the most common and are typically accompanied by some act of indiscriminate homicide (CP V), as indicated in the case studies. They also generally lend themselves to some predictability based on the behavior of the perpetrator and the interaction between the perpetrator and coworkers or supervisors. There are common behavioral characteristics that are seen repeatedly in workers who act out violence in the workplace against coworkers or supervisors, the most common characteristic being an elevated frustration level. In addition to the behavioral characteristics of the perpetrator, there are often repeated patterns of behavior on the part of workers, managers or supervisors that enable, or fail to avoid, the eventual violence. These two elements—behavior of the perpetrator and reaction of managers and staff—create an interplay that can actually increase the probability of workplace violence. In a contrary sense, a prepared and knowledgeable employee, supervisor or manager can go far to change the rules of this interplay and prevent or minimize a violent result.

A review of the Summary of Key Case Studies (Table 3.1) provides a starting point for developing a new profile of the potentially lethal employee. In the majority of instances, the perpetrator was a male in the age range of 25 to 55 years. In most incidents, the individual committed indiscriminate homicide, and in more than half the cases in which one or more behavioral warning signs was identified, one of them was "elevated frustration." Also, most incidents involved multiple behavioral warning signs.

This sample hints that the likely profile of a potentially violent individual may be a male of working age who is frustrated with his current situation and is giving vocal evidence of mounting dissatisfaction. Also implied by careful examination of the case histories are the probabilities that the perpetrator (1) is familiar with weapons, (2) will most likely use a gun as a weapon, (3) will have displayed one or more of the identified behavioral warning signs over some period of time, and (4) may kill indiscriminately. Based on the general profiles found in the literature as well as the data gathered from these case studies, a new profile of the potentially violent employee can be offered.

An analysis of the case studies addresses the general nature of occupational homicide as well as four particular areas of concern designed to assist in the mitigation of the crime across a broad variety of work environments: (1) the introduction of a system to categorize incidents of occupational homicide in a manner consistent with the knowledge and experience of workplace managers and staff (the Category Profile or CP system); (2) the development of a workable method to profile potentially violent individuals that can be practically utilized by managers and staff based on their common experience and knowledge; (3) an evaluative methodology for the study of incidents of occupational homicide that accounts for the interplay of perpetrator, organization, management, staff and others rather than the traditional view of analyzing only the actions of the perpetrator; and (4) a compendium of prevention methodologies designed to specifically address the need to mitigate potential workplace violence across a variety of work environments.

General Findings about Occupational Homicide

The case studies and earlier history of occupational homicide lead to the following general findings about the crime:

1. It is an issue that has received little previous research, despite its pervasive nature in the American workplace.
2. Incidents of occupational homicide have been on the rise annually for over a decade, an upward trend that can be expected to continue. Data from the various sources cited in earlier chapters of this book forcefully demonstrate a continuing increase in the annual rate of occupational homicides since 1980, the first year for which statistics were gathered.
3. Occupational homicide can occur in a wide variety of industries, professions, organizations and geographical venues. An examination of the NIOSH data provided earlier, as well as a review of the case studies, indicates that occupational homicide can strike virtually any industry or occupation. An examination of Tables 2.5 and 2.6 validates the assertions that (1) there is no industry or occupation of consequence that is exempt from occupational homicide, and (2) in the majority of industries and occupations recognized for study by NIOSH, occupational homicide is either the most prevalent or next most prevalent cause of worker death.
4. Many work environments in America are unprepared for the possibility of occupational homicide. This alarming finding is demonstrated by the statistical evidence of (1) an increasing number of annual occupational homicides and, (2) examples of a common lack of organizational preparation outlined in the case studies, specifically in the subsections entitled "Implications for Prevention."
5. There does not yet exist a formalized prevention program accessible to workplace managers or staff to assist in protecting the work environment against the specific threat of occupational homicide.
6. Incidents of occupational homicide are not simple events but rather consist of complex webs of interactions that involve the perpetrator, management, staff, and others. The case studies often demonstrate a deep interplay of individuals and situations, which supports this finding.

7. Workplace managers and staff must take a lead role in the prevention or mitigation of occupational homicide because they are directly threatened by the crime and have the opportunity to minimize or eliminate its impact within an organization. The analysis method utilized in this study was designed to elucidate the role of workplace personnel in incidents of workplace homicide. In addition, these case studies indicate that managers and staff are the primary victims of occupational homicide, often in an indiscriminate manner. They have both the motivation (as potential victims) and opportunity (as members of the work group) to enact ways to mitigate this crime within their own environment.
8. The judicious use of prevention techniques may be of help in mitigating future violent incidents based on an analysis of historical occurrences.
9. Some forms of occupational homicide seem to defy analysis and are not conducive to the implementation of prevention techniques, indicating that more research is needed to fully understand the issue and provide meaningful methods of mitigation.
10. Despite the uncertainty surrounding the issue of occupational homicide, it may be possible to provide tools to workplace managers and staff that educate and inform them, thereby increasing the likelihood of intervention and prevention. These tools will generally be found in the behavioral and management sciences until the knowledge of the issue is further developed.

The Category Profile (CP System)

The Category Profile (CP) system was designed to provide a methodology of categorizing and interpreting occupational homicide in a manner consistent with the common understanding of workplace managers and staff. The CP system utilizes terminology consistent with the general knowledge inherent in a typical work environment (utilizing terms such as "employee," "supervisor," and "client"). Such terminology can be applied to perpetrators or victims with equivalent common understanding. In addition, the CP system accounts, in a broad sense, for actions that may pertain to interpersonal conflicts from within or outside the organization (CP I, CP II, and CP III, for example) or to motivations that may emanate from sources beyond the work environment (CP IV, for example).

The question of the validity and applicability of the CP system to an incident of occupational homicide (or workplace violence) has been demonstrated in the case studies offered here. It is hoped that these case studies have adequately demonstrated that the methodology in question is broad enough in scope to apply to many, if not all, such events. The efficacy of this system lies in its ability to be easily understood by managers and staff and in its ease of communication and applicability for training and education purposes. It is anticipated that additional use of the CP system to categorize and identify future incidents of workplace violence will support the hypothesis that the system is capable of accounting for the issue in a manner that is understandable to the target audience. Nonetheless, it must be noted that the case studies included in this work represent only a fraction of the number of incidents identified statistically. The CP system must be validated over a longer period of time with a much greater number of actual incidents in order to truly judge its effectiveness and applicability.

A Working Profile of the Potentially Violent Employee

The sciences of sociology and psychology have long studied the causes of violence, the motivations of individuals prone to violent acts, and behavioral patterns associated with violent individuals. Much of this knowledge can be applied to the issues of workplace violence and occupational homicide. In addition, some risk management and human resource management organizations have recently started to focus on the issue in an attempt to understand the causes of workplace violence. Some of this research has resulted in several general profiles of the potentially violent employee (mentioned previously): From resources such as these, in combination with the data derived from the case studies outlined here, it is possible to further refine the profile of a violent employee. The most appropriate and accurate composite of a potentially violent employee must rely on observable behavioral characteristics that are known to precede acts of violence and which can be readily identified in the workplace by managers or staff.

Despite the implied uncertainty of the process, the practice of profiling a potentially violent employee is an important component in any prevention program. It must be realized, however, that any profile can be improved on as knowledge and understanding of the issue increases. This profile relies heavily on the behavioral characteristics common to potentially violent individuals, as examined in the case studies. This approach, in turn, relies on the fact that workers are typically familiar with their coworkers (and, perhaps, clients), and therefore have an opportunity to observe behavior that may prove threatening to themselves or others.

In each case, a probability has been assigned to the general characteristic that may be observed. These probabilities are useful as general guidelines; of course, exceptions will occur. It is important to note that the probabilities are drawn from a review of incidents and literature dealing with a sampling of actual occupational homicides. The sample was not complete because of the large number of incidents and the general unavailability of sufficiently detailed case studies. The probabilities are estimates and thus offered to assist in understanding the most likely scenario. Conservative probabilities have been used in order to minimize the effect of an inadvertent exclusion of other possibilities or characteristics. As is the case with all other attempts to profile the violent individual, exceptions must always be kept in mind:

1. male (80% or better probability);
2. white (75% or better probability);
3. working age (90% or better probability);
4. will display one or more of the following behavioral warning signs (90% or better probability of at least one, 50% probability of two or more):
   A. a history of violence,

B. evidence of psychosis,
C. evidence of erotomania or similar obsession,
D. evidence of chemical or alcohol dependence,
E. evidence of depression,
F. a pattern of pathological blaming,
G. evidence of impaired neurological functioning,
H. an elevated frustration level,
I. an interest in weapons, or
J. evidence of a personality disorder.
5. will vocalize, or otherwise act out, violent intentions prior to committing a violent act (probability uncertain, but common);
6. over a sustained period of time, will exhibit behavior that is interpreted as strange, bizarre, or threatening by multiple coworkers (probability uncertain, but common).

It must be emphasized that this profile must only be considered a working outline which should remain subject to improvement and change as more is learned about the issue of occupational homicide. Of primary importance in recognizing potential violence is the test of common sense and the availability of employee feedback.   Coworkers are typically the first to recognize a behavioral warning sign, even if they are unable to identify it precisely. This profile relies on the caveat that the work environment must be managed in such a way as to encourage a cooperative approach to identifying potential violence through the early recognition of behavioral warning signs by managers and staff.

In testing this profile against case studies both included and excluded from this work, it was found that the profile elements were consistent and provided a sound methodology for evaluating potentially violent behavior where sufficient information about the incident was available. This profile is, of course, theoretical. The practicality of field testing the profile is a limitation inherent in the unpredictability of the issue of occupational homicide. For now, the validity of the profile must rest upon its use in the analysis of incidents after they occur.

An Evaluative Technique for Incident Analysis

Throughout the case studies offered here, an effort has been made to demonstrate the fact that occupational homicide cannot be understood solely in relation to the actions of the perpetrator of the crime. In each case study, a brief analysis was offered that attempted to focus on the actions or inaction of organizational personnel as a contributing factor to the crime discussed. Through these analyses, it can be seen that an act of occupational homicide is typically the result of an interplay among the perpetrator, managers, staff, and (possibly) others. This is a view of occupational homicide not found in the literature, but which is of vital importance in a practical, prevention sense. An understanding of the fact that occupational homicide is not merely a singular act of violence but rather the result of a convergence of actions from multiple sources not only provides broader understanding of the issue but also opens up possibilities for prevention that may have been previously unrecognized. Thus, an analysis undertaken in this way leads naturally to the recognition of prevention possibilities.

This method for analyzing actual incidents of occupational homicide provides a technique for the evaluation of other incidents with a view to examining all contributing factors and not merely the actions of the perpetrator. Once again, the nature of this methodology is theoretical, and it has obviously only been applied to a limited number of actual workplace incidents. As can be seen from the case studies, however, it does provide a technique for holistically interpreting the facts surrounding a violent workplace incident. Much additional work with this analysis technique would be helpful in determining its ultimate value as a research and teaching technique.

Prevention Methodologies

Occupational homicide is a significant and growing threat to the workplace. However, knowledge of the issue is, in itself, insufficient—it is also necessary to offer practical prevention methodologies to accomplish the purpose of this work. There are numerous sources of information about general workplace safety extant in the literature. None, however, has attempted to introduce prevention techniques directed specifically at the mitigation of occupational homicide or addressed proactive management and staff action that can be undertaken on a routine basis. Consistent with the view that occupational homicide is generally an interplay of perpetrator and management action or inaction, this work will offer a compendium of prevention techniques designed to mitigate violence in the work environment. In Chapter 4, a discussion of the broad imperatives for a violent work environment will be offered to lay the foundation for a subsequent series of practical prevention methodologies. Finally, as the perpetrator of occupational homicide was profiled, so is the healthy organization in Chapter 5.

NOTES

1. Eugene D. Wheeler and S. Anthony Baron, *Violence in Our Schools, Hospitals and Public Places*, (Ventura, CA: Pathfinder, 1994), 89.
    2. Wheeler and Baron, 96.
    3. Wheeler and Baron, 118.
    4. Wheeler and Baron, 118.
    5. Associated Press, wire news release, 1 Dec. 1992.
    6. Wheeler and Baron, 127.
    7. Wheeler and Baron, 128.
    8. "2 Women Shot Dead in Seattle Courthouse," *San Francisco Chronicle*. 3 March 1995, A4.
    9. Wheeler and Baron, 128-129.
    10. Wheeler and Baron, 136-137.

11. Wheeler and Baron, 137.

12. Smith, S. L., "Violence in the Workplace: A Cry for Help," *Occupational Hazards*, 1 Oct. 1993, 29-33.

13. Wheeler and Baron, 129-130.

14. H. H. Goldman, ed., *Review of General Psychiatry* (Norwalk, CT: Appleton & Lange/Prentice Hall, 1988), 654.

15. George Hackett, "Settling a Score," *Newsweek*, 21 Dec. 1987, 43.

16. M. Satchell, "Airline Security: Mass Murder in the Clouds," *U.S. News and World Report*, 21 Dec. 1987, 14.

17. Satchell.

18. "3 Killed at Trucking Office," *San Francisco Chronicle*, 16 Dec. 1995, A4

19. Reuters News Service, Internet, 11 Jul. 1995.

20. Reuters News Service, Internet, 19 May 1995.

21. Reuters News Service, Internet, 5 Apr. 1995.

22. Peggy Stuart, "Murder on the Job," *Personnel Journal*, 71, no. 2 (1992): 72.

23. Stuart, 72.

24. Stuart, 72.

25. John Wookfolk, "Peninsula Man's Trial Begins," *San Francisco Chronicle*, 14 Aug 1994, A5.

26. Don Terry, "Chosen One Accused in Dahmer Case," *San Francisco Chronicle*, 28 Nov. 1994, A8.

27. *Chronicle News Services* (San Francisco), 23 Nov. 1994, A15.

28. G. L. Bledsoe, *Occupational Homicide: Alaska, 1993* (Anchorage: Alaska Department of Health and Social Services, 1994, Internet).

29. Andrew Bilski, "Tragedy in Texas," *Maclean's* 104, no. 43 (1991): 34.

30. Richard Woodbury, "Ten Minutes in Hell," *Time* 138, no. 17 (1991): 31.

31. S. Anthony Baron, *Violence in the Workplace* (Ventura: Pathfinder, 1993): 33-39.

32. Reno *Gazette-Journal*, 11 Sept. 1994, 6A.

33. Independent Committee of Inquiry into Academic and Scientific Integrity, *Integrity in Scholarship: A Report to Concordia University*, Apr. 1994, Scott Cowan, *Lessons from the Fabrikant File: A Report to the Board of Governors of Concordia University*, May 1994, Internet, Scott Cowan, *Lessons from the Fabrikant File: A Report to the Board of Governors of Concordia University*, May 1994, Internet.

34. Tom Fennel, "Guilty as Charged: Valery Fabrikant Gets Life for Four Murders," *Maclean's*, 106, no. 34 (1993): 14.

35. Baron, 85.

36. *San Francisco Chronicle*, 12 Dec. 1994, A8

37. Baron, 85-88.

4

Violence Imperatives and Prevention Techniques

To work at a meaningful occupation is crucial to the well-being of the individual and, consequently, society. Sigmund Freud, the founder of psychoanalysis, identified two primary human needs: the need for love and the need for work. Abraham Maslow, the father of humanistic psychology, ranked self-esteem through work as high in the hierarchy of human needs. Alfred Adler, founder of the school of individual psychology, defined work as one of the three crucial components of a successful life, the other two being love and friends. Work is an activity that defines an individual's role in society. It is the vehicle by which societal contributions are typically judged. Work is the foundation of self-esteem for many American citizens. It also represents reward, both monetary and nonmonetary, as well as an opportunity to learn and grow.

In the same way that work is crucial to the sense of happiness and well-being for an individual, it is vital to society as a whole. Employment provides for a united and economically healthy nation that is able to progress and improve living conditions for all citizens. In the same way that an individual gauges his or her well-being by a sense of success in the workplace, so also is there a national wellness that arises, in good measure, from the quality of work.

When an individual's ability to work is disrupted or denied, there may be dire and violent consequences. The purposeful activity of work is so fundamental to personal health that many individuals are not able to cope with its absence for any significant period of time. In this same sense, a nation cannot survive without a strong, productive, and healthy workforce. When situations arise that threaten the ability to work, on either an individual or societal basis, a danger to the nation's well-being ensues. Such situations set the stage for violence and upheaval.

SOCIOLOGICAL FACTORS

There are a growing number of opinions in print that attempt to define the precise causal factors contributing to violence in the workplace and the broader issue of violence in American society. It would be impractical, and not necessary, to enumerate each of the nominated influences, since the focus of this study is more narrow than the broad issue of violence in general. Many of these contributing factors ebb and flow with the near constant change inherent in American society and the economy. These factors are subject to significant modification over time. There are, however, trends of influences to be discerned and gathered as probable major contributors to the problem of workplace violence in general and occupational homicide in particular. These identifiable influences have dramatically degraded the safety of job sites in the past decade and are likely to continue this effect into the future without the implementation of effective intervention and prevention methodologies.

Occupational Hazards magazine, as an example, identified five contributing factors viewed as fundamental to an understanding of violence in the workplace and occupational homicide:[1]

1. a sluggish economy,
2. a societal desensitization to violence,
3. availability of technologically advanced weapons,
4. drug and alcohol problems, and
5. domestic problems that flare up in the workplace.

There are, of course, many other factors that contribute to violence at work. The effect of violent programming on television and in the entertainment industry, corporate reorganizations resulting in mass layoffs, organizational downsizing in search of profits and stability, business reorganizations due to changing markets and technology, and substance abuse are but a few, easily identified factors. Each of these enhance the potential for violence at work and in the home.

Workers often no longer feel secure in their jobs and frequently feel unsafe even in their own homes. Domestic disputes have begun to reach into the workplace. There is a pervasive mistrust in management, and often, mistrust among coworkers. Anxiety and stress are rampant in many organizations. All these problems combine to create a sense of frustration and anger among workers which, at times, can turn into violence.[2]

This part of the study of occupational homicide will investigate several of these elements—those considered to be primary trends of influence toward violence. However, a focused view is needed to properly identify those factors that directly impact workplace personnel responsibilities in a typical American organization. This volume will account for influences most likely to be encountered by workplace personnel and the clients they must serve. In this way, it is hoped that employees, managers, and supervisors will develop a more than rudimentary understanding of the unique and contemporary forces that impact each worker, most clients, and ultimately, the entire organization.

Factors that contribute to violence in society and the workplace are many and diverse, as are the complex cultural influences that continuously define and redefine America. Many of these forces for change are recognized by workers, managers, and supervisors, even if they are not completely understood in scope or impact. In examining the sociological factors that contribute to workplace violence, this work focuses on the forces that have most fundamentally influenced American business and have made the practice of managing staff more complex than ever before. The first and most fundamental force for a potentially violent response to a changing environment is the pervasive nature of change itself.

THE IMPACT OF CHANGE

Since the end of World War II, American society has been challenged by societal changes on a scale previously unknown in its history. Many of these changes have been global; others have been uniquely American in nature. Although change can translate into growth for a society, it can have untoward and devastating effects on an individual when the rate of transformation outpaces the ability of an individual to manage it effectively. Greater harm can result when many changes that directly impact individuals or families are too complex or remote for their understanding or acceptance. Radical or accelerated change on a national scale may leave many members of society isolated, afraid, and hostile. Some citizens may be unable to effectively compete in a changing society in which they were once prosperous and successful but can no longer operate effectively. Of course, some individuals, who are prepared and fortunate, may benefit beyond their expectations from significant social or economic changes. These individuals are typically not in the majority, however.

As the pace of social and economic transformation accelerates, the number of individuals who benefit may dwindle, while the number who are unable to keep pace suffer a variety of hardships for which they are not prepared and that they cannot accept. Although the negative impact of change is usually most significant at the individual or family levels, society also suffers in the long term. Such a scenario may eventually lead to a society of "haves" and "have-nots" which, as history shows, can ultimately result in revolution, war, and the disintegration of a nation.

In the 1960s, a key phrase of the "baby boomer" generation,[ix] as it began to experience the struggle to integrate into a rapidly changing society, was "turn on, tune in, drop out."[x] This was both a rallying cry to solidarity for a generation that had its own vision of a new world order and a plea for help to understand a nation and a world that was moving too fast and in directions too little understood.   The same generation that once cried out for a more understandable, less frenetic society is now responsible for the management of organizations in which change is even more rapid and incomprehensible. The individual and societal stresses inherent in this situation are enormous and costly.

Rapid and, often, confusing societal changes are so pervasive and commonplace in America that they are difficult to categorize. Moreover, many are so subtle as to be unrecognized. Despite this, it is important to be aware of the more obvious elements of change that affect all Americans. Although most of these changes were never intended to have a negative impact on society, the results of their rapid onset and acceleration have transformed the United States significantly. Sadly, taken together, many of these changes define root causes for the violent society that has become a modern American tradition. In such a violent society, who can expect a nonviolent workplace?

This work examines several elements of change that have transformed America. These elements have combined to accelerate violence in society and in the workplace. They each have played a role in isolating individuals from each other and from the social institutions upon which they have traditionally relied. They lie at the root of the drive toward violence that has invaded the American workplace.

POLITICS, WAR AND SURVIVAL

In less than 50 years, Americans have experienced an unprecedented upheaval in the political and social order of their nation and the world. For two generations, the awesome horror of possible total global destruction has been a daily reality. Americans have recently experienced the unprecedented changes brought about by the establishment of democracy in many countries formerly considered hostile. The past two generations, particularly, have learned to accept a national fear of nuclear war that demanded the building of back-yard bomb shelters and left the legacy of an incredible arsenal of weapons of mass destruction; they must now look toward former enemies as allies and friends, somehow learning to set aside 50 years of fear and mistrust.

---

ix. That generation born at the end of, or just after, World War II.
x. This phrase was derived from a lecture given by Timothy Leary in 1967 entitled, "Turn On, Tune In, Drop Out."

Leaders of major nations sometimes threatened the survival of the entire world for reasons not understood at the individual level, and often not made public. American citizens have seen, firsthand, the unspeakable waste of life left in the wake of new and incomprehensible weapons exercised in localized wars across the globe. Often, war and death have been electronically delivered into the home and workplace, encapsulated in a technology that makes deadly violence seem almost game-like.

Many times, since the end of World War II, America has been involved in military actions against other nations whose cultures were far away and foreign. In keeping with the American tradition of an open society, individuals once viewed as enemies later immigrated to this country to compete in the domestic workplace. The American worker, who was once motivated to hate as a form of national conscience, was now required to instantly forgive, forget, and subscribe to the equally strong imperative of fair play. Sadly, but often, the anger and bitterness arising from such a national conflict and abrupt change in political climate cast a shadow of discrimination across an entire generation of workers.

Frequently, the true purpose of an international conflict was not understood by the citizenry, or the conflict itself became a cause of social disruption at home. National leaders, both domestic and foreign, directed their citizens in acts of aggression or terrorism that seemed senseless, and for which there was no clear motive. American politicians often tore apart families, businesses, and national institutions in a witch-hunt kind of search for unseen and ill-defined enemies.[xi] These same leaders convinced the citizenry that those who desired the destruction of American society were to be found everywhere—even next door, even in the workplace. The trust that once went unquestioned between neighbors and coworkers was successfully ripped away, and today is rarely evidenced in society or the workplace.

American citizens now seem unwillingly convinced that they live in a perilous and hostile world in which they must fight with any means necessary to ensure survival. Many Americans appear to believe that nearly everything and everyone they encounter poses a potential threat to their well-being. Competition often translates into an unbridled attempt to win at any cost. The world and society are viewed by many as being comprised of enemies, both subtle and overt. Overcoming competition on every front is encouraged and rewarded, even if it results in aggression. It is all too clear that fear and mistrust have been the constant companions of more than one generation since

---

xi. The primary example is McCarthyism. This is defined by the American Heiritage Dictionary as: (1) The political practice of publicizing accusations of disloyalty or subversion with insufficient regard to evidence; (2) The use of methods of investigation and accusation regarded as unfair, in order to suppress opposition. After Joseph R. McCarthy [1909-1957].

the end of World War II. Unfortunately, this attitude continues to be passed on to each succeeding generation as an unquestioned legacy.[xii]

Given the state of affairs in American society for the past 50 years, it could only be expected that many individuals would react with fear and aggression in situations that should never engender these reactions. Often such fears are vague and diffuse and, as a result, the ensuing retaliation can be indiscriminate and senseless. Often, the individual displaces anxiety and fear on to symbols of authority such as the government, large organizations, or corporations. Sometimes, there are perceived threats from individuals who are suspected of acts never committed or even contemplated; sometimes, there is hatred and violence without motivation or purpose. With sufficient fear, given the mandate of survival and prosperity at nearly any cost in American society, indiscriminate or unwarranted violence can, and does, result. The homes and streets of America have become the backdrop against which a predisposition to aggression is transformed into a criminal act of violence. More often than ever before in American history, this violence tends to occur in the workplace—the arena where so many Americans spend so much of their lives, witnessing so many changes.

CULTURAL INFLUENCES OF AGGRESSION

There are many cultural influences on American society, but few have had more impact than the entertainment industry—particularly television. The A. C. Nielson company reported that by January 1, 1991, it was estimated that 98% of American households had at least one television set, while approximately 64% of households had two or more. Over 237 million Americans had access to television programming in their homes on a daily basis. These televisions were operating for an average of four to eight hours each day.[3] Obviously, this medium has a tremendous and ongoing cultural influence on American society. Unfortunately, this impact has been negative in many ways.

The American Psychological Association (APA) estimates that the average seventh grade student has witnessed over 8,000 murders and 100,000 other acts of violence on television. The APA has also determined that children's cartoons portray a violent act once every 90 seconds. This incredible figure has increased 10% in the past ten years alone. Finally, the APA warns

---

xii. The argument can be made that this is a matter of perspective and that the view expressed here emphasizes the negative exclusively. One should consider, though, the American traditions of self-protection and might against threat. This country was founded in revolution and, to this day, treasures its ability to "stand tall" against threat.

that even children as young as 14 months of age can, and do, adopt behavior they have seen on television.

Discounting other forms of entertainment traditional to American society that may glamorize violence (such as the film industry and sporting events), consider the impact on our society as it witnesses an unrelenting flood of violent television images. America is a violent nation because, in part, each individual accepts violence into his or her own home as a form of entertainment. This acceptance is passed on to subsequent generations, often without question. Very young children play at violent games that involve toy weapons modeled after the weapons portrayed on television or elsewhere in the entertainment industry. Within the structure of this play, which should be a vital and positive process of teaching each child how to successfully integrate into society, there are mock acts of violence and murder taken directly from popular television programming. Parents often accept these games of violence as normal play, not questioning the long-term effect on their children and the society they will inherit.

Homicide in every conceivable form, including at the workplace, is often aired during prime television viewing hours. The violence seen on television is typically graphic and voluminous. A constant barrage of violent images—particularly murder, in its countless manifestations—creates a tolerance for violence in the viewer or, worse, engenders emulation of the acts witnessed.

What of the other side of the issue of violence on television? It is a rare event when this medium denounces violence or teaches prevention with any enthusiasm. Practicing the avoidance of violence is viewed as weak and not in the American tradition; it is rarely seen on television. With the unlimited opportunity for learning that television technology provides, it is a frustrating and sad situation for America when murder, mayhem, rape, and other violent acts occupy so much leisure viewing time.

Thankfully, in the past few years, a new awareness of this problem has come to the attention of some national leaders due to the grass roots efforts of organized citizen groups. Sporadic congressional hearings have been held, and some efforts have been made by the entertainment industry to forewarn viewers of particularly violent forms of entertainment. Control of this issue, however, is still primarily in the hands of the television industry. This huge economic force is driven by commercial advertisement fees which, in turn, lie within the economic control of each citizen by his or her choice to purchase, or not purchase, a given product. Should Americans decide they desire a new, less violent, form of entertainment for themselves and their children, they could exercise this control. Surely, there has been enough violence in the homes, streets and workplaces to show Americans the right choice.

THE EFFECT OF TECHNOLOGY

Consider the technological innovations that have deeply impacted the daily lives of most Americans since the end of World War II, as shown in Table 4.1.

Table 4.1: Important Technological Innovations

Innovation/Discovery	Year	Inventor/Discoverer
Transistor	1947	Shockley/Bardeen
Panoramic Movie	1952	Waller
Fiber Optics	1955	Kapany Co.
Integrated Circuit	1959	Texas Instruments
Mini-Computer	1960	Digital Corp.
Video Disk	1972	Phillips Co.
Compact Disk	1972	RCA Corp.
Video Game	1972	Buschnel
Video Home System (VHS)	1975	Matsushita/JVC

Although these are but a few of the incredible number of technological advances that have occurred in the past five decades, they are easily ranked among those with the most significant social impact ever experienced in history and they represent technologies that have completely transformed the American workplace and home. Several of these innovations have reoriented the way in which individuals receive information and, more importantly, the quantity of information to be processed. Others have formed the basis for the most fundamental necessities in business, travel, education, and work activities. Many provide the structure for nearly all modern systems in today's communication and entertainment industries.

One of these inventions alone, the integrated circuit, has transformed virtually every office machine in the nation, created entirely new enterprises, reorganized or established a variety of aerospace and defense industries, and laid the foundation for an information management explosion that was unprecedented in human history. This innovation has been responsible for both mass employment and mass layoffs, new opportunities and workers left without jobs, the making of youthful millionaires and the elimination of careers. The integrated circuit has become indispensable to the workings of America, and has also become an icon of transformation—both beneficial and harmful. It is the premier representation of the advantages gained, and the prices paid, for late-twentieth-century technology.

The integrated circuit, though, does not stand alone at the center of technological change. The other innovations listed above are equally important and have had similar effects upon the face of American business and employment. Without question, there are few residences in America that would function acceptably without one or more of these innovations; and fewer workplaces still. Many of the products demanded by Americans as necessary for a comfortable life would not be available, or acceptable, without one or more of these innovations.   Innumerable industries and businesses would disappear without these technologies. Transportation, as we know it today, would cease; defense and government activities would come to a halt. In short, there is an unprecedented national reliance on these innovations—a reliance so pervasive that contemporary society would be unrecognizable in their absence. These are also innovations that have arisen within the lifetime of the majority of today's workers and have transformed both the worker and the workplace on a national scale.

Vital as these technological wonders are, they represent rapid and aggressive change for most Americans. Many of these innovations provide the basis for highly complex systems found in the workplace and in the home. In many instances, the systems designed around these innovations are complicated and may be intimidating.   They are often desired in their final form as consumer products; sometimes they are the cause of stress or frustration as individuals compete to master their complexities or acquire their rewards. Emerging systems, derived from mass technological improvements, require different skills and a broader understanding of their purposes and use. Often they make a job easier, but sometimes it becomes more difficult. At times, they make familiar jobs unrecognizable or, worse, obsolete.

Each of these innovations holds out a singular characteristic that has affected the lives of Americans in a powerful, but subtle, way. They each have the quality of imparting an increasing (sometimes exponential) speed to any process or system of which they become a part. In many instances, these new systems do highly complex things at an inconceivable rate of speed. They have transformed American society into a nation of individuals who must meet the intricate, ever-accelerating demands of changing systems in order to be successful at home or in the workplace.

There is no question that these innovations have proven advantageous in an incalculable number of interconnected ways. The high standard of living and many advances in the United States are due, in large part, to these innovations. However, there is a cost attached to this race toward technological superiority. The presence of countless products based on these innovations creates a competitive, sometimes frenzied, demand among citizens for their perceived benefits.   Workers in vast numbers have been required to learn unfamiliar skills, change occupations, or reorient their careers. For individuals not educated in the ways of technology, life has become more complex and the workplace seems more foreign and difficult to manage. For some citizens, such change has brought on unexpected opportunities; for others, there has been unacceptable loss.

For all Americans, though, there has been unparalleled change in virtually every aspect of their lives. These innovations, and many others not mentioned, have recreated the most basic structure of America. Technology has demanded a new pace of learning, living, and working in order to master its use and meaning. In the race for technological innovation on every front, the individual has often been left behind in skill acquisition, education, or understanding.

National focus has been clear and effective on the technological frontier; its success is apparent. Often, however, less effort has been directed toward helping American citizens, who are the intended beneficiaries of technology, to cope with pervasive technological change. Instead, isolated communities of specialists have arisen. The members of these esoteric communities create, manage, and implement technological change, and they are usually well rewarded for doing so. Often, these creators and purveyors of technology stand exclusively apart from the users of their systems. An increasing schism has developed between the artisans of innovation and their clients as technology has moved well beyond the mastery of its users. For some individuals this represents a frightening vision of the future as they struggle to keep up with the rapid change of today.

Inevitably, given the pace of technology in this country, vast numbers of individuals continue to be left behind and without understanding in the unceasing American technological race. Often subtle, and regularly dismissed in importance, this modern social direction can translate into separateness and alienation for many individuals. Given sufficient discomfort and frustration, some turn unwittingly to aggression or violence.

When a worker is unable to comprehend, or cope with, changes in the workplace brought on by technological innovation, the employer must make whatever efforts are necessary to assist that individual to succeed. Long term, successful workers may often fear change and eschew even the appearance of failure. If they are faced with rapid technological change, without strong support to accommodate the new work environment, employees may feel bitter and isolated. If such change in the workplace causes a once-successful employee to suffer economic loss or a loss of self-esteem, an aggressive or violent reaction cannot be excluded. On the other hand, a strong program of retraining or education that emphasizes the employer's commitment to long term employees can validate management's role as caring individuals who can be trusted in the workplace. Such trusted members of management will benefit, not only from emerging technologies, but from a workplace that is more unified, increasingly productive, and less violent.

OCCUPATIONAL STRESS

Occupational stress has become a dominant concern in many American organizations. A recent survey of workers indicated that nearly half perceived their job as very stressful; over a third had considered quitting their job during the 12 months preceding the survey because of stress; 70% of the workers felt that stress had negatively impacted their health and caused them to be less productive on the job; and one-third of the workers felt they were close to job "burnout."[4] These responses are not only staggering when considered on a national scale, but indicate that more workers currently perceive a negative impact from occupational stress than was previously recognized. It is safe to assume that virtually every American is at least fleetingly familiar with the effects of stress in his or her life—even those misinformed individuals who refuse to accept the very real nature of this national disorder.

The effects of stress on an employee can be devastating for both the individual and the organization if intervention is not available or is provided too late. With sufficiently long periods of unrelenting stress, an individual will become increasingly angry and hostile, eventually becoming incapable of functioning effectively or objectively. With significant stress over an extended period of time, violence will often result. Sometimes this violence is vehement and indiscriminate; occasionally, the result is deadly. It is therefore imperative that staff and managers be versed in recognizing the indicators of stress and be trained in obtaining appropriate and early intervention for the employee who exhibits relevant warning signs. Stress can be managed if it is recognized in a timely way and proper treatment is made available.

This disorder is so pervasive, and brought on by such a wide variety of life experiences, that it cannot be attributed solely to the workplace but must be considered in the context of an individual's life style and circumstances. It is therefore important to briefly diverge from the main theme of this work to examine the most significant indicators of stress and offer recommendations for workers and managers who must deal with this issue on a daily basis.

Some of the symptoms of stress are readily apparent; others are more subtle and difficult to recognize. The most notable feature of stress is that individuals typically exhibit multiple symptoms which are predictable and recognizable, given sufficient observer training. Some of the more obvious symptoms of stress include:[5]

1. hypertension,
2. nervousness and a tense demeanor,
3. excessive worry,
4. inability to relax,
5. abuse of drugs and/or alcohol,
6. excessive cigarette smoking,
7. sleep disorders,
8. aggressive, hostile or uncooperative attitude,
9. feelings of insufficiency,
10. emotional outbursts or emotional instability, and
11. digestive disorders.

Should an employee exhibit several of these symptoms, it is possible that stress is the causal factor and intervention may be indicated. Since stress can be caused by occupational and non-occupational forces, it is best to arrange for professional intervention for any employee exhibiting these warning signs. An employee assistance program (EAP) is often the best starting point to aid employees suffering from stress.

The causes of stress are many and varied. Although stress can be caused by a single factor or situation, this is not the typical situation. Stress most often results from a variety of pressures emanating from both home and work. Managers must typically deal with an array of pressures experienced by employees—pressures that frequently affect the workplace even when they are not related to the job. Clearly, however, management must focus primarily upon reducing workplace stressors to every extent possible.

Occupational stress can be minimized by sound management strategies and a healthy work environment. Any effort to reduce stress, however, must first identify its causal factors in the workplace. Some causes of stress are subtle and often overlooked, while others can be perceived and addressed directly. Typical causes of occupational stress include:[6]

1. an excessive workload,
2. inadequate time to complete the workload,
3. poor supervision,
4. uncertain organizational climate,
5. insufficient authority to meet job responsibilities,
6. unclear responsibilities or job functions,
7. philosophical differences between the organization and employee,
8. unexpected or significant change at work or at home, and
9. unanswered or unresolved frustrations.

Many of these causes can be removed, or at least mitigated, by sound management; others, such as change, can never be completely eliminated.

On a practical basis, the responsibility of stressor identification and mitigation belongs primarily to the manager or supervisor. Unfortunately, managers are often the first victims of stress and are therefore not always quick to recognize peers or employees in difficulty. Stress is a pervasive problem in the workplace and therefore requires the diligence and coordinated effort of all employees to assist in recognizing its presence and providing proper intervention. A proactive program of employee counseling and monitoring can provide an organization with effective countermeasures, even in the most stressful occupations. Such a program anticipates stress by identifying its causal factors and providing a methodology to seek out those employees most susceptible to its effects. Again, an employee assistance program may provide just such a stress management program. Health maintenance organizations (HMO) and other medical professionals often provide stress management programs which may be covered by employee medical benefits already available within the organization.

Employees can also do much on their own to relieve stress. The use of techniques such as humor, social support systems, meditation, hobbies, biofeedback, exercise, and personal wellness programs can provide a good deal of relief from occupational stress.[7] Individuals may often relieve stress by a combination of practical activities such as these:[8]

1. Develop an awareness of personal stress reactions.
2. Affirm self-worth through positive statements.
3. Be aware and conscious of achievements and positive personal qualities.
4. Do not engage in negative or useless competition.
5. Reinforce positive, assertive self behavior.
6. Accept personal limitations.
7. Be aware of the uniqueness of the self.
8. Learn to relax through enjoyable activities and hobbies.
9. Engage in a daily regimen of exercise.
10. Eat regular, balanced, and healthy meals.
11. Learn to use time well by planning ahead, avoiding procrastination and not rushing.
12. Set personal goals realistically.
13. Set priorities realistically.
14. Practice frequent periods of relaxation.

Many of these activities can be undertaken on a group basis in the workplace as well as on an individual basis at home. A combination of these techniques can provide a powerful arsenal against most stressors in the workplace and in the home.

Managers may also help reduce stress in the workplace by ensuring certain stabilizing factors within the organization. The following management actions are considered important steps in reducing workplace stress and employee burnout:[9]

1. Allow workers to communicate openly with each other.
2. Use conflict resolution techniques to minimize employee conflict on the job.
3. Ensure that workers have sufficient authority to perform their jobs.
4. Ensure that staffing and budget is adequate for the work to be performed.
5. Communicate frequently and honestly with employees.
6. Provide a supportive work environment that recognizes the efforts of employees.
7. Ensure that vacation benefits are adequate and competitive.
8. Ensure that the overall employee benefit program is adequate and competitive.
9. Work at reducing bureaucracy within the workplace.
10. Recognize workers for their accomplishments and contributions.

The behavioral sciences acknowledge that sufficient stress over a prolonged period can lead to aggression and violence. With the large numbers of employees who perceive high levels of stress related to their jobs, this is a workplace problem that must receive adequate and continuing attention by managers. Fortunately, if recognized and treated in a timely manner, stress can be reduced significantly through counseling and a program of personal wellness. The key is to recognize stress as early as possible, admit that it is a genuine disorder that affects both the individual and the organization, and arrange for appropriate intervention.

FINANCIAL STRESS

Financial stresses resulting from economic changes have become common in the past few decades; they rank high among the many stressors encountered by the average worker in the United States.   American workplaces are undergoing trying and substantial transformations as corporations and businesses adjust to rapidly changing technologies, shifting national and global markets, and a host of economic pressures.   On an individual basis, unemployment is a fear that strikes at the heart of most Americans since organizational downsizing and mass layoffs have become commonplace.

Although the federal government often expresses unemployment statistics in terms of a percentage of the work force, this is not a complete or fully accurate assessment of the problem.   There are twice as many Americans without employment today as there were in 1960.   In terms of raw numbers, this is a staggering eight million individuals (see Figure 4.1).[10] Each of these citizens faces the enormous financial and personal stress of being without work in a society which values work as one of the basic necessities of life.

Figure 4.1: Millions of Americans Unemployed

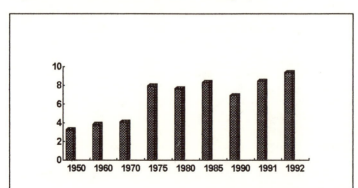

Due to the general cost of living, escalating housing prices, the cost of medical care and higher education, and the economic burden of other necessities in American society, there are more working partners, or two-income households, than ever before in the nation's history. Despite this extra income, many Americans are finding it increasingly difficult to attain economic stability. Increasing taxes, high costs to maintain a modest living standard, and the growing price of leisure pursuits have all combined to force families to require more income in order to obtain perceived necessities and compete for the comforts they desire. For many workers, this financial burden has become onerous.

Personal bankruptcies (both filed and pending) took a sharp upturn in the 1980s, and the trend has accelerated into the 1990s (see Figure 4.2).[11] This increase in the number of bankruptcies is proportionally higher than the increase in the general population of the United States. Owing to expanded financial pressures faced daily by Americans from a broad front, many have felt there was no option but to take this step to protect their dwindling assets. The option of bankruptcy, in itself, translates into long-term financial hardship as it makes the future use of credit problematical.

Balancing the budget and putting some money away "for a rainy day" has been a tradition in the American family for many generations. With the financial pressures of today, however, this activity is foremost on the minds of many and the cause of family disruption for a significant segment of society.

Figure 4.2: Personal Bankruptcies

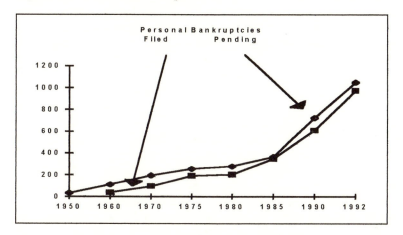

Figure 4.3: Millions of Americans Below the Poverty Level

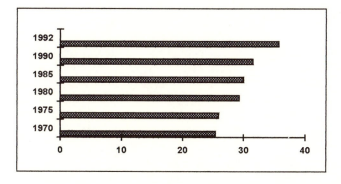

The U. S. government calculated the poverty level in 1990 at an annual income of $13,359 for a family of four. Millions of citizens are severely impoverished while living in the richest nation in the world (see Figure 4.3).[12] Many are employed part-time at menial jobs that pay a minimum wage. Some are migrant workers or other casual labor workers who earn even less.

These citizens are painfully aware of the opportunities, comfort, and security attained by so many other Americans; yet, they are unable to obtain many of the basic necessities for themselves. For some of these individuals the economic and social pressures of the their situation have become intolerable. Many have become understandably angry with their continual frustration and lack of progress. A growing number of these individuals have turned to aggressive or criminal behavior in order to obtain some perceived relief. For some of these individuals, the daily frustrations and hardships they endure have become a focal point for violent retaliation.

In comparison with those citizens known to be below the national poverty level, there are many more millions of Americans who earn enough to keep them out of this classification but not enough to provide a comfortable or secure life. The number of citizens in this near-poverty situation is statistically uncertain, but it is estimated to be at least twice the number of those at, or below, the poverty level. These individuals typically work at low-paying jobs and struggle to support family members. They share many of the same frustrations and hardships of their impoverished fellow citizens, yet remain uncounted and unrecognized by the government. These citizens are one paycheck away from poverty and desperately need to maintain their ability to work. They may often suffer from inadequate medical care and educational opportunities, yet they must endure the same high expenses and meet the same employment demands as their more financially successful counterparts in the vast and politically powerful American middle class.[xiii] These large numbers of citizens are extremely vulnerable to a changing economic climate and are often subject to mass layoffs as organizations shift strategies. When unemployed, these individuals may have difficulty obtaining work, even at a low pay scale, and a.e in constant danger of financial disaster. With only an overburdened and unpopular government sponsored safety net standing between them and absolute poverty, the uncertainty and frustration of their life circumstances is understandable.

With the strains of economic change that have swept the United States in recent years, many individuals who could not conceive of a life at or near the poverty level have found themselves in just that situation. Mass layoffs and corporate downsizing strategies have left countless Americans without jobs and in the ranks of the long-term unemployed. Many of these individuals are well educated and highly trained. Often they are middle-age males who have spent most of their lives working at a single trade or in a single career, and who suddenly find themselves without work. They have typically not planned for such an eventuality and, because of their age and pay status, are not as likely to

---

xiii. The American Heritage Dictionary defines this term as "that part of the U. S. middle class thought of as being average in income and education and conservative in values and attitudes."

be readily employed as their younger counterparts in the same profession. These individuals typically view success in the workplace as crucial to their well-being and are devastated by a period of unemployment. In many cases they are not financially prepared for unemployment and cannot continue to support themselves or their dependents in a way that is acceptable to them. James Alan Fox, dean of the College of Criminal Justice, Northeastern University, commented in this way about the impact of unemployment for workers in this group: "If a 25-year-old gets laid off, he looks at it like it's a job and goes and gets another one. A 45-year-old man may think there are no other job opportunities out there for him, and in this economy, he may be right. He feels he should be at the top of his career, not at the bottom."[13]

With so much of their perceived self-worth torn away, and with little hope for a future as promising as the past, it is not surprising that some react with anger and violence.

A University of California psychologist, Ralph Catalano, released a report in August 1994 in which he stated that layoffs were one of the most prevalent causes of workplace violence and occupational homicide. In his study, Catalano found that those who were laid off were six times more likely to commit an act of violence or murder in the workplace than other employees. In his view, the fact that an individual lost his or her job was actually a better predictor of violence than such factors as age, sex, economic status, ethnicity, marital status, mental disability, or a history of violence.[14] Although Catalano's statement disputes the long-held assertion that a violent past is the best predictor of future violence, the results of this survey cannot be ignored. Clearly, employees who are terminated for any reason represent a potential risk to coworkers and the organization.

Finally, even those individuals fortunate enough to weather the recent economic storms in America have not fared all that well. The 1990 census reported that median household income fell in the census year by 1.7%, to $29,943 annually. The primary decrease occurred in the category of white males in the workforce—the single largest group of employees and the classic profile of a workplace murderer. The average annual salary of a white working male fell 3.6%, to $27,866 annually. This same group of workers experienced a decline in average salaries for the three years preceding the 1990 census. Other working groups, such as African-American males and female employees, experienced a slight increase in median income; but, this was as a result of the decline in white male worker salaries and not by direct salary gains for these other categories. Overall, on a per capita basis, real income for all Americans in 1990 declined by 2.9%, to $14,387 annually.[15]

The financial stresses to which these various economic groups are subjected can be both unforeseen and unbearable. Particularly onerous is the fact that each individual who suffers financial misfortune is fully aware of those who have been more fortunate. They are constantly reminded, through the media and the advertising industry, of their own plight and of missed opportunities. As this pattern continues in the United States, the nation becomes more economically stratified and individual citizens find more reasons to stand apart than to unite. The anger and hostility that can ensue, although understandable, is a burden that will continue to be shared by each member of society for as long as the situation remains unchanged.

Changes in the Family

The once-traditional nuclear family in America has also experienced significant change in the past three decades. The number of single-parent households has increased dramatically as the number of divorces has risen steadily since 1960 (see Figure 4.4).[16] The annual number of divorces in 1990 was nearly 1.2 million, or three times higher than the number of divorces recorded in 1960. In 1990, only 26% of American households with children under the age of 18 included two parents or adults. The number of single-parent households increased by 2.8 million in the ten year period of 1980-1990 alone.[17] The traditional family structure, with which many members of today's work force were once comfortable and familiar, has been radically altered in less than two generations.

Figure 4.4: Number of Divorces

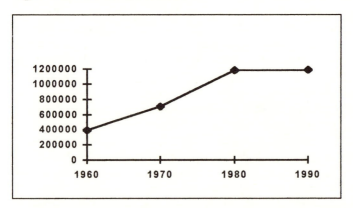

With so many disintegrating relationships and changes in the traditional structure of the family, there are enormous resulting financial and emotional hardships on former partners. Single parents are burdened with additional financial obligations, such as child care expense, that compound the heavy responsibilities involved in rearing young children. Many single parents are women who do not receive adequate child support from their former spouses, often earn less than their male counterparts in the workforce, and who face the prospect of trying to earn a living while maintaining their obligations as a parent. Husbands are sometimes angry and bitter about the breakup of the traditional family or the additional financial obligations they incur. It should not be surprising that some of these individuals react aggressively in social or work situations given the stressors they experience in their personal lives.

The disintegration of a relationship often negatively impacts family relations and friends, sometimes causing a "take sides" type of reaction that can be bitter and hostile. Frequently, a divorce may result in a nearly complete realignment of relationships that may extend beyond the social circle into the workplace. The emotional distress of divorce unfailingly extends to all members of the immediate family and can have a lasting effect on both adults and children. Resulting financial and emotional stresses compound already difficult living situations and can place individuals in what they perceive to be an untenable position. Recent information about homicide in the workplace indicates a dramatic increase in spillover violence that originates outside the job site. An increasing number of workplace murderers are acting out aggressions that stem from the disintegration of personal or family relationships. Many of these individuals will murder their spouses, as well as other workers on the job site, in response to domestic difficulties they are unable to resolve.

PREVENTION METHODOLOGIES

Workplace violence or occupational homicide can impact any individual or work environment, despite significant prevention efforts. Violent incidents may erupt with apparently little or no warning, even in the most secure environments. However, the apparent spontaneity of such occurrences is often a myth that can be exposed by a close examination of the circumstances leading up to the violent incident. In many of the case studies previously reviewed, there were early warning signs of potential violence; unfortunately, but frequently, these warning signs were ignored or not completely recognized for their importance. This is a common situation that can sometimes be rectified with proper violence prevention techniques.

If one blindly accepts the assumption of spontaneity, scenarios for possible workplace violence seem limitless and difficult to define from any point of view. Possibly a once trusted coworker, unable to cope with difficulties apart from the office, will bring a handgun to work and begin shooting. Perhaps, a customer with severe psychological problems will carry a weapon with him on his next visit. Possibly, a terminated employee with a grudge will lash out against the organization in an act of indiscriminate violence. Without sufficient consideration of the subject, there may seem to be little staff can do to foresee all possibilities. There are, though, many real opportunities for action and prevention if the issue of workplace violence is given adequate study and understanding.

With the dramatic increase in occupational homicide over the last decade, an argument can easily be made that virtually every American worker is potentially at risk. An equally strong argument can be made that every employee in every organization in America can, and should, be prepared to ensure his or her personal safety and minimize violence in the workplace. With an overburdened law enforcement system and a judicial system stretched to the breaking point, it makes good sense for each individual to do what he or she can to sustain their own well-being. This implies an understanding of how violence erupts and what measures can be taken to protect the individual worker as well as the organization.

These arguments appear obvious, but they are often overlooked in favor of seeking outside protection services. Often, the individual worker would simply rather not deal with a subject as unsettling as occupational homicide. Prevention is, however, an issue that must ultimately succeed or fail at the individual level, since each worker is at risk.

The recent trend in the rate of occupational homicide is both clear and frightening. This is a problem that, it seems, will worsen significantly over time unless proactive measures are taken soon—and at the worker level. Each member of an organization is a potential victim, but also a possible source of prevention. The critical point is to implement a preventative approach to workplace violence that is unified across organizational lines and integrates a multitude of skills, knowledge, and options.

When dealing with a potentially lethal employee or client, a manager or employee is dealing with the personality, behavior, and unknown intentions of another individual. Managers are typically trained in matters of organization, motivation, teamwork, supervision, and goal setting; they are not often trained to be therapists or behaviorists. Although it is true that an effective manager learns, through experience, how to somewhat judge the motivations and character of others, the matter of predicting and preventing violence challenges both the assumptions and expectations of what management is all about. A manager has traditionally been viewed as a leader and motivator, not as a predictor of mayhem or interpreter of the hidden intentions of another. The manager of today, however, must possess all these skills and a good deal more to be effective in the workplace. The manager of today must integrate a wide variety of · knowledge and experience, along with a greater-than-average blessing of common sense, to be the workplace leader of tomorrow. Integrating what is known about workplace violence into a comprehensive program of prevention that is accessible to managers and staff may be the ultimate answer to eradicating this management crisis.

The effective prevention of occupational homicide requires a strong commitment to preparation. An organization must be prepared to recognize the possibilities of workplace violence, organize the workforce through communication and training, and establish a work environment that emphasizes safety and mutual concern as primary considerations. The single most effective methodology in violence prevention is a focused program of intervention.

This section of the study of occupational homicide will bring together a variety of components that are integral to a comprehensive and practical violence prevention program. Each of these components emphasizes the primary concept of intervention as the most efficacious method of violence prevention. A series of topics will be presented, each of which contain several components important to this integrated approach.   Some of these topics are broader than the subject of workplace violence itself and are intended to create a positive, safe, and productive work environment in which the general possibility of violence is minimized.   Other topics deal directly with the issues of workplace violence and occupational homicide.   It is important to know that each topic is a vital piece of the prevention puzzle.   These elements work together to create the kind of work environment where the possibilities of unanticipated or uncontrolled violence become small or insignificant.

Many organizations, because of their own desire to provide a healthy work environment, will have already made progress in violence prevention by utilizing some of these elements.   Other businesses may need to add procedures to their existing methodologies.   Hopefully, many organizations will be able to develop a comprehensive and integrated program for violence prevention and intervention through the combined use of these components.   This kind of integrated approach to the workplace will surely yield benefits throughout the organization in many ways.   The major prevention topics and their emphasis can be summarized as shown in Table 4.2.

The most effective violence prevention program must be especially tailored for a specific organization.   This is particularly true when considering such issues as physical security, staffing of safety or security functions, and the creation or modification of a written violence prevention plan.   It is impossible to refine all the following suggestions to the point that would allow for their immediate and universal implementation in a specific organization.   What follows, though, will provide the basic groundwork for developing an effective violence prevention program for most organizations.   The key is the integration of these components into a comprehensive organizational strategy that takes into consideration the unique nature of the subject organization.

EMPLOYMENT PROCESS

The first step in a successful violence prevention program is to ensure that the organizational hiring process is effective, reliable, and consistent.   The obvious, and best, methodology for avoiding the potentially lethal employee is to not employ him or her in the first place.   In many organizations, however, the employment process is handled in a routine fashion that belies its importance and may actually put the workplace at risk.   There is no better place to halt the possibility of occupational homicide than at the front door of an organization.

The process of recruitment, screening and employment can easily become an exercise designed for consistency rather than result.   In great measure this is due to a single, common misperception held by those in the organization who do the hiring. These individuals may believe that complex regulatory requirements mandating equal opportunity, and therefore equal processing of all job applicants, minimizes their ability to strengthen the employment process.   In reality, equal opportunity regulations do not conflict with an employer's ability to ensure a safe workplace through rigorous hiring practices. The intent of these regulatory measures is to eliminate prejudicial treatment of applicants, not to compromise the workplace or the safety of workers. In order to combat this misconception, each employer should be completely familiar with the pertinent legislation that effects and regulates the hiring process. At a minimum, individuals responsible for the hiring process within an organization should be familiar with the following legislation:

1. Title VII of the Civil Rights Act of 1964,
2. Age Discrimination in Employment Act,
3. Equal Pay Act,
4. Executive Order 11246,
5. Americans with Disabilities Act,
6. Rehabilitation Act of 1973, and
7. Vietnam Veteran's Readjustment Assistance Act of 1974.

Two other factors that tend to dilute the efficacy of the hiring process are time and habit. The hiring process can often be lengthy and staff intensive. This is particularly true if a successful recruitment produces a large number of applications. In such a situation, employment procedures often take on a kind of "mindless processing" methodology wherein insufficient thought is given to hiring the most suitable individual in favor of an emphasis upon completing the employment process itself. Staff responsible for these vital human resource activities often feel intense pressure to fill an open position as quickly as possible. This can easily result in employment activity that gives insufficient attention to such vital aspects as background investigation and individual suitability to the existing work environment.

A hurried approach to the hiring process is understandable given the competitive nature of the activity, but it can prove to be costly in the extreme. Many times, individuals are employed who are not suited for the open position or who cannot "fit in" appropriately with the existing workforce or work environment. With the rush to meet growing or complex staff requirements, much can be overlooked. Decisions are made in haste or selections are made based on assumptions rather than facts. After an individual is employed and becomes known to coworkers and management, the expectations of both parties may be shattered.

Employing the right worker for the right job is the single most critical activity for any organization. It is the employer's goal to attract an employee who is skilled, loyal, and able to become an effective member of a team. The invitation to work for an organization should be thought of as opening the door of the company to a new family member. Both parties expect skill, trust, fairness, respect, and the willingness to work for a mutual goal. In an ideal, full-time employment scenario, both parties are seeking a long-term relationship that will benefit both the organization and the employee. Unfortunately, however, in the haste to fill open positions, many employers simply fail to consider the importance of the potential relationship as it will develop over time.

Table 4.2: Violence Prevention Plan Components

General Topic	Purpose
Employment	Refine the employment process to minimize the possibility of hiring an individual prone to violence.
Terminations	Explore the process of terminating an employee so as to minimize the potential for violence.
Training	Build skills in communicating, teamwork, safety, crisis management, management of change, conflict resolution and recognition of potentially violent employees.
Security	Examine general security methods, physical security systems, and security through preparation.
Safety	Examine general safety issues, safety programs, the role of the Safety Officer and Safety Committee, safety meetings, and employee suggestions and recommendations to prepare staff to deal with violence.
Communications	Build communications skills to link employer and employees, deal with conflict resolution, and exchange information about violence issues and potential.
Management	Point out the importance of managing change in the workplace; the importance of management commitment to violence prevention; establishment of violence prevention work groups; keeping abreast of issues; contacting public officials and leaders for support and assistance; establishing employee assistance programs.
Crisis Management	Explore the purpose of crisis management, crisis plan development, monitoring, and updating the crisis plan procedures in the event of, and after, a violent incident.
OSHA	The role of the Occupational Safety and Health Agency.
Regulatory Issues	The importance of dealing with regulatory agencies, evaluations, and investigations.

The employment process is much more than "offering a job"; it is the mutual exchange of a very serious commitment. When a job offer is about to be made, expectations for success are naturally high on both sides. There is the anticipation of a new beginning for both parties. Typically, there is the hope that a relationship will develop which can last for decades, perhaps a lifetime. It is not uncommon for both parties to be less than objective about each other as the process of selecting the final candidate begins to finalize. These are serious considerations for both parties that far outweigh the day-to-day responsibilities of either, and which often may reshape an entire organization. These matters are frequently lost in the more mundane activities of the hiring process.

Even though the prevention components that follow provide a head start on violence prevention by strengthening the hiring process, they are not sufficient by themselves. The personnel staff responsible for each step in the hiring process must be fully aware of the nature of the mutual commitment about to take place. Throughout the rather long process of recruitment, application processing, screening, interviewing, and selection, there are many opportunities to ensure that the right individual is employed. There are also innumerable opportunities to make a poor choice if the hiring process becomes routine or is viewed as anything less than vital. It is therefore imperative that the hiring process benefit from a good deal of planning. The recruitment of a new employee should never be rushed or given token attention. It can literally make the difference between the success or failure of an organization.

Personnel staff should be highly trained to deal with employment functions in a way that elevates their activities to the level of importance they truly warrant. Employers must always keep in mind that hiring an individual is a mutual commitment that will change both parties, for better or worse, possibly forever.

PREEMPLOYMENT TESTING

The question of the efficacy and legality of preemployment psychological testing remains unanswered, although the national trend favors abandoning reliance upon such methods. Except under specific circumstances, preemployment testing can create an additional liability for an employer and, in the end, may not be an effective means of eliminating potentially violent workers. If an organization decides to use this method for screening job applicants, it should never be undertaken without a good deal of legal research and staff support.

The state of California, in 1992, determined that certain methods of preemployment testing can both invade the privacy of individuals and be discriminatory in nature. Dayton Hudson Corporation, owner of Target Stores, was using a preemployment psychological screening test called Psychscreen. This test was a combination of two well-established psychological screening methods, the Minnesota Multiphasic Personality Inventory (MMPI) and the California Psychological Inventory (CPI). The organization used Psychscreen to evaluate all applicants for the position of store security officer (SSO). The use of this test was appealed by job applicants in a class action brought against the corporation when a number of individuals were rejected on the basis of test results. The California Court of Appeals ruled that the use of such a test violated California's constitutional guaranty to individual privacy and existing statutory regulations by inquiring about the applicant's religious beliefs and sexual orientation. The court also noted that the corporation failed to establish that the use of Psychscreen related to an applicant's ability to successfully perform the job of store security officer.[18] Although the California decision in this case was groundbreaking, a national trend has developed that tends to support the concept that preemployment testing is fraught with legal problems and, in some situations, may violate the rights of job applicants.

The use of psychological testing has also been determined illegal by the Americans with Disabilities Act (ADA), by implication, in that the act assumes this type of examination to be medical in nature. Although the Americans with Disabilities Act does not specifically address psychological testing, medical examinations that can discriminate against individuals with disabilities are prohibited. Recent court decisions tend to support the concept that many forms of psychological testing constitute a form of discrimination prohibited by the ADA when used to determine job suitability.

In addition to the questionable legal status of preemployment testing, there is the uncertainty of its efficacy. It has not been proven that such testing is effective in screening out individuals who are potentially violent. There is a good deal of divided, and heated, opinion on this matter, with little evidence to prove the infallibility of preemployment psychological screening. The situation is somewhat different if the testing takes place after an individual is employed. This, however, defeats the intent of preemployment testing.

Employers may condition a job offer on the results of an examination made after the job is offered so long as two conditions are met: (1) the examination is required of all employees in the same job category; and (2) a decision to revoke a job offer because of the results of the test is strictly job related and necessary for the business. The ADA also allows employers, under some circumstances, to reject job applicants who pose a clear and direct threat to the health and safety of coworkers or clients. This latter exception is difficult to establish and carries strict requirements of proof.

In general, the ADA requires employers to make reasonable accommodations for individuals with disabilities. In this sense, it is difficult to exclude an applicant on the basis of a psychological test alone. Much more evidence would be required to conclusively prove the case that employing a questionable applicant would create a hazardous situation for other individuals in the workplace. In addition, many states, such as California, have very strict right-to-privacy legislation that makes the use of psychological testing problematic or impossible. Testing that includes questions about sexual orientation, religious preferences or similar privacy issues is prohibited by law. Finally, the use of a compulsory lie detector test to screen applicants is prohibited by federal law.

In general, it is difficult, at best, to embark upon a program of preemployment testing without risking liability on several fronts. In addition, the usefulness of the method is uncertain. It is safer, and often more effective, to use rigorous methods of interviewing and background checking to eliminate potentially violent individuals unless the organization is well grounded in the legalities and techniques of preemployment testing.

SCREENING AND INTERVIEWING

The employment interview is a crucial element in preventing workplace violence. This interaction is an opportunity to evaluate the candidate for a job and share information about the organization and the position being offered. A detailed interview undertaken by a skilled interviewer can yield vital information not available elsewhere in the course of the hiring process. The interview is, however, an activity that is both art and science; it is also subject to a variety of federal and state legislation.

Questions to be asked in the interview must be carefully constructed and adhere to federal guidelines. In a general sense, questions must be job related and deal with such aspects of the candidate's background as experience, ability to perform the job, and qualifications needed to perform the job successfully. Questions dealing with race, religion, national origin, marital status, family arrangements, sexual orientation, age (if over 18), arrest records, or financial condition should usually be avoided since they rarely deal with job-related issues. Nothing that takes place in the interview should invade the right to privacy of the applicant or allow discrimination to occur.

Despite complex and sometimes confusing legal restrictions, questions may be posed if they deal with job-related qualifications, abilities, and suitability for the position offered. Qualifications and abilities are typically easy to determine through skill testing, background investigation and the interview itself. Suitability, or personal characteristics, are usually not simple to determine, but are vitally important in the hiring process. Determining the suitability of the individual for the organization is critical to avoiding individuals who may become violent after they are employed. Therefore, the ability to evaluate the true personality of the applicant is necessary to successful hiring. This is an aspect of the interview process that is not hampered by legislation so long as the object is to determine job-related suitability and protect current employees.

There are two fundamental concepts to keep in mind when attempting to evaluate the suitability of a job applicant. The first is that personality characteristics remain generally consistent over the lifetime of most healthy individuals. Because of this, there are patterns of behavior that can be discerned. These patterns will generally be apparent throughout the course of an applicant's history, and likewise, will be consistent throughout the interview process. Through a combination of multiple interview sessions and thorough background investigation, it is possible to build a fairly accurate portrait of an applicant's personality and behavioral traits. In attempting to eliminate an individual who is prone to violent reactions, this is often a crucial process.

Clearly, an individual who demonstrates aggressive behavior, is negative and argumentative, or demonstrates any of the behavioral patterns known to be warning signs of violence should be avoided.

The second primary concept is that of using multiple interviewers. It is best to have as many different coworkers as reasonable interview the job applicant. A number of organizations undertake the first interview on a panel basis in which a number of employees interview the candidate collectively. This is later followed by two or more separate interviews, undertaken at different times with different interviewers, to further evaluate the individual. The collective experiences and opinions of all interviewers are then gathered to form a more comprehensive profile of the applicant. This process should allow each of the interviewers to separately rate the applicant on a standardized interview form. A composite rating can then be derived from each interviewer's input. Such a process is much more likely to result in an accurate and objective assessment of the job candidate than would be available from a single interviewer. Carefully documenting and retaining these rating forms also provides necessary compliance with legislative requirements.

Throughout each interview there must be consistency and focus. Each interview must consistently abide by legislative requirements and focus on an exchange of information that allows both the organization and applicant to make an informed, objective decision. In this sense, the interview should be broad in scope and not simply confined to only a preconceived script of questions. Although it is important that interview questions be prepared in advance, show consistency, and be thorough, they should not dominate an interview to the point where the free flow of information is impeded. One of the most efficacious ways of determining suitability in the interview process is the interviewer's ability to follow the changing direction of a conversation in order to disclose new information. In this process, too, there must be consistency and focus: consistency in gathering information through prearranged interview questions and a focus on the changing dialogue so that it can be used to learn more about the applicant and share appropriate information about the organization and the offered position.

One of the most effective techniques to be used in drawing out a profile of applicant suitability is the open-ended question. Using open-ended questions not only disallows short, yes-or-no, replies, it provides the applicant with an opportunity to expand upon an issue and disclose his or her genuine reactions to it. Questions that require the applicant to provide personal reactions or opinions are typically very valuable in assessing an individual's personality. When open-ended questions are used with "echoing," the likelihood of gathering significant information increases. Echoing is the technique of providing signals to the applicant to gather additional information. Through the use of body language or short responses such as "I see" or "I understand," followed by a pause in the conversation, the applicant is encouraged to provide additional feedback and information. The point of echoing is to prompt the candidate to offer as much information as possible during the interview process.

Echoing can be used with appropriate periods of silence, which is also designed to lead the applicant to share information openly.

Although it is often impossible to precisely determine whether or not an individual will react violently in the future, it is quite possible to disclose behavioral warning signs. Important behavioral warning signs were examined at length in Chapter 2 and it is in the interview, as well as on the job, that such indicators become important. Should a candidate display behavior that can clearly be interpreted as potentially violent, and should this behavior be consistent in several interviews with different employees, there is evidence of potential future violence.

Sometimes, however, potentially violent behavior will not be readily apparent during the hiring process. This is to be expected and generally cannot be avoided. A job applicant is usually highly motivated to acquire an offered position and will therefore do his or her best to make a good impression. This means that the behavior witnessed by the interviewer is most likely the most appropriate behavior the applicant can muster in responding to the situation he or she is experiencing. This is an important point for each interviewer to keep in mind. It is often the case that an applicant will be somewhat guarded and careful throughout the interview process. Thus, any indications of behavioral warning signs during the interview will generally be even more evident if the applicant is successful in the hiring process. For this reason alone, it is imperative that the interview process be as thorough as possible. The more time and opportunity the applicant has to express his or her true personality, the more a prospective employer will learn about suitability. The primary function of the interviewer, then, is to discern as much information about the candidate as possible. The more effective an interviewer is at encouraging the applicant to share significant information about him or herself, the better the opportunity to prevent a violent incident in the future.

Finally, the interviewer must be an expert listener and observer. Often, interviews are rushed and overly scripted. In such a situation it is inevitable that the interviewer will not listen closely and not observe sufficiently. The interview process should never be rushed and must always allow at least as much time for open-ended dialogue as it does for a scripted question-and-answer period. The interviewer should be careful to truly listen to the applicant and understand what is being said. There is often much information exchanged in what, on the surface, appears to be casual conversation. In addition, observing the candidate's body language and methods of expression can provide significant insight into his or her personality. Once again, consistency and focus are the keys. An interviewer must be consistently attentive to each and every applicant response and focus on information provided by the individual in order to pursue a better assessment of his or her suitability.

BACKGROUND INVESTIGATIONS

A complete background check should be performed on any individual who is seriously considered for employment. This must take place before a job offer is tendered. Information provided by the applicant on a standardized employment application should be the primary basis upon which the background check is undertaken.

One of the most important areas to check is that of prior criminal convictions. Most states allow an employer to inquire about felony convictions and, in some states, even misdemeanors. Many states, however, will not allow inquiries about arrests that did not lead to a conviction. This same prohibition is applied to court-sealed conviction records. It should be kept in mind that if an individual who has a conviction for a violent felony is hired and later commits a violent act in the workplace, the employer may be found liable through negligence. Thus, thoroughly checking on prior convictions, particularly if they involved a violent crime, is essential.

There are several reasons why an employer might legitimately want to inquire into an applicant's criminal conviction record. Such motives are upheld by legislation and encompass a reasonably perceived threat to the loss of company assets, employee-bonding requirements, and potential liability incurred by hiring an individual who is known to be violent.

If information about a prior conviction becomes known before an applicant is employed, this fact should not necessarily bar the individual from being hired. Some states prohibit excluding an applicant simply because of the existence of a prior conviction. This is usually the case with many government jobs. The bottom line is that the employer must evaluate each applicant upon his or her own merits, including, but not limited to, information about prior convictions. The decision to hire or not, would necessarily depend on the nature of the conviction and the job for which the individual is applying. Clearly, it would be unwise to employ an individual to work at a day-care center when he or she had been convicted of child molestation and currently no legislation would prohibit barring the individual in this situation. Such an obvious situation is not typical in the employment process, however. It is more likely that a situation will arise in which it is unclear as to whether a prior criminal record can constitute grounds for an automatic rejection of an applicant.

Since each case will be unique, the employer must always remember that it is of utmost importance to protect current employees and clients while not discriminating against a job applicant. This can sometimes prove to be a difficult situation to resolve; however, if it is obvious that the applicant poses a threat to the well-being of others in the workplace, he or she should be eliminated from consideration. Such difficult decisions should be resolved only after consultation with a human resources expert and, as an added precaution, with legal counsel if practical.

An extensive and detailed background check should be undertaken with all prior employers listed on an the job application. The results of this background check should be committed to writing for future reference. Such a background check can be of enormous assistance in protecting the workplace from a violent employee as well as protecting the potential employer from future liability. In addition, this is one of the best methods of determining the applicant's qualifications. Previous employers, knowing that they too face liability, may sometimes offer only superficial information or only verify hard data offered by the candidate on the current application. This is normal and, from a liability point of view, advisable. Despite this difficulty, each element recorded by the applicant about his or her previous jobs should be researched in detail. Particular attention should be paid to dates of employment, job duties, and reasons for leaving the prior positions. Gaps in employment should be investigated and inconsistencies noted for follow-up with the applicant. Whenever possible, ask the job applicant to provide certified copies of pertinent background records.

The application form itself should carry a statement informing the applicant that any false statements on the document could be grounds to reject the applicant or, later, to terminate the employee. With the combination of such a disclosure and a complete background check, the employer will reduce the possibilities of hiring an unsuitable employee or incurring future liability.

Although resumes are of assistance in determining qualifications for a job, they should never be used in place of an application form. The application form is a standardized document, which, in itself, requires certain legal disclosures and must meet strict regulatory requirements in the hiring process. In addition, an application form provides for a uniform way of evaluating all job applicants in a fair and consistent manner. If possible, however, it is preferable to also obtain a resume from the applicant. The resume can provide supplemental information to the application and should also be used as the basis for a thorough background check. If an applicant offers a resume for consideration, the information contained on that resume may be checked as thoroughly as the information presented on an application form.

Letters of recommendation may also be helpful, although many employers either do not require or do not rely on them. If letters of recommendation are obtained, permission from the applicant to discuss the letter with the writer should also be sought. Follow-up telephone calls to those who wrote the recommendations is another important safeguard in the screening process.

It is best to gather as much information as possible directly from the applicant. An application on the organization's standard form is mandatory. If this can be supplemented with a resume, letters of recommendation, evidence of prior work history, or any other information the applicant is willing to offer, so much the better. All information, however, should be verified as completely as possible and subsequently documented with detailed notes.

TERMINATION PROCESS

That the act of terminating an employee can be a dangerous undertaking, even after the actual termination itself has taken place, can be demonstrated by an event which took place in the small town of Sparks, Nevada, on January 18, 1995: "Jim Teller, a supervisor at the KMart distribution center in Sparks, says revenge prompted a fired employee to come looking for him with a gun. Teller, 52, was wounded in the leg. Gunman Gary Provance took his own life during an 8-hour standoff with officers. He was fired for sleeping on the job and I'm the one who verified it, Teller (said)."[19]

This incident of workplace violence, culminating in suicide, could have been much more devastating except for the prompt actions of store managers in notifying other employees of a crisis on the premises and the superlative response of local law enforcement officials. Occupational homicide, or other forms of violent retaliation, resulting from terminations, must be of significant concern to all workplace managers.

The process of terminating an employee is, at best, difficult for both parties. To an employee, the termination process can be emotionally and financially devastating. To the organization, a departing employee may represent a significant threat to the well-being of the workplace. It is not uncommon for a terminated employee to be bitter, angry, and confused. How management handles the termination process can often make the difference between a peaceful or violent end to the relationship. Because the act of terminating an employee is fraught with legal complications and is often the scene of intense emotional reactions, managers must be thoroughly trained to deal with terminations from the employee's perspective as well as within the guidelines of their organizational responsibilities. Without a good deal of diligence and sensitivity in the process, the act of terminating an employee may evolve into a lawsuit or, at worst, a violent incident in the workplace. It is also important to keep in mind than the initial reaction of an individual to the termination process may not at all represent that individual's final reaction. As many incidents of occupational homicide reveal, individuals who remain relatively calm during the termination process may later react with unpredictable violence. It is therefore important to consider the potential effects of the termination process on the individual well after he or she has departed the workplace for the last time.

The termination process will always severely test the skill and sensitivity of a manager; but it is vital to keep in mind that the process is typically much more painful for the departing employee. Even experienced human resource professionals find the act of terminating an employee stressful and difficult. Managers, who may have developed a strong relationship with the departing employee, are sometimes significantly affected by the actions they must undertake. There are, however, guidelines that can minimize the potential for violence and make the transition as smooth as possible for all parties to the termination. Some of these guidelines are:[20]

1. The employee must be treated with respect, sensitivity, and dignity throughout the termination process.
2. If the termination involves a performance issue, the organization must ensure that performance standards are applied equally to all employees, without exception.
3. The timing of the termination process is critical. Try to avoid terminating an employee when he or she is undergoing stressful life situations such as a divorce, illness, or the recent death of a close friend or family member.
4. Two members of management should always be present at the termination meeting, one of which should be a human resource professional, if possible. In some cases it may be advisable to have a member of the security staff present at the meeting. This is particularly important if the departing employee is known to have a history of aggressive or violent reaction to change.
5. Expect the terminated employee to react emotionally. Try to understand the shock and pain of the process from the employee's point of view. Regardless of the emotional nature of the meeting, remain objective and calm. Try to keep the meeting focused on the issue at hand, always using a dignified, sensitive approach.
6. Act professionally in the termination meeting. Confine conversation about the termination to the business reasons motivating the organization's decision. Ensure that the employee understands what is happening and why it is happening. Do not assess blame or react in a judgmental manner.
7. Be honest with the employee and ensure him or her that the matter will be handled in a confidential manner. Provide straightforward answers to questions important to the employee.
8. If there is reason to suspect a violent reaction from the employee, be sure to have security personnel present at the termination meeting and in the presence of the employee when he or she is leaving the premises.
9. Be prepared for the meeting. Have all documents ready for presentation to the employee. Have all benefit information ready for review and immediate delivery to the employee. Ensure that arrangements have been made for the employee to gather personal belongings and return company property after the meeting. Prepare and rehearse the meeting in advance so that all points important to the employee are covered.
10. Take any follow-up action necessary to ensure the continued security of the workplace (involving keys, passwords, etc.) after the departure of the employee.
11. Ensure that an effective outplacement program is available to the employee. A strong outplacement program often makes a significant difference in the transition process.
12. Ensure that the physical departure of the employee from the workplace is handled with dignity and in a confidential manner. There should be no possibility of embarrassment or undue stress involved in the departure process.

Of critical importance to the termination meeting is the approach and attitude taken by the members of management present. Departing employees must not be stripped of their dignity and, if possible, they should be given reasonable assistance to help them reenter the workforce as quickly as possible. Managers must always keep in mind that termination represents one of the most painful transitions an individual is likely to experience. Honesty, understanding, and sincerity should be the keynotes throughout the termination process.

TRAINING STAFF, SUPERVISORS, AND MANAGERS

Training is an investment that is often given minimal attention in American organizations. Properly training an employee should encompass far more than simply providing job skills necessary to carry out a required function. Ideally, each employee should be trained in a comprehensive manner, with the ultimate goal of enhancing, not only current skills, but also the skills and qualities necessary to future responsibilities the employee may encounter. In addition, training should be made available on subjects that enhance organizational efficiency, aid in personnel management, and encourage team building. Although these subjects are less tangible than traditional skill training, they are equally important to the overall success of both the worker and the organization.

Managers and supervisors, as well as potential supervisors, should be the recipients of specialized training programs designed to enhance their role in the organization and aid in violence prevention efforts. Intensive training for managers and supervisors who are charged with safety and violence prevention in the workplace should include subjects such as the following.

1. *Communicating effectively.* This should be a program that teaches how to listen effectively, convey accurate and meaningful information, be concise and precise in conversation and written communication, and analyze and interpret verbal and nonverbal information.
2. *Teamwork concepts and team building.* These should impart the concepts of working as a group for common goals, managing work groups, understanding and encouraging the individual to participate in directed efforts, understanding the value and importance of the individual worker as part of a team, and understanding group contributions to the organization.
3. *Safety and crisis management.* This training should impart the important concepts of prevention and intervention. Employees and managers should be made familiar with organizational safety procedures, potential workplace hazards, and violence prevention techniques. The organization's crisis management plan should be the subject of considerable focus, along with skills necessary to manage a crisis in the workplace.
4. *Managing change.* This familiarizes individuals with the inevitability of change, techniques for anticipating the effects of change, strategic planning and preparation for known change. The manager or employee should be encouraged to recognize change as opportunity, share information about change with peers and staff, and develop a forward-looking attitude about the future.
5. *Conflict resolution.* Perhaps one of the most crucial elements in personnel management, conflict resolution is a skill that is needed by all members of the workforce, especially managers. The training program should develop skills in the area of communications, understanding opposing points of view, negotiation, intervention, and diffusing hostile or violent situations.
6. *Recognizing the behavioral warning signs of potentially violent individuals.* Recognition should focus on the early recognition of characteristics known to be related to subsequent violent behavior. This training should lay the foundation for skill enhancement in intervention and assistance.

7. *Employee intervention and assistance training.* Such training should cover skills needed to provide (or acquire) assistance to diffuse a potentially violent situation and organize aid for an employee in need. Employee assistance programs (EAP), and their role in aid and intervention, should comprise a part of this training.
8. *Workplace security.* Security should focus on the physical infrastructure of the organization. Attention should be paid to monitoring the workplace and enacting enhancements to ensure employee safety and organizational security. Security procedures and policy should be an important subject in this training program.
9. *Regulatory and compliance training.* Such training should familiarize managers with safety issues subject to laws and regulations applicable to their organization. Other areas of compliance, such as the hiring process, should also be covered.

A working knowledge of topics such as these can prepare staff or managers to effectively succeed in a modern, complex, and rapidly changing workplace. This kind of comprehensive training, however, demands a significant commitment from any organization. In daily practice it is often difficult, and expensive, to undertake such a comprehensive training regimen. Nonetheless, this training is a true investment in the future of the organization. Individuals who receive this broad array of skill enhancement are much better prepared to deal with the eventualities of workplace violence than those workers who receive little or no preparation. If an organization decides to make a commitment to violence prevention, training such as this is fundamental to the success of its program.

AWARENESS AND PARTICIPATION AS PREVENTION GOALS

The goal of maximum employee participation in any violence prevention program implies a commitment to continuing education in the workplace. This education should be oriented to a universal, objective awareness of the problem on the part of each member of the staff. Employees should be especially trained to be aware of changes or deficiencies in the work environment which may prove hazardous. Individuals should be given the skills to be cognizant of their coworkers, clients and environment as a routine matter. Awareness of this order should extend from such "soft" topics as behavioral warning signs to "hard" topics such as the physical security of the office or plant. Certainly, it is not the purpose of such training to create an unnecessary and artificially heightened sense of insecurity among staff; but rather, to impart a vigilance based upon the objectively recognized possibilities of violence. This form of vigilance is of the order of what would be expected by the implementation of any effective safety program within any organization.

To the degree that each worker is aware of the possibilities of workplace violence or occupational homicide, the overall security of the work environment is improved. Naturally, awareness alone is not sufficient to afford reasonable protection. However, without adequate worker awareness, there can be little, if any, security in the workplace. It is the role of the manager to ensure an adequate awareness of the problem without inducing anxiety among the staff.

As with any other form of education, this is best accomplished by presenting all sides of the issue in an objective, informative manner and allowing ample opportunity for individuals to express any concerns and articulate questions. When sufficient awareness of the problem is imparted to the staff, taking action to protect the work environment becomes a more effective, less complicated next step.

PHYSICAL SECURITY

Successfully achieving adequate physical security in any work environment is a task that can range from relatively simple to virtually impossible.   There are a number of factors that define, and limit, an organization's ability to provide effective physical security. Considerations that weigh heavily upon any decision to increase workplace security include:

1. the existing physical infrastructure of the office, business or plant;
2. how title to the property is held and the necessity for leasehold improvements to common areas;
3. the complexities of the physical work environment itself, including size, location and accessibility;
4. the current state of physical security, if any;
5. the level of security to be attained;
6. the constraints of cost incurred by establishing or increasing security;
7. the demographics and opinions of the staff and their anticipated response to new or additional workplace security systems;
8. reliance on outside contractors and service providers to establish and maintain new or improved security systems; and,
9. the impact of new or increased security on clients and others in the business community.

In fact, this is but a limited list of the many factors to be considered when planning for a secure work environment.   Establishing effective physical security in the workplace can be an extremely expensive, and nearly limitless, commitment.   Since the possibilities for violence are so broad and diverse, a commitment to the maximum physical security attainable is typically beyond the means of most businesses. Management must be aware of the fact that a commitment to physical security will most often be modulated by the test of reasonableness and therefore always be somewhat of a compromise for most organizations. This is not, however, a reason to withdraw from establishing a reasonable program of physical security in the workplace. It is vital that every organization take steps to make the work environment as safe and secure as it can manage; such a commitment is not only fundamental to good management, it is required by law.

One approach to an initial consideration of installing or enhancing workplace security is to use the services of a security consultant. A recognized, professional security consultant will be able to tour an installation and, for a reasonable fee, prepare an initial report for management. Such a report can provide the basis for determining the current state of physical plant security and allow management to define new goals for improved security systems. For larger organizations, this may, in itself, be an expensive procedure but for smaller businesses, the cost should not be excessive for an initial consultation. For some organizations, existing employees may have the skill and training necessary to provide an initial assessment of workplace security. In any case, the organization should make an objective initial assessment of existing security systems to identify major areas of weakness and pinpoint needed improvements. Once a security program is in place, this kind of workplace assessment should be accomplished on, at least, an annual basis.

The implementation of a physical security program must encompass a view of the organization from many different aspects. It is simply not sufficient to focus on limited areas such as offices, plant workshops or customer service counters. In assessing the need for security, the evaluator must examine diverse geographical constituents of the business such as parking lots, entrance and exit facilities, escape systems, storage areas, surrounding businesses and offices, nearby services and facilities, shrubbery and pathways, and a host of other possible points of vulnerability. Often overlooked are such crucial elements as the arrangement of chairs and desks in an office, or even the items on a desktop, which may offer a weapon of opportunity for an intruder. Communications systems, data storage and retrieval systems, and transportation systems must also be considered. In short, assessing the state of security within any organization is a complex task that requires an evaluator who is well trained and insightful. This is a responsibility that, because of its importance and complexity, is best relegated to a recognized professional.

There is another, equally important, aspect to physical security that falls within the scope and responsibility of each manager and employee. This is the issue of personal safety. The practice of personal safety procedures is one that should be instilled in every member of the staff. Managers who train their employees in fundamental, personal safety practices are providing an excellent and much-appreciated benefit for the organization and the individual. Workplace violence or occupational homicide are sometimes crimes of opportunity. Effective personal safety procedures minimize these opportunities throughout the workplace. Managers should arrange for periodic employee training in the workplace on the subject and techniques of personal safety. The training should be provided at the expense of the organization and offered to groups of employees of reasonable size so as to allow for effective interaction. This is an extremely effective form of empowering employees to unite in a concerted effort to improve workplace safety and eliminate violence.

CRIME PREVENTION THROUGH ENVIRONMENTAL DESIGN (CPTED)

The concept of crime prevention through environmental design (CPTED) was first offered by author C. Ray Jeffrey in 1971.[21] The term was subsequently adopted as a project title for grants issued by the Law Enforcement Assistance Administration of the United States Department of Justice.[22]   CPTED is an applied system of workplace crime prevention that focuses on the work environment as the basis for a secure environment. It is considered to be a proactive model for workplace design in that CPTED attempts to directly manipulate the physical work environment in an effort to emphasize violence prevention.

Managing a work environment by CPTED techniques implies the use of four environmental components:

1. *natural surveillance*, or the capacity to be aware of events and personnel in and around the work environment;
2. *access control*, or the ability to control access to the work environment and personnel;
3. *territoriality*, or the capacity to recognize and define secure areas in the work environment; and,
4. *activity support*, or the ability to bring together staff and clients in appropriate ways to increase the possibility of a secure environment.

These components are used at three different levels of implementation:

1. the primary intervention level, at which the component is used to develop prevention policy and workplace design;
2. the secondary level, at which the workplace is analyzed and responses are made to areas of the workplace that appear to be at risk for violence; and
3. the tertiary level, at which the components are used to respond after a violent incident has occurred in the work environment.

Using CPTED in a formalized fashion, an organization can undertake workplace security assessment, security systems design and implementation, and workplace retrofitting in an organized manner. An organization using CPTED concepts would be able to design and implement a variety of systems to enhance the physical security of its operations.   If an organization is constructing a new work site, CPTED techniques allow for the provision of "designing in" the most effective physical infrastructure applicable to the business. In fact, the use of CPTED at the earliest stages of planning for a new physical plant can provide security systems which are quite effective against workplace violence. Managers interested in learning more about the applications of CPTED are referred to Jeffrey's book of the same title and to the U.S. Department of Justice for more information.

THE TEMPORARY RESTRAINING ORDER (TRO)

A relatively new tool in the arsenal of violence prevention is the use of a temporary restraining order (TRO) against an individual who has threatened the safety of the workplace. However, the use of a TRO has traditionally been constrained in that this remedy required a potential victim, acting as an individual, to seek judicial restraint. Due to this requirement it was often impossible for an employer to use the TRO as an effective or timely prevention technique on behalf of employees. Often, the employee, who would be required to act alone to secure a temporary restraining order, was reluctant to do so for fear of embarrassment or retaliation. This situation is, however, beginning to change in some states.

On September 21, 1994, Governor Pete Wilson of California signed the Workplace Violence Safety Act, to take effect on January 1, 1995. This act allows employers to obtain a temporary restraining order against any individual who threatens violence against an employee, employer or the workplace. It is important to note that this act deals with any legitimate threat to the workplace that could reasonably be expected to result in violence. Such a broad definition permits an employer to act quickly in using the TRO methodology so that the potentially violent conduct of any individual can be addressed. The California law amends the previous requirement that the individual target of the threat must obtain the TRO. The new legislation allows employers to obtain a TRO on behalf of any, or all, employees who are harassed or threatened.

Although the efficacy of using temporary restraining orders is a matter open to debate, there is a growing interest in this methodology as one component in an overall violence prevention plan. The liberalizing of regulatory requirements in obtaining a TRO, such as occurred in California, is an important step in allowing employers to incorporate an additional method into a comprehensive violence prevention program.

ISSUES OF WORKPLACE SAFETY

Every organization should have a strong safety, or illness and injury prevention (IIP), program in place. The primary goal of such a program is to eliminate, to every extent possible, potential hazards in the workplace. One of the legally recognized workplace hazards is employee or client violence. It is therefore necessary to incorporate this subject into any existing IIP as well as make it a key subject for newly developed plans.

An effective safety program will benefit an organization in subtle but powerful ways, which far exceed the specific topics actually addressed in a written plan. A work environment that is clean, comfortable, and safe can dramatically improve employee morale and productivity. An environment in which little attention is given to working conditions can be not only unacceptably hazardous, but may become a breeding ground for discontent, poor productivity, and even violence.

In the workplace of today, violence is one of the primary safety hazards that must be addressed. The ramifications of a murder or serious injury in the workplace can be enormous and can include both monetary and nonmonetary elements. Demoralization of the staff, high medical and worker compensation costs, regulatory sanctions, and civil and, even, criminal penalties can all result from a violent incident in the workplace. Employers are obligated, both legally and morally, to ensure that safety issues are given proper attention throughout the work environment, including safety from coworker or client violence.

The Occupational Safety and Health Act of 1970 is the fundamental federal legislation that regulates health and safety in the workplace. This act contains a general duty clause that requires virtually every employer to provide a workplace which is free from known hazards that can cause physical injury or death. The act mandates compliance with industry-specific, recognized hazard avoidance recommendations and regulates the behavior of employees by requiring them to adhere to health and safety standards.

Violations of provisions of the act can bring both civil and criminal penalties which, in some cases, can be severe. Employers who fail to document safety procedures, or fail to post appropriate safety notices, may be fined up to $7,000 for each violation or for each day the violation continues. Willful or repeat violations can bring a penalty of up to $70,000 for each violation (OSHA, 1995).

Many states have also enacted similar legislation to ensure workplace safety. California, for example, has passed extremely tough legislation in this area.[xiv] Under these laws, an employer, or even an individual manager, may be fined up to $5,000 and sentenced to six months imprisonment for safety violations. Failure to notify employees of serious or hidden dangers in the workplace can result in fines up to $1 million for corporations as well as individual fines of up to $25,000 and up to five years imprisonment. Beyond the sanctions imposed by federal or state legislation, there is the matter of civil penalties. These penalties can be imposed in virtually any amount by a judge or jury.

To further complicate matters, there are any number of other agencies that regulate employee safety and health within particular industries or within certain workplace environments. An example of such an agency is the U. S. Department of Transportation, which regulates safety and health issues under more than 20 different legislative acts.

Employers are legally obligated to take proactive measures that provide a safe workplace for employees. This obligation extends to a prevention program established by employers to eliminate workplace violence. In various court decisions, organizations have been found liable for injuries or death caused by the violent behavior of employees.[23] The precedent of employer liability in this area has been well established and should be given careful consideration.

The bottom line is that an effective safety program, which includes an effective violence prevention component, is mandatory for every organization. Such a program should be a combined effort of management and staff to ensure its maximum effectiveness. Employees should not only be encouraged to participate in the planning, documentation and implementation of a safety

---

xiv. California Labor Code 140-175 and 6300 *et seq.*

program, they should also be fully familiar with its contents and required to comply with its provisions. Managers and supervisors should be trained to monitor safety issues and ensure compliance. The most successful safety program will find unanimous support and commitment from all levels of the organization.

The Safety Program

The safety program must be a living document if it is to be of use. This means that the safety program must be practical in implementation and complete in documentation. Documentation is crucial to the effectiveness of a safety program and to ensure evidence of compliance for regulatory agencies having oversight in this area. The written safety program should be available to all employees and should constitute a ready and constant reference for managers and supervisors as well as employees. A well-prepared safety manual provides the basic tool for safety training, monitoring, and compliance on a continuing basis. Procedures to ensure that the plan is updated regularly are of vital importance.

Material in the safety program may include public information, regulatory information, brochures, informational pieces, instructional information, reporting procedures, medical information and even video or audio presentations. Staff should be assigned to ensure that information in the plan is maintained and kept current as safety regulations change and additional workplace hazards become recognized. The safety program should also include "how to" sections for each major work area so that individual employees are best able to implement safe work practices in their daily activities.

Since each organization will require specific safety measures and procedures, it is difficult to outline a detailed program in this book. However, at a minimum, the written safety plan should touch on the following subjects:

1. a management policy statement and commitment to safety and nonviolence in the workplace for all employees and the public;
2. a listing of individuals responsible for safety matters in the organization;
3. a compendium of required safety notices, disclosures, and regulatory information, including reference to centralized safety files;
4. a section on how to respond to, and report, occupational illnesses, injuries accidents, or violent situations;
5. intervention procedures and emergency communications;
6. emergency medical and evacuation information, including basic first aid procedures;
7. a section on how to identify and report hazardous situations, including how to recognize and report potentially violent behavior in the workplace;
8. safety training, communications, meetings and access to the organizational safety library and training material;
9. handling and care of equipment, machinery, and vehicles;
10. handling and care of chemical substances or other hazardous substances used in the workplace;

11. a section dealing with general office and shop safety, including machinery, equipment, tools, substances and work environment;
12. tips and "how to" information about personal safety in the workplace; and
13. safety documentation and recordkeeping.

A methodology should be established to ensure that updates to the plan are transmitted to all departments and employees on a regular basis.   The plan itself should include provisions for employee feedback and suggestions in an effort to increase participation in, and commitment to, the safety program.

The subject of workplace violence should play a prominent role in any documented safety program. This is the forum in which to lay down prevention techniques as well as outline personal safety recommendations. Such a plan should clearly describe how to recognize potential violence as well as methods to minimize injury or death in the event of a violent incident in the workplace.

One area that should always be included in the safety program, but in fact is often neglected, is the issue of personal safety.   There are several basic commonsense procedures that can go a long way to improve safety, both on the job and elsewhere. Although not strictly in the realm of workplace violence prevention, matters of personal safety are important for every individual and deserve a place in the safety program. Employee training in personal safety procedures is highly valued by workers and demonstrates a strong management commitment to staff wellness.

Role of the Safety Officer

The role of safety officer in an organization is complex and challenging. For larger organizations the safety officer will be a full-time position; for smaller businesses this role may be assumed by a member of the staff who has other primary assignments. In either case, the function of the safety officer can be crucial to the design and implementation of a comprehensive safety and violence prevention program.

The safety officer is primarily responsible for program development, compliance, safety program documentation, safety training, and monitoring of the workplace. This individual should be knowledgeable in compliance matters and safety procedures applicable to the specific organization or industry.   In addition, the safety officer must be capable of organizing and writing a safety plan, training other staff, keeping abreast of regulatory issues, and preparing informational reports for management and staff.   Practical safety work experience may be essential in some work environments where a high technology environment exists or where complex machinery is present.

The safety officer should be the organizational expert on the practical methods of violence prevention. This individual must be familiar with the issues surrounding workplace violence as well as capable of training others in prevention techniques. Since violence prevention is a rapidly changing issue, the safety officer must be capable of keeping abreast of the subject on a proactive basis as well as preparing written reports for management. He or she must also be committed to keeping managers, supervisors and staff informed of the most efficacious prevention techniques and ensuring that they are enacted in the organization.

In order for the safety officer to be successful, the individual must have the full support of management and the authority to create, implement and enact safety and violence prevention methodologies throughout the workplace. The responsibilities of the safety officer range broadly across an organization and can deal with such diverse issues as ergonomics, machine safety, office safety, vehicles, and countless other areas of risk. Since the safety officer must also be knowledgeable in the recognition, intervention, and prevention of violence at work, he or she must be knowledgeable about the behavioral warning signs of impending violence and appropriate intervention techniques.

In creating a position description for a safety officer, at least the following key responsibilities should be incorporated:

1. Develop and implement written safety and violence prevention procedures.
2. Ensure compliance with the existing safety plan, as well as state and federal regulations applicable to the organization.
3. Interface with staff, management, outside regulatory authorities, and the public on matters of workplace safety and violence prevention.
4. Monitor employee actions and the workplace for unsafe conditions; take corrective action as needed.
5. Prepare reports for management and staff on safety and violence prevention issues and the status of safety and violence prevention techniques in the workplace.
6. Organize safety and violence prevention training programs for personnel.
7. Participate in the development and implementation of a Crisis Management Plan and Disaster Recovery Plan as applicable.
8. Investigate accidents, incidents and hazards with a view to prevention of future occurrences. Prepare management reports and recommendations about incidents.

All of these responsibilities, especially in combination, can translate into a significant demand upon the safety officer. Larger corporations will find there is a need to support the safety officer with staff in order to ensure that vital programs are carried out and required documentation is always fresh. Smaller companies may find that a safety officer can spend less time on projects and that coworkers may be the best method of supporting a safety program. In either case, it is important that there be an individual in the organization who is able to organize and implement a workable safety program and who will remain responsible for its efficacy.

Safety Committee

The Safety Committee functions as an advisory panel to management and the safety officer. It is best to have a Safety Committee composed of both supervisors and staff from a variety of workplace environments. The safety officer may act as chairperson for the committee, or the chair may be selected by vote or on a rotational schedule.

The most effective committee will be one that relies heavily on worker input and participation. The observations, suggestions and recommendations of workers, through their representatives on the Safety Committee, provide an invaluable source of information about workplace conditions. The presence of management and supervisors on the committee indicates the level of support an organization is willing to provide to matters of safety.

The Safety Committee can be an exciting forum for improving workplace safety and establishing a strong violence prevention program. It is typically a dynamic environment and, if properly constituted, a trusted forum for the exchange of information. With this potential for getting things done, it is important that the Safety Committee operate in an environment where all suggestions are welcome and no topic is off limits. It should be thought of as both a working group for suggesting improved or new policies and a "think tank" for examining possible workplace hazards. This last function is where the Safety Committee can provide leadership in the area of violence prevention.

In constructing an effective Safety Committee, the following concepts should be kept in mind:

1. The committee should not be so large as to be unwieldy, yet it should be comprised of sufficient numbers to adequately represent all major areas of the work environment.
2. The chairperson can be the safety officer; however, consideration should be given to a rotational or elected chair if this leads to more active participation and a better flow of ideas and improved communication.
3. All workers should have access to the committee through its representatives.
4. Management must actively support the work of the committee.
5. The committee should be encouraged to be proactive in safety matters and in issues of violence prevention. They should not just respond to known workplace hazards or violent incidents.
6. The committee should produce documentation of its meetings, decisions and recommendations to be provided to management.
7. The committee should have a method of communicating its activities to staff. Likewise, the committee should solicit suggestions and recommendations from workers.
8. The committee should meet at regular times. Sufficient allowance should be made in work schedules to permit committee members to pursue the work of the committee without haste or interference.

Since an effective Safety Committee will be comprised of workers from a variety of organizational levels, brought together for a common purpose, there are strong possibilities for positive change. Topics such as workplace violence and occupational homicide will be viewed as an organizational problem, not simply a departmental one, if properly presented. Such companywide issues can bind diverse workers together, encouraging them to freely share ideas and information. Through such a process, the members of the committee are able to look beyond jurisdictional concerns and work together to improve workplace safety and quality at all levels.

Of primary importance to the effectiveness of a Safety Committee is management support. Organization leaders must not just passively support the committee but should be proactively involved in its operations. If management makes it clear to all employees that the Safety Committee is important to the organization, a wider interest and level of participation will result. An active Safety Committee will, in the end, immensely benefit the workers and the organization through aggressive prevention and safety activities. In addition, strong management support confirms for each employee that the organization is truly one that cares for, and about, its staff.

Safety and Violence Prevention Meetings and Workshops

Safety and violence prevention meetings provide an opportunity to share information with employees and to gather feedback about general conditions in the workplace. Meetings can, and should, take place on a variety of organizational levels and on a regular basis. For workers involved in maintenance or service, or those working in an environment subject to regular changes in working conditions, a short, weekly safety meeting dealing with a new topic at each session is effective. For employees who do not deal with dangerous equipment or tools or whose work environment is stable and not subject to change, less frequent meetings would suffice. New or revised safety and violence prevention issues should be the topic of special meetings devoted to that particular subject for all workers.

Although the most effective method of safety and violence prevention training is one-on-one instruction from a knowledgeable coworker or professional, safety meetings provide a reasonable and effective forum for employee education. Training aids such as video presentations, work books, informational pieces, and handouts help make the meeting more interesting and provide the employee with reference material for later study and use. A good practice is to provide each worker with a binder of safety and violence prevention training and reference material; this binder should be reviewed periodically by supervisors to ensure it is complete and up to date.

It is important to invite experts from outside the organization to address employees on safety matters of a complex nature; this is particularly effective in a high technology or industrial environment. Safety meetings should be interesting, informative, and allow for worker input and feedback.

An especially effective method of holding a safety and violence prevention meeting is to allow employees to conduct sessions dealing with specific issues. It is not unusual for certain employees to develop a keen interest in matters of safety and violence prevention if management supports a strong safety program. Many of these employees become quite knowledgeable in specific safety or violence prevention issues and are willing to share this information with coworkers. These individuals, if carefully selected as safety meeting leaders, are typically quite effective trainers in that they are often highly regarded by their peers for their practical knowledge and skills. Employee leadership in the area of safety and violence prevention also builds morale and emphasizes that management entrusts workers with issues important to the organization and themselves.

The safety meeting can be a crucible of innovative ideas about violence prevention possibilities. Workers often exchange information at such meetings, which would otherwise remain unknown. By comparing notes and exchanging experiences on the job, workers are able to identify areas of potential violence and suggest prevention methodologies. At the heart of this concept is a key component of any successful violence prevention program—the exchange of ideas through open communication. Discussions surrounding areas of concern for personal safety, as well as ideas for prevention, should be encouraged at safety meetings as a matter of routine. It is important for management to take the leading role in encouraging this kind of information exchange. Managers should be aware of the natural reluctance of workers to discuss subjects such as workplace violence or occupational homicide. Efforts should be made to encourage workers to face the possibilities of violence and work together to protect themselves and the work environment. In this sense, a regular safety meeting provides an excellent forum for such open communication.

Employee Suggestions and Recommendations

With proper encouragement, employees can provide significant information about workplace hazards and suggest methods for improving workplace safety and violence prevention, which may frequently be more detailed and effective than those obtained by other means. Since workers are typically quite familiar with the work environment as well as with each other, they can offer detailed recommendations that lead to early management intervention, thereby preventing injury or death and decreasing employer liability. The employee must, however, feel secure in offering a suggestion, knowing that this kind of feedback is taken seriously by management. In order to be effective, this form of upward communication must be nurtured and encouraged on a continual basis.

Whether by suggestion box, formal recommendation or employee work groups, management should ensure that workers are comfortable when offering suggestions about any safety or violence prevention issue that may arise. Workers should never be concerned that issues surfaced by their recommendations have the potential to negatively impact their jobs or careers.

Formal recognition of important employee recommendations is a crucial element to encourage the flow of information from staff to management. Such recognition need not be of a monetary nature and, in fact, is often more effective if it is not. Management should emphasize that safety and violence prevention recommendations provide the basis for a caring work environment, which benefits the entire staff as well as the organization. An employee who is honored for his or her suggestions and who recognizes that the recommendation has been acted on, will often encourage other workers to offer their opinions.   This kind of practical recognition enhances loyalty to the organization and publicly places a high value on employee opinions. Workers who are recognized for their leadership in enhancing the safety and security of their peers receive important encouragement to expand their efforts to look beyond their own function within the organization and view the workplace as an area of shared responsibility.

If possible, an open process of reviewing all recommendations should be enacted; each recommendation should be answered so that the employee understands management's position on the issue. If a recommendation is not enacted, an explanation should be provided to the employee, along with an expression of gratitude from management.   At a minimum, employee suggestions should be openly encouraged by management and, when appropriate, enacted in the workplace. This kind of communication loop not only provides an added measure of workplace safety and security, but it will enhance morale and team building throughout the organization.

Often overlooked is the fact that employees tend to know each other quite well. If a worker is experiencing difficulties, his or her coworkers are typically among the first to be aware of the problem. Should a worker begin to display behavioral warning signs that may indicate a violent outcome, it is often coworkers who are first aware of the situation.   In an environment where employee feedback is valued by management and employee confidence is assured, information vital to the safety and security of the workplace can be found flowing from staff to management in the form of suggestions or recommendations.   Whether the information constitutes the suggestion of specific intervention for a coworker or a more general recommendation about prevention possibilities, employee feedback may open an opportunity for intervention to prevent potential violence in the workplace.

A good deal of emphasis has been placed on establishing an effective safety regimen within an organization. Although the consistent practice of safety and violence prevention is of tremendous importance unto itself, there is another motivation for its emphasis when dealing with violence in the workplace. The concept of personal safety is one that is of significant interest to all employees in any organization. In this sense, the subject of safety can easily provide a common meeting ground for diverse groups of workers to come together for a unified purpose. Bringing all employees together for a common purpose is crucial to an effective workplace violence prevention program.

Eliminating occupational homicide requires the concerted effort of all employees, with each caring about the safety of their coworkers. If employees feel isolated and apart from their coworkers, they are not only more likely to ignore the possibilities for violence but, for those who are prone to acting out their own aggressions, more likely to commit violence themselves. Workers who are committed to personal safety for themselves and their coworkers are more likely to become involved in seeking assistance from management to intervene in a potentially violent situation before it becomes disastrous. The issue of workplace safety, then, provides a common forum for an important element in uniting any staff against violence—open communication.

Conflict Resolution

Conflict in the workplace is inevitable and can arise from many sources. The genesis of conflict can be volatile and swift or painfully slow to develop; it can be predictable, or sudden and unexpected. Whatever the process, or source, every workplace will experience conflict from time to time, and it is generally the role of the manager or supervisor to resolve conflict before it escalates into violence.

The traditional view of conflict defines four possible results for the involved parties:[24]

1. The *lose-lose* result, in which neither of the parties benefits from the conflict.
2. The *lose-win* result, in which one of the parties loses, the other wins.
3. The *win-lose* result, in which situation (2) is reversed.
4. The *win-win* result, in which both parties benefit from the outcome of the conflict.

In each instance of conflict in the workplace it should be the goal of the manager or supervisor to produce a win-win result that benefits both parties and the organization. It is a common misconception that a win-win result is virtually never attainable. The fact is that a manager experienced in conflict resolution can often produce a win-win result in many workplace conflicts. A manager who is able to effectively implement conflict resolution techniques in the workplace can often avert violence that would otherwise ensue without intervention.

Conflict resolution strategies are complex and require a good deal of experience and skill to be implemented effectively. Key managers should be extensively trained in conflict resolution and all supervisors should have at least a working knowledge of the process. Training should emphasize role playing in combination with a solid grounding in the four basic conflict resolution strategies:[25]

1. *Avoiding* the conflict by withdrawing physically or psychologically.
2. *Smoothing* the conflict by accommodating the interests of the parties.
3. *Forcing* issues in order to resolve the conflict.
4. *Confronting* the issues comprising the conflict in order to arrive at a mutually beneficial resolution.

Training must emphasize the win-win resolution as the goal of the conflict resolution process.

Many successful managers already possess the fundamental skills necessary to successful conflict resolution by virtue of their experience on the job. Unfortunately, not all managers view this as an important or necessary responsibility. The reality is, however, that conflict resolution is one of the most efficacious ways to prevent violence in the workplace. An astute manager will be able to intervene at an early period in a developing conflict and, through the use of conflict resolution techniques, assist in a resolution that benefits all parties.

EMPLOYEE BEHAVIOR AND PERSONNEL POLICY

Each organization should concentrate on adopting fair and effective personnel policies, in writing, to guide managers in their supervisory responsibilities.   A comprehensive personnel policy manual provides an effective tool for consistent supervision and also codifies a variety of issues important to all employees.   There are many components that, together, comprise a practical and useful personnel policy.   One of these components should state organizational rules and views dealing with workplace violence, violence prevention, and activities that may lead to violence in the workplace.

It is important that the organization take a firm position on such unacceptable activities as harassment, intimidation, and physical or verbal violence against employees in the workplace. Potentially violent individuals typically display a number of behavioral warning signs prior to physically acting out their aggressions and may embark on a course of harassment or intimidation against coworkers, supervisors, or clients prior to engaging in a violent act. Should such a situation develop, it is imperative that management intervene immediately to stop the aggressive behavior. If left to run its course, this kind of behavior sometimes results in physical violence and may result in homicide. Intervention implies the consistent use of a codified personnel policy along with human resource skills appropriately applied by a supervisor or manager.

The first step in controlling acts of harassment or intimidation in the workplace is a strong, written policy prohibiting such behavior.   The organizational personnel policy should make it quite clear that employees who harass or intimidate others will not be tolerated and that this type of behavior can result in dismissal from the organization.   In other words, the written personnel policy should take an extremely firm stand on the issues of harassment and intimidation in the workplace. Obviously, this policy should be known to all workers.

As a practical matter, harassment and intimidation of workers may take place without the knowledge of management or even front-line supervisors. In fact, this occurs frequently in some industries and organizations. Clearly, then, a strong personnel policy statement is not sufficient to manage the problem. Beyond the act of establishing a strong prohibitive policy, an organization must create an environment in which harassed or intimidated workers feel comfortable in reporting the situation to a supervisor or manager. Reporting this type of behavior is naturally difficult for an employee, who will often fear retaliation and the worsening of an already difficult situation. In order to overcome this understandable reluctance on the part of the victim, it is necessary for management to overtly support any written policy by taking immediate action to protect the harassed employee and stop the inappropriate behavior of the perpetrator. In order to accomplish this, it is necessary for management to react without delay to investigate any complaint of harassment and intimidation and, further, to take immediate action to stop the activities of the perpetrator. Actions against the perpetrator may range from counseling or referral to an employee assistance program, to suspension or termination from the job. Whatever action is taken, the situation must be so resolved as to ensure that the victim of harassment or intimidation is protected from the perpetrator.

If management accepts disruption in the workplace by ignoring acts of harassment or intimidation, they are setting the stage for inevitable violence or, perhaps, homicide. Even if the source of harassment or intimidation is outside of the workplace, the employer, and potentially others, may be held responsible for any resulting violence. Should an employer fail to take prompt corrective action when harassment or intimidation is occurring, significant and unexpected liability can result: "For example, in 1982, several workers were shot in a San Francisco office building by the husband of one of the victims. The wife had alerted her employer to threats made by her husband several months earlier, but neither the company nor building management took any special steps to protect its employees. In their suit for negligence, the victims recovered about $7 million total [damages] from the employer and building management company."[26]

Clearly, acts of intimidation or harassment are taken seriously at the judicial level, regardless of their genesis. Employers should be keenly aware of this issue and take strong, proactive measures to ensure that this kind of behavior does not affect the workplace.

Contacting Peers, Public Officials, and Political Leaders

Workplace violence and occupational homicide are subjects that are still insufficiently understood and infrequently given proper emphasis in many organizations and by many public officials. Some government agencies, however, are demonstrating an increased interest in this subject. Agencies such as the National Institute for Occupational Safety and Health (NIOSH), the Occupational Safety and Health Administration (OSHA), the Department of Labor (DOL), and the Department of Justice (DOJ) support activities designed to inform the public about workplace violence and, in some cases, provide prevention recommendations. At the state and local levels there are a growing number of agencies that can provide support for managers active in violence prevention techniques. Finally, a few private organizations have been established to provide information, training, and recommendations for prevention. In some cases, these private organizations charge significant fees, whereas government agencies are likely to provide information for little or no cost.

The subject of workplace violence has yet to benefit from a comprehensive and widely accessible program designed to benefit the majority of American organizations. This is due, in part, to the fact that occupational homicide has only been recently recognized as a major challenge facing American businesses. There is also a natural reluctance for managers to deal with the subject since it is, by its nature, not a welcomed topic in the workplace. Nonetheless, it is a subject that cries out for a comprehensive solution.

There does not appear to be a great deal of interest in the subject at the congressional level of the U. S. government. Although agencies such as NIOSH and OSHA are active in the area, new legislation designed to help managers protect their employees in the workplace has originated only at the state level, and even there, only infrequently. There is a need to expose the problem on a much wider basis to gain the support of public leaders and influential community and national leaders.

At the local level there is an obvious absence of a unified approach to workplace violence by business leaders. Even if an organization, itself, is well-prepared and committed to violence prevention, it is extremely rare that the organization will share its knowledge or resources, even in the nearby geographical area. Clearly, occupational homicide is a crime that can impact any business. It is a challenge apart from the considerations of business competition. Although it would not be advisable for a well-prepared organization to openly share all its prevention techniques with others, there is much room to share information, training opportunities, and knowledge. To accomplish this in an effective way it would be best to establish centralized clearing houses through which businesses of all types could share information and, where appropriate, services. The expense of such a centralized service could be shared among member businesses on, say, a sliding-scale basis to ensure that even small organizations could benefit. The key is a commitment to a business-community sharing approach to the prevention of workplace violence and occupational homicide.

Business leaders should also bring the subjects of workplace violence and occupational homicide to their representatives at both the state and federal levels of government. Although regulations imposed by the government are often anathema to business owners, there is a proper function to be fulfilled by governmental support and, where appropriate, legislation. With a broader, national perspective on workplace violence and occupational homicide, it would be possible to afford greater protection for business owners and employees as well as a more generally accessible resource base for prevention techniques. At a minimum, a more significant commitment on the part of government agencies to providing information and training to American organizations would save lives and economic resources.

There must first, however, be a heightened level of interest within the business community, with such interest brought to the attention of public officials and politicians. The effects of workplace violence and occupational homicide are drastically changing the nature of many American organizations.

This is the appropriate time for organizational leaders to be proactive in managing this change in the workplace.

Employee Assistance Programs

The lives of most Americans are complex and subject to unforeseen challenges and change. It is impossible for a worker to completely separate his or her personal challenges from those encountered daily in the workplace. Every manager must be aware that each employee is a total human being, who is affected by a wide range of dynamics that originate from both within and outside the workplace. Supervisors are only truly effective when they manage workers from a holistic perspective and regard each individual as unique, yet subject to a variety of stressors common to most individuals. This holistic understanding of staff is essential when assembling and implementing a program to address violence in the workplace. Although it may often be inappropriate for a manager or supervisor to interject him or herself into a volatile and very personal employee concern, it is undeniable that difficulties outside the workplace frequently have an impact on the work environment. The manager is, however, not without tools to assist an employee under these circumstances.

It can happen that occupational homicide or other forms of workplace violence occur as a result of situations which are wholly, or mostly, unrelated to work. The contemporary term for this type of workplace incident is "spillover violence"—aggressions that takes place at work despite a genesis outside the workplace. It is often difficult for a manager to know if an employee suffering distress emanating from outside the work environment is nearing the point at which he may become a threat to coworkers or clients. Even in such complex situations, though, there often exist strong interpersonal connections within the workplace that could prove helpful. It is not unusual for employees to form relationships with their peers at work—individuals with whom they may share their deep, and sometimes very personal, concerns. These relationships are extremely important to the well-being of an employee, and can help to form a key component in a violence intervention program. Many day-to-day personnel and personal difficulties of a minor nature are handled within these interpersonal networks, usually without the knowledge or intervention of management. Such a network of trusted colleagues can also assist a worker by directly encouraging him or her to accept positive intervention from a supervisor or manager. Despite this advantage, however, there are certain situations that arise when an employee faces personal or work difficulties too onerous to surmount or too complex for the direct assistance of a coworker or supervisor. This is when an employee assistance program (EAP) may prove to be the most effective form of intervention.

Employee assistance programs are designed with one important concept in mind—positive intervention. Their purpose is to assist an employee and his or her family through a difficult period in order to return that individual to a positive, productive place in the organization. A strong employee assistance program benefits both the employee and the organization in diverse ways. An EAP is perceived by employees as a valuable benefit, indicative of an organization's willingness to invest in the wellness of its workers. From an organizational point of view, an effective EAP can save a valuable employee and return him or her to the workforce with a fresh and positive outlook. If well designed, strongly staffed, and managed in a caring way, an EAP can provide invaluable and cost-effective services to any business.

Large organizations may support an employee assistance program with both in-house staff and outside assistance from counselors or therapists who specialize in a variety of issues. Smaller businesses may provide an EAP that is comprised totally of outside services and maintains only an arm's-length relationship with management. In short, employee assistance programs can be designed in any number of ways so long as they (1) provide positive intervention services to employees and (2) provide these services in a confidential, professional manner.

Intervention services typically deal with issues such as substance abuse, behavioral or performance problems, financial difficulties, legal matters (in some cases), domestic issues, or conflict resolution arising from workplace or domestic interactions. In everyday practice, however, an employee assistance program must be ready to deal with any matter brought forward by an employee or supervisor that effects the individual or the organization.

The most effective employee assistance programs will have characteristics highly valued by both employer and employee:

1. strong organizational support for the EAP and, in particular, for the confidential nature of the intervention process;
2. assistance to the employee and his or her family;
3. assessment, counseling, and referral to other assistance as needed;
4. a strong conflict resolution component;
5. a commitment to follow up with each employee in order to ensure the maximum benefit;
6. an education and training component to help employees develop interpersonal skills useful at work and away from the workplace;
7. technical assistance to management on personnel matters which deal with issues of intervention; and,
8. service that is available to employees and managers on a 24-hour-a-day basis.

Managers should be trained in the process of making appropriate referrals to an employee assistance program; they should know when a referral is indicated, how it should be handled, and be aware of any organizational policies or procedures applicable to a referral. The EAP should also be available to all employees without referral, on a confidential and direct basis.

Intervention is crucial to diffusing situations that can lead to workplace violence. A proactive employee assistance program, combined with a management team that strongly supports the EAP concept, is an excellent addition to any violence prevention program. As an additional benefit to the organization, employee assistance programs can reduce operational expenditures more than sufficiently to pay for themselves; they accomplish this by reducing absenteeism and helping to hold down costs often attributed to overuse of the health care plan.

CRISIS MANAGEMENT: PREPARING FOR THE WORST

A recent survey of businesses in the Atlanta, Georgia metropolitan area revealed the following information about crisis planning and management:[27]

1. 76% of those businesses surveyed believed that a crisis in the workplace was inevitable.
2. About this same percentage of businesses had no crisis management plan.
3. 73% had no training in dealing with crisis situations.
4. 72% lacked a crisis management team.
5. 57% reported they were not satisfied with their crisis response capabilities.

Other sources have also indicated that crisis planning by American businesses may run as low as 2 or 3 percent of all workplaces.[28]

American organizations are simply not often prepared for a workplace crisis. When an organization is ready for a crisis, the focus of preparation is most often directed at preserving data, not personnel. However, an effective crisis management plan must cover a wide array of possible disruptions, not the least of which is violence or murder in the workplace.

The objectives of a crisis management plan are to save lives, minimize injuries, protect organizational assets, and provide the most expeditious, effective response to emergency situations. In meeting these objectives, the crisis management plan must address a wide array of possibilities yet remain focused on the two most important elements: saving lives and reducing injuries. The best crisis management plan must account for the worst of possibilities in the workplace.

Although a written crisis management plan is vital, it cannot be effective without a good deal of management commitment and continuing practical support. Teams of individuals must be assembled and trained to handle emergency situations; communications protocols must be established and outside agencies must be organized into a comprehensive program of response techniques. Emergency drills and training sessions must also be a regular part of crisis management. Trauma plans must be put into place, and staff must be trained in a variety of skills to overcome severe workplace disruption. A crisis management plan should, at a minimum, deal with such issues as fire, explosion, hazardous materials, civil disturbance, violence in the workplace, natural disasters, or other common threats to the safety of employees, clients, or property.

Organizing and implementing a crisis management program can be an expensive and resource-intensive exercise; nonetheless, it is fundamental to the health of an organization. Unless a plan is given continuous management support and encouragement, there is a risk that it will become outdated and ineffective. An effective crisis management program must be constantly refined and tested to ensure its efficacy when workplace disruption occurs.

Developing a Crisis Management Plan

Developing a crisis management plan requires a proactive, committee-oriented approach; the subject is much too complex and exhaustive for a single employee to effectively organize and implement a successful program. For some organizations the safety committee can provide the most efficient vehicle for plan creation and implementation; for larger organizations, a special crisis management committee would be more appropriate. The committee should be staffed with a representative from each major organizational unit along with representatives from security, personnel and key management staff. If the organization supports a safety officer, or equivalent, this employee may be appointed to chair the committee. This committee should be charged with researching crisis management plans from other organizations, developing a plan, coordinating services with external agencies, and implementing the training and simulations necessary to make the plan workable.

Each organization will require a unique plan that is applicable to their physical plant, location, and employee demographics. Broad issues, such as natural disasters and available emergency services, vary according to geographical location. The size of an organization will determine the level of employee training and participation in actual crisis management exercises. Larger organizations may rely heavily on staff for specific emergency roles, while smaller organizations will require coordination with outside services.

In developing the crisis management plan, an organization should consider the following factors:

1. The types of workplace disruption to which the organization may be subjected should be determined based on experience, foresight, and sharing of knowledge with other organizations in the area. Community emergency service organizations and law enforcement officials should be consulted for additional information and participation in the planning process. The workplace violence component of a crisis management plan should address such areas as physical threat, hostage situations, armed intruders, and telephone threats.
2. Staff is an integral part of a crisis management plan. Employees should be assigned key coordination roles in the event of an emergency and staff should be trained in areas such as emergency medical intervention, emergency communications, services coordination, and other areas in which individual participation can prevent injury or loss of life. Employees should be fully familiar with the organization's crisis management plan and they should participate in regular crisis simulations.
3. A network of resources outside of the organization should be established and maintained. These resources should include medical services, law enforcement, communications, counseling and other staff support, and media management. An

organizational evacuation plan should play a prominent role in crisis management procedures and should account for individuals with disabilities.

4. An employee assistance program (EAP) should be in place and part of the crisis management plan.

5. Staff should be assigned to research changes in regulations and examine workplace disruptions at other organizations so that the crisis management plan is kept current and forward-looking.

There are many ways to approach the development of a crisis management plan and crisis management strategy for an organization. An effective method of initiating the planning process is to assemble a working design group to focus on defining four main objectives:

1. crisis events that could impact the organization,
2. an action or response plan to the events,
3. coordination activities during and after the events, and
4. simulations and training sessions important to preparation and response.

Moving toward these objectives, a crisis management working group should be able to develop a written crisis management plan to accommodate foreseen workplace emergencies. The plan could include an individual event sheet for any recognized workplace crisis. This event sheet should detail the nature of the event, action to be taken, and coordination of resources necessary to meet the workplace emergency. Using this methodology, the crisis management working group should then be able to assemble a crisis management plan that would encompass the majority of possible workplace crises. This plan would provide the basis for staff training and crisis simulations. A proposed event sheet for crisis planning purposes can be found in the Appendix.

When a working plan has been developed and implemented, staff should be trained and a regular schedule of emergency simulations enacted. Employees should be fully familiar with the plan and active in all simulations; they should be encouraged to share suggestions for improvement in the plan or its procedures. Outside agencies should be encouraged to participate in simulations, if possible, and to comment on the crisis management plan to improve its effectiveness.

Crisis management planning should be a shared process. Local organizations, or businesses with similar profiles, should come together to share their experiences and their plans in order to strengthen individual emergency programs. Several organizations, in combination, may be able to provide mutual resources and information that can make the difference between an effective crisis management plan and chaos when an emergency strikes. If practical, a network of support services shared among several organizations should be implemented. This kind of coordinated cooperation can be of immense benefit to smaller organizations unable to commit needed resources to crisis management but capable of committing staff to a combined organizational program.

OCCUPATIONAL SAFETY AND HEALTH AGENCIES

The Occupational Safety and Health Administration (OSHA) is concerned with all aspects of workplace safety, including occupational homicide and other forms of workplace violence. This agency functions as both a source of information and as regulatory authority for safety issues. The state of California, Department of Industrial Relations, has a division known as Cal/OSHA, which functions as the statewide agency in charge of workplace safety regulations. Cal/OSHA is considered to be among the most progressive of state-based agencies, being known for its hard-line commitment to worker safety.

In April 1994, Cal/OSHA initiated a conference on workplace security in Los Angeles. The focus of this conference was to assess the current state of workplace security and provide recommendations for employers to minimize future violence in the workplace. On August 15, 1994, Cal/OSHA released a report entitled *Cal/OSHA Guidelines for Workplace Security*. This report summarized key elements of the Los Angeles conference and was made available to the public.[29] Although the details of this report deal with workplace violence issues in California, the trends identified, and the recommendations put forth, are applicable to organizations in other states.

A statistical profile of workplace fatalities in California closely resembles the one offered by NIOSH for the United States. In 1993, Cal/OSHA reported that "the category of assaults and violent acts became the leading cause of occupational fatalities in California."[30] From 1992 to 1993, the number of homicides in the workplace increased 22.6%. Death by a transportation accident, long the leading cause of workplace fatalities, had been relegated to a secondary cause in California.

The state of California found that the high-risk occupations originally identified by NIOSH were reflected accurately at the local level. Consistent also was the fact that most victims of workplace homicide were male, even though occupational homicide was the leading cause of death for female workers (48.2%). Throughout each category surveyed, Cal/OSHA found results comparable to the NIOSH national data.

Incidents of workplace violence in California were categorized as *event-types*.[31] Although more narrow in scope than the category profiles used in this study, the event-type method is helpful in promoting safety recommendations. Cal/OSHA recognizes the following event-type categories:

1. A *first-type event* is one in which the perpetrator has no relationship to others in the workplace or to the organization itself. He or she will usually enter the workplace for the purposes of committing a crime. This type of event is often viewed as a general form of violence prevalent in society since the act of aggression is likely to take place during the commission of another crime. Employers are legally required to take measures to protect employees to a reasonable extent against this type of violence, as they are with other forms of workplace violence. Cal/OSHA takes the following position on employer obligations in this area: "Employers are required to address workplace security hazards to satisfy the regulatory requirement of

establishing, implementing and maintaining an effective Injury and Illness Prevention (IIP) Program. See Title 8, California Code of Regulations."[32] This is a clear problem for employers in that first-type event violence is difficult to predict and even more difficult to prevent. Nonetheless, there are guidelines that can assist an employer to at least minimize risk and avoid regulatory liability:

A. Ensure that workers and managers are in compliance with existing state and federal safety regulations. Since these regulations undergo continuous change, it will be necessary for management to keep in contact with both state and regulatory safety authorities. State agencies, such as Cal/OSHA in California, are typically willing to provide as much documentation as needed to enable employers to remain in compliance with local and federal regulations. This information is usually free of cost.

B. The organization must maintain a system in the workplace so that information about safety issues can be disseminated to employees. Employees must be advised of all workplace hazards, without exception. In addition, employees must be provided with a way to inform management of workplace hazards so that corrective action can be taken.

C. A system must be put into place that provides for periodic inspections of the workplace. Hazards, including those that may contribute to workplace violence, need to be identified, documented, and corrected. Records should be kept to minimize employer liability and provide evidence of compliance in the event of an audit by a state or local agency.

D. There must be a procedure in place that provides for an investigation of all workplace injuries or deaths. All such investigations must be thoroughly documented.

E. A system must be in place to correct all discovered workplace hazards or potential violence, and to protect employees from retaliation in the event they disclose a workplace hazard to management or others outside of the workplace. Employees must also be protected by the employer, to every reasonable extent, from threats, harassment or intimidation in the workplace.

F. Employees must be trained in recognizing workplace hazards, potential violence, risk factors, crime awareness, diffusing hostile situations, and assault/rape prevention.

G. The workplace must provide adequate physical security for employees.

Each of these requirements apply to all three event types. Employers should be aware, however, of the special difficulty of providing adequate protection for first-type events.

2. A *second-type event* is one in which the perpetrator is a "current or former client, patient, customer, passenger, criminal suspect or prisoner."[33] Much of this book is devoted to what Cal/OSHA terms second-and third-type events. State and federal safety agencies are particularly concerned with such matters as (1) physical security, (2) training, (3) reporting, and (4) documentation. These key areas should be addressed by each employer in relation to the work environment and needs of the employees.

3. A *third-type event* is one in which the perpetrator is a current or former employee; a current or former spouse/lover of an employee; a relative or friend of an employee; or another person who has a dispute with an employee. As evidenced by the case studies, the third-type event has become common. Both second- and third-type

events can often be minimized by early identification of potentially violent individuals. This form of prevention is crucial to a workplace safety program. An employer who fails to account for threatening actions by an employee against others may be liable for any subsequent injuries or death.

Agencies such as Cal/OSHA require that employers provide a safe work environment. Each employer must be aware of safety regulations and reporting requirements in order to successfully operate his or her business in compliance with the law.   These agencies also provide an excellent resource for recommendations and assistance in order to ensure that the workplace is safe. Many such agencies will provide free consultative services to an employer on any safety related issue.

Regulatory Evaluations and Investigations

Many agencies, such as Cal/OSHA, may judge workplace safety by means of an on-site evaluation.   Such an evaluation will typically result from an allegation of unsafe work conditions made by an employee or client or, in the worst case, because of a violent incident.   Although onerous, such evaluations are designed to enforce reasonable workplace safety measures for employees. On-site inspections have recently encompassed the specifics of workplace security and violence prevention as important components in evaluating the overall condition of a site.   Many areas of an organization's operation will be evaluated, such as:[34]

1. The workplace must have an illness and injury prevention program (IIP) or safety program in place. This program must address the subject of workplace security and the prevention of workplace violence.
2. The organization's program must be effective in identifying workplace security hazards and provide for a method of investigating and correcting such hazards. Such hazards include conditions that could lead to workplace violence or occupational homicide.
3. The organization must provide, and document, effective workplace violence prevention training to employees.
4. The workplace must provide effective physical security, appropriate to the needs of the employees and clients.
5. An agency evaluation will usually review prior incidents of workplace violence to ensure that corrective action was taken in a timely manner.   Procedures for investigating incidents and reporting them properly will be emphasized.
6. An evaluation will provide recommendations for improving workplace security. These recommendations will be reviewed in subsequent evaluations to ensure compliance.

An astute employer will be in early contact with local safety agencies to obtain the precise requirements of an on-site evaluation. These requirements can provide a good starting-point for in-house inspections of the workplace. Employers should also be aware that agencies such as Cal/OSHA are required by law to investigate workplace assaults that involve serious injury or death. In

California, for example, the California Labor Code requires Cal/OSHA: "To investigate all industrial accidents which are fatal to one or more employees or which result in a serious injury or illness or a serious exposure, unless the Division [Cal/OSHA] determines an investigation is unnecessary, in which case the Division shall summarize the facts indicating that the accident need not be investigated and the means by which the facts were determined."[35]

Agencies that regulate safety in the workplace are typically given broad powers to investigate incidents and enforce corrective measures. With the increasing rate of workplace homicides in America, agencies such as Cal/OSHA are taking proactive measures to minimize the risks to employees. Employers should expect these agencies to react swiftly to any workplace incident that involves violence.

AVOIDING CLIENT VIOLENCE

It must be recognized that an organization's client base can also be the source of violence in the workplace. This is particularly true when the organization deals with a large number of different clients or is involved in some form of social or government service. The interactions between staff and clients can be either a flash point for violence or an excellent line of first defense in a violence prevention program.

An organization can do much to avoid workplace violence by ensuring that client interaction is professional, sensitive and consistent. As some of the case histories have shown, client violence has become increasingly lethal in recent years. There is no reason to suspect that this trend will diminish over time unless appropriate and effective prevention measures are enacted by employers.

In many instances, the potentially violent client is not recognized as such by employees, or the obvious warning signs of impending violence are ignored. Without a positive approach to client service, an organization may put employees and other clients at risk with each interaction. There are several specific areas of client interaction that are crucial to preventing or minimizing a violent reaction by a client who is distressed or contemplating a violent act.[36] These important client service principles should be made part of any violence prevention program:

1. Never keep a client waiting without adequate explanation or feedback. No client appreciates waiting—particularly an angry or frustrated client. It is imperative that clients are given prompt recognition and, if possible, prompt service. Under no circumstances should a client who is clearly distressed be ignored or kept waiting. If it is impossible to assist the client quickly, be sure that he or she is informed of the cause of the delay; allow the client an opportunity to express his or her needs and accommodate them if possible and reasonable. Keep in mind that inordinate waiting for assistance is the most frequently cited reason for a violent client reaction.

2. Be exceptionally wary of individuals who are under the influence of alcohol or other substances. If a client is clearly under the influence of alcohol or some other

substance, never deal with him or her alone if at all possible. On a similar note, as an employee, never deal with a client after consuming alcohol. The recognizable presence of alcohol can trigger hostile reactions from an individual who is already distressed. Alcohol or other behavior altering substances can frequently lead to unexpected or violent reactions. It is crucial that clients are shown respect and provided the attention they feel they deserve. The presence of drugs or alcohol in a client-employee interaction is unprofessional and potentially dangerous.

3. Avoid intruding into the personal affairs of a client. Remember that this activity is often a matter of perception on the part of the client. If it is necessary to gather personal information from a client, do so with care and sensitivity. The client should never be made to feel embarrassed or sense that his or her personal affairs are subject to unwarranted scrutiny. Seek only the information that is truly necessary to fulfill the job at hand. Demonstrate an awareness of the client's right to privacy by ensuring confidentiality and putting him or her at ease.

4. Be alert to signs of emotional or mental instability. If a client is exhibiting behavior that indicates stress, or is otherwise communicating or acting in a bizarre manner, do not engage the client without assistance. Be aware of the behavioral warning signs of a potentially violent individual and use them to your advantage by seeking assistance as needed.

5. Avoid judgmental comments or conversation. Never express assumptions about a client or his or her activities. Never engage in a "shouting match" with clients; never engage in argumentative behavior.

6. Express understanding and sensitivity in each interaction; never deal with a client as an intrusion or without recognition of his or her uniqueness. Mutual respect should be the keynote of each interaction.

7. Be alert to the behavior of clients in groups. An individual member of a group may behave quite differently than an individual client. Be aware of the dynamics of the group.

8. Be aware of the impact of such symbols as uniforms, badges or other official artifacts of the business. These symbols can be threatening to some individuals and may provoke an unexpected response. In other situations these symbols may have a calming or reassuring effect. The key is to be aware of the fact that such symbols will almost always have some impact on the client's reaction and receptivity.

9. Avoid bureaucracy. Never use rules, policies and regulations as the sole reason for avoiding a client's needs. If a reasonable policy prohibits client satisfaction, it is important that the client understand the rationale for the prohibition. Take the time to explain the reasons for any decision that impacts a client.

These client service principles are especially important in dealing with individuals who are distressed. It has been often demonstrated that ignoring these principles can provoke an angry or frustrated client into an act of violence. Beyond the obvious benefits of prevention, adherence to these guidelines will enhance any customer service program in a variety of ways.

A SELECTION OF ORGANIZATIONAL RECOMMENDATIONS

A number of organizations have compiled recommendations for violence prevention in the workplace. Some of the following suggestions are applicable to specific industries; others are more general. All these recommendations are sound, although some may be impractical or undesirable for certain industries or environments. Together, however, they provide a comprehensive checklist of possible prevention techniques. The best of the compiled recommendations are provided here as a further basis upon which an organization can develop their own violence prevention program.

NIOSH Violence Prevention Recommendations

The following recommendations were made by the National Institute for Occupational Safety and Health (NIOSH). These were released on October 25, 1993, in the *NIOSH Update*, publication number 93-109. A review of these recommendations will reveal that many are directed to the prevention of homicide during the course of a robbery or other crime. In this sense, they focus on security issues almost exclusively. For those involved in the retail, sales, transportation or restaurant industries, these NIOSH recommendations should prove particularly helpful:

1. Make high-risk areas visible to more people.
2. Install good external lighting.
3. Use drop safes to minimize cash on hand.
4. Carry small amounts of cash.
5. Post signs announcing that limited cash is on hand.
6. Install silent alarms.
7. Install surveillance cameras.
8. Increase the number of staff on duty.
9. Provide training in conflict resolution and nonviolent response.
10. Instruct workers to avoid resistance during a robbery.
11. Provide bulletproof barriers or enclosures.
12. Have police routinely check on workers.
13. Close establishments during high-risk hours (late at night and early in the morning).

High-Risk Activities

NIOSH has also identified six workplace activities that significantly increase the risk of being murdered on the job. Each organization should review these activities and apply strong violence prevention measures appropriately:

1. exchanging money with the public,
2. working alone or in small numbers,
3. working late at night or in the early morning hours,
4. working in high-crime areas,
5. guarding valuable property or possessions, and
6. working in community settings.

Psychological Perspective

The following recommendations appeared in the January/February 1994 issue of *Psychology Today*.[37] Although general in nature, many of these recommendations express the best of management goals and techniques from a psychological perspective. Some of these recommendations, the first for example, may not be permitted by law in certain states.[xv] Others require serious cost considerations and better definition of scope. Nonetheless, the goals of these suggestions are quite worthy:

1. extensive psychological screening for all potential employees,
2. continual training for supervisory teams to help them detect early warning signs of emotional upset,
3. implementing a "golden rule" attitude at work, wherein employees feel a sense of reward and recognition for their achievements,
4. educational programs aimed at teaching workers how to respond to conflict in personal situations,
5. counseling services for employees and their families for either job or personal problems,
6. proper security measures to protect the organization and its employees, and
7. counseling and stress debriefing in the aftermath of violence in the workplace.

Recommendations for Larger Organizations

These recommendations were offered by authors Wheeler and Baron, specialists in workplace violence, in 1994.[38] They represent a cross-section of methods that are applicable to a wide variety of larger organizations able to provide departmental support as needed. Some elements may be utilized in smaller organizations with appropriate modification:

1. Conduct training to identify potential sources of violence. Familiarize employees with the profile of the potentially violent individual.
2. Train employees to be alert to warning signs and to avert violence by reporting any threatening remarks or situations.
3. Train employees and management to observe—to know the basic levels of human needs and how to recognize stress.
4. Conduct training of managers/supervisors on hiring, downsizing and termination procedures.
5. If not already in existence, consider establishing an employee assistance program (EAP).
6. Define the organization's assets that need protection.
7. Establish priorities for providing protection.
8 Develop sound physical security plans and systems; identify any problem areas; have written security procedures.
9. Assess the organization's capability to respond quickly to workplace violence.

---

xv. California, for example, prohibits certain forms of preemployment testing.

10. Establish written policies so there are clear lines of communication between employees and management concerning veiled or overt threats.
11. Provide training programs and tools for adequate preemployment screening and potential behavioral problems.
12. Establish written policies concerning terminated or laid-off employees, or when downsizing.
13. Establish psychiatric resources or outplacement services for former employees.
14. Train managers and supervisors to use appropriate intervention procedures when dealing with employees.
15. Train all employees in methods of self-protection, both verbal and nonverbal.
16. Form a Crisis Management Team with individuals from human resources, legal, security, social services and other departments.
17. Establish a telephone team from the human resources department to call family members and to notify employees of when to return to work, where to find help, etc.
18. Establish a second source of communication, if possible, in case the telephone system should be destroyed.
19. Establish a plan to provide information about trauma and post traumatic stress.

Recommendations for Public Offices

The California State Employment Development Department (EDD) established a task force in 1986 to study the problem of violence in the public workplace and make recommendations to increase safety. A summary of some of the EDD recommendations, with a few modifications to apply to the general office environment, is presented below. A review of these recommendations will disclose that they may be applied to a wide variety of office environments and, with few exceptions, without a great deal of expense:

1. All clients should be escorted to and from work areas.
2. Any situation that is thought to be dangerous should be immediately reported to the local law enforcement agency.
3. Records should be kept regarding threats. Notations should be made regarding potentially hostile clients so that workers are aware of potential danger.
4. Supervisors should be prepared to assist workers with hostile or difficult clients.
5. Clients should be helped without undue waiting and with courtesy.
6. Staff should be trained to identify potentially violent behavior.
7. Staff should be trained continually in effective interviewing techniques.
8. The offices should be comfortable and attractive to clients, with sufficient seating.
9. Attempts should be made to limit public entrance to a single entryway.
10. Hazardous objects that could be used as weapons should not be available in the work area.
11. Protective counters ("bank counters") should be used where feasible. Counter openings should be gated with a buzzer control.
12. Alarm buzzers should be installed at every desk where interviews are held. This system should be capable of alerting a supervisor for intervention, if needed.
13. Multiple exits should be available to workers.

Personal Safety in the Retail Trades

The following recommendations were made in a trade journal in 1993.[39] These suggestions are oriented towards personal safety for workers in the retail or restaurant industry. They embody an emphasis on violence in the course of a criminal act, particularly robbery, and include directives about ex-employees. Although these recommendations are general, and have been somewhat abbreviated from the original, they are of value from a common sense point of view:

1. Always do everything a criminal tells you. Once a criminal has been antagonized, your personal danger increases.
2. Try to be perceptive enough to help the police capture the perpetrator. Remember details.
3. When an employee or ex-employee is upset on the job, management should always take the situation seriously. Employee assistance programs should be advertised and available to all employees.
4. Employers should always take special note of disgruntled employees or ex-employees. If an inclination toward violence is demonstrated, proper procedures should be immediately taken.

OSHA Recommendations for the Retail Industry

The California Division of Occupational Safety and Health (Cal/OSHA) released the following retail industry recommendations in late 1994:[40]

1. All store counters should have an unobstructed view of store windows.
2. Parking lots should be well illuminated.
3. Report suspicious activity occurring immediately outside the workplace to local authorities.
4. When no customers are in the store, keep busy at tasks away from the cash register.
5. Post emergency services telephone numbers by the telephone.
6. Mount mirrors on the ceilings to view hidden corners of the workplace; consider surveillance cameras.
7. Post signs stating there is limited cash on the premises.
8. Use a time access safe for valuables or large amounts of cash.
9. Limit the amount of cash on hand to small bills in the cash register.
10. Use only a single cash register after dark and leave the other cash registers with their open drawers plainly in sight.

GENERAL RECOMMENDATIONS FOR PERSONAL SAFETY

Workers should be aware of general safety procedures, not only in the workplace, but moving to and from job sites. The issue of personal safety is broad and, upon first examination, seems to stray from the primary subject of workplace violence. Still, a good violence prevention program should address issues of personal safety since they do apply so broadly. An employee who is aware of, and practices, personal safety measures will be naturally more aware of potentially violent situations in the workplace.

Many of the following personal safety recommendations have been offered by such organizations as the Chicago-based Citizens Against Crime and were summarized in *Safety and Health* magazine in 1993.[41] These recommendations are valuable to every American, but are often overlooked in workplace violence prevention programs. They are of such importance, however, that they should be offered to each employee as part of an overall violence prevention plan or company safety program:

1. There is safety in numbers. Car-pool with someone you trust or use the company van pool if one is available. Walk to and from your car with another person or a security officer.
2. Keep purses and other valuables out of sight in your car when it is parked and when you are driving.
3. When you approach your car, have your keys in hand ready to unlock the door. Check in, around and under the car before you get in.
4. Always keep your car doors locked, even when you are in your car.
5. Do not get on an elevator if you are suspicious of someone on it. If you are in an elevator and a suspicious person gets on, get off. Stand close to the floor-selection buttons and if someone threatens you, press as many buttons as you can. The elevator will stop often and you will have more chances to escape or get help.
6. Consider carrying pepper spray for self defense (but learn how to use it correctly and safely).
7. Lock anything of value in your desk drawer.
8. Avoid stairwells in parking garages. The auto ramp is less isolated and if you have to scream for help you are more likely to be heard. Walk as far from parked cars as possible (but, of course, be careful of traffic).
9. Do not open the door to a stranger before or after regular business hours.
10. When you work early or late, let security guards know so they can check on you.
11. If anyone calls while you are alone in the office, never mention that fact to the caller. If you are faced with a criminal with a gun, do not resist. If the criminal wants your money, give it to him or her unless the criminal wants to take you hostage, in which case refuse to surrender the money.
12. At the first sign of trouble, immediately call security or local emergency services. Get help on the way.
13. Stay alert. Notice everyone and everything. Criminals can be anywhere, and you need to be ready for them.

BASIC PERSONNEL SECURITY RECOMMENDATIONS

The following points were offered by *Security Management* magazine in 1992 and are presented in summary form.[42] These are basic security concepts that can, with few exceptions, be applied to most organizations. The recommendations deal primarily with the personnel aspects of security in the workplace:

1. Take all threats seriously and take action quickly.
2. Have a safety program that addresses workplace violence.
3. Know the employees.

4. Always do an in-depth background investigation before hiring.
5. Recognize trigger situations such as terminations, strikes, and reorganizations.
6. Discipline and termination should be handled by a different manager than the one to whom the employee reports on a daily basis. Such actions are best undertaken on a Friday to allow a "cooling off" period for the employee.
7. Handle personnel problems immediately.
8. If a threat is real and imminent, contact law enforcement immediately.
9. Employees who make threats should be interviewed immediately by an individual trained in psychology or personality analysis to evaluate the risk.
10. Provide armed security personnel for key managers and executives, if possible.
11. Increase access security for parking areas and building perimeters.
12. Keep employees informed of situations as they develop.

DIFFUSING VIOLENCE IN THE WORKPLACE

The respected journal *Management Review* provided a series of general recommendations regarding workplace violence in 1994.[43] These recommendations are applicable to virtually any organization and provide a "mind set" of violence prevention for management. The following summarizes the most important of these suggestions:

1. Every organization should have a written policy prohibiting violence, threats, and intimidation. This policy should require that employees and supervisors report potentially violent activities, threats, or acts of intimidation to management.
2. All reports of threats, intimidation or violence should be promptly and thoroughly investigated and documented, followed by management action to eliminate further similar activity.
3. Every organization should have some kind of employee assistance program designed for intervention in order to help prevent violence.
4. Every organization should have a safety program and an emergency plan which is written and known to all workers.
5. Every organization should have adequate security measures protecting the workplace.

ORGANIZATIONAL PREVENTION PLAN SUGGESTIONS

These recommendations focus primarily on the process of organizing a violence prevention program. Unlike some of the previous recommendations, these take an organizational view of the process of violence prevention and offer methods of bringing individuals together to form a cooperative and integrated program:[44]

1. Establish a violence prevention team that includes representatives from personnel, security/safety, legal counsel, staff and management. This team should undertake the following tasks:
   A. Perform an assessment of potential violence in the workplace by reviewing organizational history and current staff activities.
   B. Perform an assessment of the organizational capability and preparedness for workplace violence.

C. Gather as much information as possible about workplace violence in order to educate team members.

D. Form networking relationships with outside agencies that may be needed in the violence prevention program.

E. Develop a written plan for violence prevention; incorporate this plan into the existing safety program.

F. Develop a training program for staff and management that emphasizes violence prevention and appropriate responses to violent incidents.

2. Assess the current level of organizational security and establish new or improved methods as needed.

3. Develop a crisis management plan that is capable of responding to any workplace disruption, including violence.

4. Implement the training program developed by the violence prevention team. Be sure that the trainees are familiar with the recognition process as well as preventative measures and post-incident response measures.

5. Implement a strong employment process that includes proper evaluation and screening methodologies.

6. Document all incidents that indicate potential violence. Have these incidents reviewed by human resources personnel and, if appropriate, legal counsel for further involvement.

7. Effectively use the employee assistance program (EAP) to assist employees in difficulty before they become violent.

8. Appoint an individual responsible for media interface as part of the organizational prevention program.

MANTELL SEVEN-STEP APPROACH TO VIOLENCE PREVENTION

Michael Mantell, assistant clinical professor of psychiatry for the School of Medicine at the University of California San Diego, identified the following seven-step factors crucial to violence prevention in his book *Ticking Bombs — Defusing Violence in the Workplace*:[45]

1. preemployment screening;
2. informed, aware management trained to see the early warning signs (of potential violence);
3. management understanding of the "golden rule" of employee treatment;
4. education programs to teach employees and the organization how to respond to threatening interpersonal situations;
5. counseling services for employees and their families for job or personal problems;
6. proper security measures to protect the organization and the employees;
7. workplace violence aftermath training.

NOTES

1. Smith, S. L., "Dealing with a Crisis," *Occupational Hazards*, 1 Oct. 1993: 30.

2. Jenny McCune, "Companies Grapple With Workplace Violence," *Management Review*, 83, no. 3 (1994): 52.

3. Eugene D. Wheeler and S. Anthony Baron, *Violence in Our Schools, Hospitals*

and Public Places, (Ventura, CA: Pathfinder, 1994), 154-155.

4. John W. Newstrom and Keith Davis, *Organizational Behavior*, 9th ed. (New York: McGraw-Hill, 1993), 457.

5. Newstrom and Davis, 458.

6. Newstrom and Davis, 461.

7. Newstrom and Davis, 466.

8. "Stress Management," State University of New York Counseling Center, 1994, 1-2.

9. United Press International, "Suggestions Offered for Reducing Workplace Stress," 3 Aug. 1992.

10. Bureau of Labor Statistics, U.S. Department of Labor, *Microsoft Bookshelf*, 1994 ed. (Redmond, WA: Microsoft, 1994).

11. Bureau of Labor Statistics.

12. National Center for Health Statistics, *Microsoft Bookshelf*, 1994 ed. (Redmond, WA: Microsoft, 1994).

13. Don Lattin, "Layoffs Called One of the Biggest Causes of Violent Behavior," *San Francisco Chronicle*, 16 Aug. 1994, A29.

14. Lattin.

15. U. S. Bureau of the Census, Department of Commerce, *Microsoft Bookshelf*, 1994 ed. (Redmond, WA: Microsoft, 1994).

16. National Center for Health Statistics, *Microsoft Bookshelf*, 1994 ed. (Redmond, WA: Microsoft, 1994).

17. U. S. Bureau of the Census.

18. Betty Southard Murphy, "Pre-Employment Test Invades Privacy," *Personnel Journal*, 71, no. 2 (1992): 22.

19. "Revenge Behind KMart Shooting, Victim Says," *Reno Gazette-Journal*, 21 Jan. 1995, D1

20. S. Anthony Baron, "Violence in the Workplace," (Ventura, CA: Pathfinder, 1993), 103-104.

21. C. Ray Jeffrey, *Crime Prevention Through Environmental Design*, 1971 reprint, 2nd ed. (Beverly Hills: Sage, 1977).

22. Janice L. Thomas, "A Response to Occupational Violence Crime," *Risk Management*, June, 1992, 27.

23. Martin B. Herman, "Planning for the Unpredictable," *Security Management*, 36, no. 11 (1992): 33.

24. Newstrom and Davis, 395.

25. Newstrom and Davis, 395.

26. Daniel Weisberg, "Preparing for the Unthinkable," *Management Review*, 83, no. 3 (1994):58.

27. Peggy Stuart, "Murder on the Job," *Personnel Journal*, 71, no. 2 (1992): 72.

28. W. Ransom, "Planning Ahead Reduces the Impact," *Industrial Engineering*, 24, no. 4 (1992): 14.

29. Department of Industrial Relations (Division of Occupational Safety and Health (Cal/OSHA)), *Cal/OSHA Guidelines for Workplace Security*, 15 Aug. 1994.

30. Cal/OSHA, 4.

31. Cal/OSHA, 7.

32. Cal/OSHA, 7.

33. Cal/OSHA, 7.

34. Cal/OSHA, 17.

35. Cal/OSHA, 18.

36. Lonnie Hayhurst, "Workplace" Violence seminar, (San Rafael, CA: based on notes by Sid Wilkins), 21 Oct. 1994.

37. "It's Personnel as Well as Personal," *Psychology Today*, 27, no. 1 (1994): 20.

38. Eugene D. Wheeler and S. Anthony Baron, *Violence in Our Schools, Hospitals and Public Places* (Ventura, CA: Pathfinder, 1994), 251-253.

39. Gary Owensby, "Violence in the Workplace," *OHIO Monitor*, Sept./Oct. 1993, 24.

40. Cal/OSHA.

41. Catherine B. Kedjihjian, "Violence at Work: Is Anyplace Safe?," *Safety and Health, 1* Oct. 1993, 79.

42. Herman, "Planning for the Unpredictable," *Security Management,* 36, no. 11 (1992): 33.

43. Weisberg, "Preparing for the Unpredictable," *Management Review,* 83, no. 3 (1994): 58.

44. Steven Terry, "Workplace Violence Prevention Checklist," *Inside Safety,* 1, no. 2 (1994): 3.

45. Michael Mantell. *Ticking Bombs—Defusing Violence in the Workplace,* (New York: Irwin, 1994): x.

5

Conclusions and Recommendations

The impact of occupational homicide in most work environments can be mitigated with sufficient understanding of the problem and attention to effective intervention and prevention strategies. Through the examination of case studies, the relevant organizational weaknesses that can be identified as contributing causes to the crime, the study of a variety of behavioral and cultural influences that can be identified as potential causal factors in workplace violence, and the presentation of a number of management techniques designed to identify safety and security concerns, it should be clear that there are avenues available to staff and managers to effectively deal with this onerous threat to the workplace.

A method of categorizing and defining incidents of workplace violence (Category Profiles) has been offered, a working profile of the potentially violent worker or client has been outlined, and a new method of analyzing and holistically interpreting violent workplace incidents has been described and utilized. Finally, a preliminary compendium of prevention techniques and methodologies has been recommended for use in a variety of work environments. These specific tools were designed for the practical use of workplace managers and staff and, hopefully, will be proven to be of assistance in that environment.

Further, by addressing the combined influences of (1) a lack of information about the nature and impact of occupational homicide, (2) the unfortunate view that the problem is beyond the scope or control of workplace personnel, (3) the understandable reluctance to address this disturbing subject within the context of existing organizational training or safety programs, and

(4) the absence of a readily-accessible, understandable program of intervention and prevention, it can be argued that the threat of occupational homicide can be reduced in many organizations by the application of effective management techniques that evolve from a comprehensive understanding of the problem.

It must be recognized, however, that there are limitations to the efficacy of any intervention or prevention program because of the sometimes wholly unpredictable and apparently random nature of the crime. This is due, in part, to an incomplete understanding of the causes of such violence and a limited ability to introduce complete safety into most work environments. Minimizing these limitations and increasing the probability of a safe and violence-free workplace will be most likely achieved by informed and committed workplace staff and managers who are willing to deal with this crime as a serious and continuing area of concern in any work environment. Much has yet to be learned about occupational homicide, and much effort lies ahead if this crisis is to be significantly mitigated in the majority of American workplaces.

THE HEALTHY ORGANIZATION

An organization, like an individual, can be healthy or unhealthy; the difference is often a matter of commitment on the part of staff and management. A healthy organization need not fear occupational homicide because it is prepared and alert. However, a poorly managed, uncaring, or unwary organization is a waiting victim.

Organizational health is, of course, not a simple subject to define. The wellness of a business cannot be judged solely by the issues raised in this book. Businesses are dynamic and complex by nature and the health of a company must be constantly monitored across a large variety of areas. Matters of economics, staffing, marketing, resource management, and many more are all vital to the well-being of a business. Vital also are the issues of workplace violence and occupational homicide. It is of critical importance that an organization function proactively in the areas of risk management to ensure the overall wellness of the work environment.

This book has attempted to focus on the issues surrounding murder in the workplace, but always with the primary goal of formulating a prevention program applicable to as many work environments as possible. It should now be clear that prevention cannot be interpreted as merely a series of recommendations, even though, in this case, that is the most effective manner of offering knowledge gained through experience. An effective violence prevention program must be a fully integrated array of concepts and philosophy, techniques, and practices. Each recommendation that has been offered is, therefore, only a component in an overall plan. That plan must be designed by workplace managers, in conjunction with staff, to apply to each unique work environment in the most efficacious manner.

An organization that is unafraid of occupational homicide, yet remains always prepared for the possibility, will be one that is consistent, fair-minded, practical, and open to change. From an employee's perspective, the healthy organization is a second home—one that is safe and secure. Within the work environment of such an organization, each employee knows that he or she is highly valued; there is no question that management cares about each member of the staff. A strong violence prevention program is evidence of this kind of management commitment.

What follows is a summary of elements that, together, can improve the health of an organization by minimizing the possibility of violence in the workplace. Managers can use these elements as a checklist to determine the health of their own organization and pinpoint where improvements might prove beneficial. The concepts presented here are practical and can be implemented in many different environments. Some may require additional expenditures or staff resources, but many do not. When taken as a whole, they constitute the basis for a strong violence prevention program which should prove workable in most environments.

Management Practices

There can be no violence prevention program without the complete commitment of management. Beyond this commitment to prevention, management must also be committed to creating and maintaining a workplace environment that fosters dignity, trust and wellness for each employee. A successful manager must view him or herself as being chiefly responsible for ensuring that the overall work environment focuses on the individual worker as indispensable to the organization. This implies a constant effort to implement excellent communication, teamwork, honesty, sensitivity to employee needs, safety in the workplace, excellent working conditions and a positive, forward-looking attitude among the workforce.

These are not easy goals to attain when a manager or supervisor is also faced with the daily responsibilities of managing change and working toward productivity goals. Nonetheless, the overall working environment can either ensure a safe and healthy workplace or set the stage for potential violence. Workplace managers and supervisors are at the center of the activities necessary to create a nonviolent organization. For this reason, it is imperative that a manager always keep in mind the higher goal of a violence-free workplace.

A management team that is committed to the well-being of the staff and the organization must be alert for the warning signs of violence. They must ensure that workers are trained in the process of recognizing these warning signs. Managers must also work constantly at creating an environment in which full and open communication between staff and themselves is the order of the day. Managers and staff must view themselves as a single unit, working toward common goals. It is the responsibility of the manager to organize individual workers into a team that is committed to each member and to the goals of the organization. Members of the team must be aware of changes in the work environment that may threaten other workers, or the organization; they must then have sufficient confidence in management that they will make this information known to those who can intervene to ensure the wellness of the group.

It is not reasonable for a manager to expect to eliminate all possibilities of violence in the workplace. The motivations for violence are too complex and numerous to attain the goal of complete safety, and consequently there may be occasions when even the most prepared and healthy organization will experience a violent incident. Sound management practices can, however, greatly reduce the possibilities of a violent incident.

A manager should always be aware of the vital role that work plays in the sense of wellness for each employee. To many employees, the organization and their job is of such importance that it cannot be sacrificed for any reason; it is a life connection that can make the difference between satisfaction and complete hopelessness. In view of the overwhelming importance of work to an employee, the manager must be always alert to the fact that he or she can greatly influence the future behavior of a worker. Handling this responsibility with honesty, understanding and fairness clearly marks the successful manager as an individual who not only can be trusted by the staff, but represents the organization in the best possible manner.

Employment

The first line of defense against violence in the workplace is a strong hiring process. An organization that is watchful and proactive in the employment process can greatly reduce the likelihood of welcoming a violent individual as a new member of the workforce:

1. Be sure that each individual involved in the employment process understands its importance. Employing a new worker is the act of entering into a commitment and a relationship that can severely impact an organization.
2. Never rush the recruitment process. Provide ample time to recruit the right individual for the right job.
3. The organization must have its own application form that complies with federal and state legislation. Have the form reviewed by an attorney and a human resource expert before it is used. Once approved, use the form consistently for all job applicants. The application provides the basis for a background investigation that can eliminate a potentially violent employee.
4. An applicant should be screened and interviewed by more than one staff member. Multiple opinions are preferable. Multiple interviews are even better.
5. Be thorough to a fault. There is limited time to learn about the applicant, so make the most of it by never ignoring details.
6. The interview process is critical. Learn what you can about the applicant and share any information about the organization or job that might make a difference in the decision process. The "no surprises" concept should be foremost.
7. If desirable, use preemployment testing to the extent allowed by law in the organization's state. Remember that preemployment psychological testing is

problematical and not proven to be effective. Legal advice should be sought if preemployment psychological testing is desired.

8. Whenever possible, give the final applicants a practical work test. This provides an opportunity to observe skills as well as individual reactions to the work and the work environment itself. It also provides the applicant with some knowledge of work standards and procedures in the organization. Remember, any testing must comply with federal and state legislation as well as with the Americans with Disabilities Act (ADA).

9. Look for fit. Always keep in mind that the employer and employee are about to embark on a relationship that will change both forever. The workforce is a team, and each member is a crucial element.

10. Thorough background checks are mandatory and effective. Check on all information provided by the applicant, but use the organization's application form as the primary basis. The more information voluntarily provided by the applicant, the better. Information received through background investigation should be recorded in detail.

11. If the background investigation discloses convincing evidence that the individual would pose a threat to workers or clients, do not employ the individual without first consulting a human resources expert and, preferably, an attorney specializing in employment law. Employers often face liability for the actions of their workers.

Termination

As the case histories in this book have shown, violence can result when an individual is improperly terminated. Like the hiring process, the act of terminating an employee is critical to a successful violence prevention program:

1. Keep in mind that the process of termination can be traumatic and emotionally charged. Maintain a professional, calm demeanor. Try to avoid terminating an employee who is undergoing major changes in his or her life.

2. Always have at least two members of management present at a termination hearing; it is preferable that one of these members be a human resource professional. Consider inviting a member of the security staff to the meeting, if appropriate.

3. Treat the departing employee with dignity, respect, and honesty.

4. Keep the meeting focused on business issues and try to answer the departing employee's questions openly and fully.

5. Be prepared for the meeting. Rehearse what is to be discussed, and have all documents and benefits forms ready for signature and delivery.

6. Make use of an outplacement program to assist the departing employee to reenter the workforce as soon as possible.

Safety and Crisis Management

Workers must feel safe in the workplace. A worker who does not feel secure can be subjected to significant stress on the job and may react with aggression or hostility. Potential violence in the workplace can be significantly reduced by a strong safety and crisis management program:

1. Appoint someone in the organization as a safety officer to be in charge of a companywide safety and violence prevention program.

2. Make the safety and violence prevention program an active, participatory process between management and employees.
3. Make it clear to all employees that management strongly supports the philosophy of safety and violence prevention in the workplace, as well as in the formal safety program.
4. Devote attention to violence prevention and possible violent scenarios in the workplace as a key component of the safety program.
5. Document the safety program and maintain it regularly. Communicate the program and its changes to all staff.
6. Establish a Safety Committee, comprised of management and nonmanagement personnel, to monitor safety and violence prevention in the workplace. Ensure that the committee is proactive and that the members are given sufficient time and management support to participate actively.
7. Be aware of the role of the local, state, and federal Occupational Safety and Health agencies. Use these agencies as sources of information about workplace safety. Ensure that the organization is in compliance with OSHA regulations and is prepared for any external safety evaluation or investigation. Maintain complete documentation on safety and violence prevention matters.
8. Develop a crisis management plan that incorporates a crisis management team, a trauma team, employee support components, and a schedule of training and crisis simulations. Ensure that the crisis management plan is reviewed regularly and updated as needed. Incorporate the elements of crisis management into the training regimen for staff.

The Work Environment

A quality work environment is crucial to staff and management alike. Management must ensure a work environment that fosters honesty, open communications and a sense of caring for each employee:

1. Establish an employee assistance program (EAP) that can help the worker and his or her family with a wide variety of issues. Ensure that confidentiality is a prominent feature of the program.
2. Emphasize effective communication across all levels of the organization as there is no single factor that has a greater impact on the health of a company. Of critical importance is maintaining an open and free flow of communication between staff and management personnel.
3. Management must genuinely care about employees. This is a philosophy that cannot be merely discussed but rather must be evidenced by practical and daily action by management. If the management of an organization simply does not care, it is unlikely that the workers will.
4. The single, most powerful resource in any organization is the staff. Involve them in the process of creating and maintaining a healthy and safe work environment.
5. Emphasize the concepts of preparation and prevention when dealing with workplace violence. Ensure that managers and staff are aware of the issues surrounding the subject. Solicit comments from staff on how best to ensure workplace security and safety. Train staff to be aware of threats to the workplace and how to report them to management for action.
6. Management should be committed to effective intervention and assistance practices at the staff level. Employees should be trained in the recognition of behavioral

warning signs and in how to access management assistance to provide appropriate intervention for any member of the staff who may be experiencing difficulties. There is simply no substitute for early intervention in order to ensure a safe work environment.

7. Management should be committed to an effective and continual training regimen on topics such as safety, security, employee assistance, communications, and conflict resolution to ensure that the workforce is informed and concerned about violence prevention. As many of the case histories have demonstrated, ineffective training and communication can lead to workplace violence that could have been otherwise prevented.

8. Strive to be aware of how workplace violence impacts other organizations. Management should make a continuing effort to understand how violence can intrude into the workplace, the many forms of workplace violence, the evolving knowledge of prevention, and how organizations can work together to share information about prevention. As knowledge of this issue is acquired, it should be shared with staff in order to encourage an organizationwide effort to improve the safety of the work environment.

Security Issues

At least minimum physical security is important to every workplace. The options for implementing security measures in the workplace are broad and can range from little or no cost to extremely expensive. Each organization must carefully analyze its ability to fund an effective security system and balance this fiscal commitment against the risks inherent in the workplace. Consideration must be given to the size and demographics of the workforce, physical plant location and construction, diversity of work sites, clientele, and a variety of other issues, some of which may be unique to the particular organization.

Since physical security systems must be customized for each work environment, the installation of a security system can be a complex and resource-intensive process. For this reason it is often wise to engage a professional consultant who can recommend the most effective security system for a particular environment. The use of a committee specifically charged with the responsibility of physical security may be beneficial to larger organizations.

Many businesses will find a pressing need for physical security systems if they deal with significant numbers of unknown clients; other organizations that enforce regulations or provide special services, such as government or law enforcement agencies, may require specialized security systems to minimize a significant potential for workplace violence. In general, physical security systems should provide for areas of refuge, methods of escape, and areas of isolation and protection in the event of a violent incident in the workplace. In addition, it is important that security systems provide for quick and efficient methods of communicating with outside assistance providers and with work groups throughout the physical plant, as well as general office warning systems.

If the organization is planning the construction of a new facility, management might consider using crime protection through environmental design (CPTED) techniques from the initial planning phase. The use of

CPTED may also be appropriate during periods of significant physical reorganization.

The planning and implementation of physical security systems provides an opportunity for management and staff to come together on issues that are important to the workplace. A committee comprised of staff and management personnel, dedicated to the review and implementation of security systems, can provide strong leadership in maintaining a secure work environment. Such a security committee can function in ways similar to an organization's safety committee, with their efforts leading eventually to the implementation of a wide range of security systems, techniques, and staff training.

Communication: The Best Prevention

There is no more effective violence prevention technique available to an organization than a commitment to effective and meaningful communication with staff. The employees of any organization can provide insightful and important information about a wide variety of conditions and events in the workplace. This information is only valuable, however, if it is heard and understood by management. In a similar way, the expert knowledge gained through the experience of managers must be shared with staff at all levels. Without a free flow of information between staff and management, a workplace may be at risk from factors that could be otherwise controlled.

Since the subjects of workplace violence and occupational homicide are unsettling for most individuals, a special effort must be made by management to ensure that these important issues are not ignored. It is to be expected that these subjects will, at first, be unwelcome in many organizations or employee groups. With management commitment and effort, however, employees can be shown that dealing with the issues of workplace violence and occupational homicide is a true indication of management's willingness to provide a safe and productive work environment. It is therefore vital that employees be brought into the process of discussing workplace violence and occupational homicide, and that they play a major role in helping to define prevention techniques appropriate to the organization.

Preventing workplace violence and occupational homicide is an exercise in improving the work environment for each employee. It is therefore important that each employee understand that management is committed to their personal safety. Educating employees about workplace violence prevention and training them in prevention techniques should be a personal and meaningful experience for each individual. To the extent that each worker feels personally committed to a nonviolent workplace, the organization as a whole will be improved and made more safe. At the heart of reaching the goal of a violence-free workplace is the commitment of management to the highest standards of open communication between and among employees and managers.

INDIVIDUAL COMMITMENT TO A NONVIOLENT WORKPLACE

There is virtually no business in America that is currently safe from workplace violence or occupational homicide. Although some organizations have made a strong commitment to the prevention of workplace violence, the majority of American businesses have not dealt adequately with the subject. It is unfortunate, but likely, that each year an increasing number of citizens will become victims of occupational homicide before employers comprehend the pervasive nature of the problem and take appropriate action. Until there is sufficient commitment on a national scale to a secure and caring work environment, many Americans will continue to be sacrificed needlessly. America's employers and organizational managers must take the lead in preventing this inexcusable waste of life—and they must do so immediately.

Occupational homicide cannot be answered after the fact. The only reasonable response to the potential for workplace violence is an effective prevention program that involves all levels of the organization.   Such a program, to be effective, must begin with workplace leaders who embrace the fundamental concepts of good management. Each member of the management team, and, through their leadership, each member of the staff, must be able to genuinely express these workplace concepts:

1. *I care.* I care about my coworkers, supervisors, the management of the organization, and its clients. I will guard the safety and integrity of others, and they will do the same for me.
2. *I am committed.* I am committed to safety, honesty, and success, for myself, my organization, and all its members.
3. *I will communicate.* I recognize that the free flow of communication across all levels of the organization is vital to every member of the group. I will do my part to keep those lines of communication open and effective. I will hear others, and ask that they also hear me.
4. *I will respect.* I will respect myself and other individuals. I will seek peaceful solutions and treat others, always, in a nonviolent way. My actions affect others and theirs affect me; therefore, I will show respect always.
5. *I will progress.* I choose to learn and grow in ways that better myself, my family, my organization, and my society. I want my organization to help me achieve my goals and I, in turn, will help the organization achieve its goals.

It is easy to dismiss these expressions as trite and inapplicable in the often-competitive and dynamic work environments so common in America. They are, however, the cornerstones of trust and caring in the workplace—elements crucial to the prevention of violence in any venue. Although the techniques of violence prevention are fundamental to the safety of any organization, they are no substitute for workplace leadership that is caring, respected, and trusted by all members of the staff. This kind of positive work environment greatly reduces the possibility of violence, enhances motivation, and engenders a group commitment to security and success.

Appendix

SAMPLE CRISIS PLANNING EVENT SHEET

This sample crisis planning event sheet is designed to be part of a comprehensive crisis management plan. The event sheet summarizes action to be taken in response to a particular workplace crisis for which staff has been previously trained. It is meant to be used as a reference for periodic review by staff and as the basis for regular training and crisis simulations.

Crisis Event

Violent individual in second floor waiting area, armed with a gun and firing rounds. Staff and clients in peril.

Staff Action

1. Use panic buttons to alert dispatch service.
2. Dial 911 if safe to do so.
3. Do not confront the intruder.
4. Use escape and evasion techniques as trained.
    A. Escort staff and any other clients to safety using preplanned escape routes.
    B. Use alternate exits as indicated on floor plan.
    C. Warn other offices on the floor and in the building.
    D. Use locked offices for safety if immediately available and accessible.
    E. Use other locked and secure areas for safety if immediately available and accessible.
5. Do not use the elevator under any circumstances.
6. Evacuate injured if safe to do so.
7. Once you have reached a secure location, do not leave that location until law enforcement officials or the on-site emergency team indicates it is safe to do so.

8. If you escape the building for safety, meet the on-site emergency team at the annex lobby as pre-arranged.
9. If you have the opportunity, and it is safe to do so, post the emergency notification cards on outside doors to advise others of the emergency condition inside.
10. Act promptly on any request made by law enforcement officials, emergency services personnel, fire personnel or members of the on-site emergency team.

Staff Coordination

1. Supervisors are to take charge of staff and client evacuation. Each supervisor should have a backup individual appointed who is also trained in emergency response techniques.
2. Expect outside assistance from law enforcement officials, medical services personnel and fire personnel.
3. As many individuals as able should be sure to activate their alarm (panic) systems or dial 911 emergency services.
4. The first priority is to evacuate the area if it is safe to do so. If evacuation is not safe, take escape and evasion measures as trained (locked offices, etc.).
5. All interaction with the media and emergency services should be handled by the members of the on-site emergency team.
6. The post trauma team should be activated as soon as the on-site emergency team is able to make contact. In this situation the post trauma team will be comprised of:
   A. the head of the on-site emergency team,
   B. a mental health professional,
   C. a medical advisor,
   D. a human resources expert,
   E. the chief attorney, and
   F. the insurance representative.

VIOLENCE PREVENTION RESOURCES

There are a growing number of national and local resources available for individuals who wish to pursue more information about developing a comprehensive violence prevention program within their own organization:

Occupational Safety and Health Administration
1120 20th St. NW
Washington, DC 20036
Telephone (202) 219-8148

OSHA Consultation Services - California
Cal/OSHA Consultation Service
Telephone (415) 703-4050

Centers for Disease Control
1600 Clifton Road NE
Atlanta, GA 30333
Telephone (404) 639-3061

National Institute for Occupational Safety and Health (NIOSH)
4676 Columbia Parkway
Cincinnati, OH 45226-1998
Telephone 1-800-35-NIOSH
Fax (513) 533-8573

NIOSH - Atlanta
1600 Clifton Road NE
Atlanta, CA 30333
Telephone (404) 639-3061

United States Department of Labor
200 Constitution Ave. NW
Washington, DC 20210
Telephone (202) 219-6666

Scripps Center Quality Management, Inc.
(Crisis Management Services)
9747 Business Park Ave.
San Diego, CA 92131
Telephone (619) 566-3472

Crime Victims Research and Treatment Center
Medical University of South Carolina
151 Ashley Ave.
Charleston, SC 29425
Telephone (803) 792-2945

American Society for Industrial Security
1655 North Fort Myer Dr.
Arlington, VA 22209
Telephone (703) 522-5800

American Psychological Association
750 1st Street, NE
Washington, DC 20006
Telephone (202) 336-5500

Society of Human Resources Management
606 N. Washington Street
Alexandria, VA 22314
Telephone (703) 548-3440

National Crime Prevention Council
1700 K Street, NW, Suite 618
Washington, DC 20006
Telephone (202) 466-6272

National Institute for Mental Health
5600 Fishers Lane
Rockville, MD 20857
Telephone (301) 496-4000

Public Health Service
DHHS Region I Office
John F. Kennedy Federal Building
Government Center, Room 1875
Boston, MA 02203
Telephone (617) 565-1439

DHHS Region IV Office
101 Marietta Tower, Suite 1106
Atlanta, GA 30323
Telephone (404) 331-2396

DHHS Region VIII Office
1185 Federal Building
1961 Stout Street
Denver, CO 80294
Telephone (303) 844-6166

NIOSH Educational Resource Center - California
Center for Occupational and Environmental Health
Richmond Field Station
1301 S. 46th Street, Building 102
Richmond, CA 94804
Telephone (510) 231-5645

Selected Bibliography

Bachman, R. *Violence and Theft in the Workplace*. Washington, D. C.: U. S. Department of Justice, Bureau of Justice Statistics, 15 Jul. 1994.

Baron, S. A. "Workplace Violence." Crisis Solutions International Seminar material, 1994. 12.

Bell, C. A. "Female Homicides in United States Workplaces, 1980-1985." *American Journal of Public Health*, 6 (1991): 729.

Bell, C. A., Stout, N. A., Bender, T. R., Conroy, C. S., Crouse, W. E., and Myers, J. R. "Fatal Occupational Injuries in the United States: 1980-1985. Journal of the American Medical Association, 22 (1991): 3047.

Bendix, L. "Number of Killings at Work Rises." *San Francisco Chronicle*, 18 Aug. 1994, A23.

Bilski, A. "Tragedy in Texas." *Maclean's*, 104, no. 43 (1991): 34.

Bledsoe, G. L. *Occupational Homicide: Alaska, 1993*. Anchorage, Alaska: Alaska Department of Health and Social Services, 1994. Internet summarized edition.

Blow, R. "A Social Disease." *Mother Jones*, Dec. 1992. Internet summarized edition.

Boxer, P. A. "Assessment of Potential Violence in the Paranoid Worker." *Journal of Occupational Medicine*, 2 (1993): 127.

California Department of Industrial Relations, Division of Occupational Safety and Health (Cal/OSHA). *Cal/OSHA Guidelines for Workplace Security*. 1994, 8.

Castelli, J. "On-the-Job Violence Becomes Epidemic." *Safety and Health*, 149, no. 2 (1994): 85.

Castillo, D. N., and Jenkins, E. L. "Industries and Occupations at High Risk for Work-Related Homicide." *Journal of Occupational Medicine*, 2 (1994): 125.

Cowan, S. *Lessons from the Fabrikant File: A Report to the Board of Governors of Concordia University*, May 1994 Internet summarized edition.

Dunkel, T. "Newest Danger Zone." *Working Woman*, 19, no. 8 (1994): 38.

Fennel, T. "Guilty as Charged: Valery Fabrikant Gets Life for Four Murders." *Maclean's*, 106, no. 34 (1993): 14.

Goldman, H. H., ed. *Review of General Psychiatry*. Norwalk, VA: Appleton and Lange, 1988.

Hackett, G. "Settling a Score." *Newsweek*, 21 Dec. 1987.

Hales, T., Seligman, P. J., Newman, S. C., and Timbrook, C. L. "Occupational Injuries Due to Violence." *Journal of Occupational Medicine*, 6 (1988): 483.

Hayhurst, L. "Workplace Violence." Seminar, based on notes by Sid Wilkins. San Rafael, California: 21 October 1994.

Herman, M. B. "Planning for the Unpredictable." *Security Management*, 36, no. 11 (1992): 33.

Independent Committee of Inquiry into Academic and Scientific Integrity. *Integrity in Scholarship: Report to Concordia University*, Apr. 1994.

"It's Personnel as Well as Personal." *Psychology Today*, 1 (1994): 20.

Jeffrey, C. R. *Crime Prevention through Environmental Design*. 2nd ed. Beverly Hills, CA: Sage, 1977.

Jenkins, E. L., Layne, L. A., and Kisner, S. M. "Homicide in the Workplace." *AAOHN Journal*, 5 (1992): 215.

Kedhdjian, C. B. "Violence at Work: Is Anyplace Safe?" *Safety and Health*, 1 Oct. 1993, 82.

Lattin, D. "Layoffs Called One of the Biggest Causes of Violent Behavior." *San Francisco Chronicle*, 16 Aug. 1994, A29.

Lissy, W. E. "Workplace Violence." *Supervision*, 55, no. 4 (1994): 20.

Mantell, M. *Ticking Bombs—Defusing Violence in the Workplace*. New York: Irwin, 1994.

Microsoft. *Microsoft Bookshelf*. MS-windows 3.1. 1994 Edition. Redmond, WA.: Microsoft, 1994. Computer software

McCune, J. "Companies Grapple with Workplace Violence." *Management Review*, 83, no. 3 (1994): 52.

"Murder at the Post Office." *Training and Development*, 1 (1994): 29.

Murphy, B. S. "Pre-Employment Test Invades Privacy." *Personnel Journal*, 71, no 2 (1992): 22.

National Institute for Occupational Safety and Health. *Fatal Injuries to Workers in the United States, 1980-1989: A Decade of Surveillance*. Cincinnati: OH.: NIOSH, Aug. 1993.

Newstrom, J. W. and Davis, K. *Organizational Behavior* (9th Ed.), New York: McGraw-Hill, 1993.

"Over the Edge." *Security Management*, 12 (1993): 12.

Owensby, G. "Violence in the Workplace." *OHIOmonitor*, Sept./Oct. 1993, 24.

Pedersen, D. "10 Minutes of Madness." *Newsweek*, 1 Sept. 1986.

"Poll Finds 1 in 3 Postal Workers Fears Violence in the Workplace," *San Francisco Chronicle*. 12 Dec. 1994, A9.

Poyner, B. "Working against Violence." *Occupational Health*, Aug. 1989.

Prince, J. J. "Fuming over Workplace Violence." *Security Management*, 37, no. 3 (1993): 64.

Quirk, J. H. "HR Managers Face Legal Aspects of Workplace Violence." *HRMagazine*, 38, no.11 (1993): 115.

Ransom, W. "Planning Ahead Reduces the Impact." *Industrial Engineering*, 24, no. 4 (1992): 14.

Satchell, M. "Airline Security: Mass Murder in the Clouds." *U.S. News and World Report*, 21 Dec. 1987, 14.

Seligman, P. J., Newman, S. C., Timbrook, C. L., and Halperin, W. E. "Sexual Assault of Women at Work," *American Journal of Industrial Medicine*, 12 (1987): 445.

Sheinin, R. *Response to the Cowan Report.* Concordia University, privately published. May 1994, Internet summarized edition.

Solomon, J., and King, P. "Waging War in the Workplace." *Newsweek*, 122, no. 3 (1994): 30.

Smith, S. L. "Dealing with a Crisis." *Occupational Hazards*, 1 Oct. 1993, 30-31,

Smith, S. L. "Violence in the Workplace: A Cry for Help." *Occupational Hazards*, 1 Oct. 1993, 29.

Stockdale, J., and Phillips, C. "Physical Attack and Threatening Behavior." *Occupational Health*, Aug. 1989, 212.

"Stress Management," State University of New York Counseling Center, 1994.

Stuart, P. "Murder on the Job." *Personnel Journal*, 71, no. 2 (1992): 72.

"Suggestions Offered for Reducing Workplace Stress," UPI Internet News Service, 3 Aug. 1992.

Terry, S. "Workplace Violence Prevention Checklist." *Inside Safety*, 1, no. 2 (1994): 58.

Thomas, J. L. "Occupational Violent Crime: Research on an Emerging Issue." *Journal of Safety Research*, 23, no. 2 (1992): 55.

Thomas, J. L. "A Response to Occupational Violent Crime." *Risk Management*, June 1992, 27.

Toufexis, A. "Workers Who Fight Firing with Fire." *Time*, 143, no. 17 (1994): 34.

United States Department of Commerce. *1980 Census of the Population: Alphabetic Index of Industries and Occupations.* Washington, D. C.: U. S. Government Printing Office, 1982.

United States Federal Bureau of Investigation. *Uniform Crime Report.* 1990.

United States Federal Bureau of Investigation. *Uniform Crime Report.* 1992.

United States Office of Management and Budget. *Standard Industrial Classification Manual.* Washington, D. C.: U. S. Government Printing Office, 1987.

"Violent Incidents on the Rise." *USA Today Magazine*, 122, no. 2587 (1994): 5.

Walton, J. B. "Dealing with Dangerous Employees." *Occupational Hazards*, 37, no. 9 (1993): 81.

Weisberg, D. "Preparing for the Unthinkable." *Management Review*, 83, no. 3 (1994): 58.

Wheeler, E. D., and Baron, S. A. *Violence in Our Schools, Hospitals and Public Places.* Ventura, CA: Pathfinder, 1994.

Windau, J., and Toscano, G. "Murder Inc.: Homicide in the American Workplace." *Business and Society Review*, 89 (1994): 58.

Woodbury, R. "Ten Minutes in Hell." *Time*, 138, no. 17 (1991): 31.

Wookfolk, J. "Peninsula Man's Trial Begins." *San Francisco Chronicle*, 14 Aug. 1994, A5.

Index

About the Author

MICHAEL D. KELLEHER specializes in strategic management, human resource management, staff education, and in threat assessment and management crisis resolution for organizations in the public and private sectors.

ISBN 0-275-95652-0

9 780275 956523

90000>

EAN

HARDCOVER BAR CODE